D0864095

Read Real Japanese

Read Real Japanese

Short Stories by
Contemporary Writers

EDITED BY Michael Emmerich

NARRATED BY Reiko Matsunaga

KODANSHA USA

Note from the publisher

All Japanese names are given in the Japanese order, sur-
name first (except on the jacket, title page, copyright page,
and recordings).
Audio files are available for download. Go to kodansha.us,
search for "Read Real Japanese Fiction."

Photo Credits: Copyright © Bungei Shunjū, pp. 15, 39, 49, 107. Copyright © Thomas Karsten, p. 139. Photo on p. 73 courtesy of Banana
Yoshimoto.

CD narration by arrangement of PSC Produce & Management. Recording and editing by The English Language Education Council Inc.

Dictionary, pp. 3–48 (starting from the back of the book), compiled
by Nihon IR Inc. Copyright © 2008, 2013 by Kodansha USA Publishing, LLC

Published by Kodansha USA Publishing, LLC
451 Park Avenue South, New York, NY 10016.

Distributed in the United Kingdom and continental Europe
by Kodansha Europe Ltd.

Printed in South Korea through Dai Nippon Printing Co., Ltd.
ISBN 978-1-56836-617-3

First published in Japan in 2008 by Kodansha International
First US edition 2013 by Kodansha USA, an imprint of Kodansha USA
Publishing, LLC
26 25 24 23 22 21   6 5 4 3 2 1

The Library of Congress has cataloged the earlier printing as follows:
Library of Congress Cataloging-in-Publication Data

Read real Japanese fiction : short stories by contemporary writers /
edited by Michael Emmerich ; narrated by Reiko Matsunaga.
    p. cm.
  ISBN 978-4-7700-3058-0
  1. Short stories, Japanese. 2. Japanese fiction—Heisei period,
1989– I. Emmerich, Michael. II. Matsunaga, Reiko.
  PL777.65.R43 2008
  895.6'30108—dc22
                                 2007052677

kodansha.us

CONTENTS

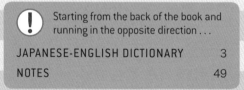

! Starting from the back of the book and running in the opposite direction . . .

PREFACE

The phrase "best-kept secret" gets on my nerves, in part because I usually turn first to the restaurant reviews when the newspaper parachutes through our mail slot, and this overdone expression seems to crop up in every third review. Sometimes, though, you simply have no choice but to use it. Take, for instance, the Japanese language. You've heard rumors, no doubt, that Japanese is an extremely difficult language for English speakers to master. Impossible, even! Well, rest assured, fellow student—those rumors are false. One of the best-kept secrets around, really and truly, is that Japanese is not actually all that hard.

Learning a language, I would suggest, is like jumping on a train without having any idea where it's headed, and staying aboard until you get there— wherever "there" is. Trips of this sort can be a bit unnerving, sure, and with Japanese you have to travel a long way before the scenery starts to change, and it can get kind of boring just sitting there, staring blankly at your flashcards. That's the rub, really—it's not that the language is *hard*, per se, you just have to take your time getting into it, and that's true of any language.

Japanese grammar is much simpler than that of German or French or, say, Punjabi, with its array of nominative, genitive, accusative-dative, instrumental, ablative, locative, and vocative cases—one for every day of the week. And you know those "three writing systems" you hear so much about? That, as our Russian friends say, is a bunch of hooey. Japanese is so wonderfully fun and rich precisely because it mixes three scripts—kanji, hiragana, and katakana, the second two of which can be learned, in a pinch, over a long weekend—into a single, very versatile writing system. It takes a while to learn the 1945 kanji identified by the Japanese government as appropriate "for general use," it's true, and the *Asahi Shimbun*, for instance, uses 66 more that aren't on this list; but when you get right down to it, how difficult is it to learn 2011 kanji, especially when they're all cobbled together from only two hundred some-odd parts? English, according to Masha Bell's spine-chilling *Understanding English Spelling*, makes use of more than 90 spelling rules, and even if you have these down pat (I certainly don't) you still have to memorize over 3700 irregular, irrational, and (to me) highly irritating spellings in order to become even moderately competent as a spellor—or rather, speller.

So you see, Japanese isn't an impossibly hard language. The problem stems from the fact that it just takes so much time to travel from here to there, the train ride gets old fast, we start to hate our flashcards, if only there were some fun way to while away the hours, a book to read, perhaps . . . and that's where *Read Real Japanese* enters the picture. The book you are holding in your hand right now is designed to be the perfect reading material for you on the linguistic trip you're taking: to help you have more fun getting where you're going, and to help you get there faster.

THE STORIES

The six stories in this collection are all amazing. I spent months putting together a list of candidates for inclusion, then mulling over the titles, trying to whittle the list down. The stories are also totally contemporary: only one, Kawakami Hiromi's "Kamisama," was first collected in a book prior to 2000; half of them were published between 2005 and 2008. And the authors, who write in all sorts of different literary genres—from horror to fantasy to mystery to avant-garde experimental fiction to children's stories to . . . well, "literary fiction," whatever that is—are all major figures, masters of their craft, writers who will leave you wanting to read more. They shouldn't be seen, though, as representative of Japanese fiction being written today, because there are just too many incredible writers producing unique, powerful works for any six figures to represent them all; despite their great stature, this magnificent six could have been augmented by any number of other writers, had the need for concision been less pressing. The dozens of stories and authors I had to cut from my original list were as fun and exciting as the ones you're about to read. Contemporary Japanese literature is, as you'll see, extremely good.

Of course, I don't expect you to take my word for it. I hope you won't—this book is only meant to tide you over until you reach the stage where you can saunter casually into a Japanese bookstore, scan the table of new releases, and pick out a book that looks like just the thing you're in the mood for. And, of course, until you have a versatile enough vocabulary and a subtle enough sense of recent trends in Japanese book design that you actually do end up with what you want, rather than something that looks eerily similar to what you want but turns out to be a recently retranslated philosophical novel about vomit or some such thing.

That said, I hope you will take my word for it, as you stand at the beginning of what may well be a rather extended commitment of energy and imagination, when I say that the stories in *this* book are all very, very good. I hope, too, that you will trust me when I tell you that it will be best not to shuffle the order of the stories too much. They've been arranged in what I believe is a good sequence, in an order that makes sense, like a well-planned meal. Which reminds me—I ought to explain each of the courses.

Soup Course

"Kamisama" by Kawakami Hiromi

This is the perfect starter. Refreshingly light and fairly easy to read, the prose has a delightful, humorous quirkiness to it that matches to a T the wackiness of the plot—not that there's much of a plot. "Kamisama" is what you might call an "idea" piece. And the idea is great! You'll find, I'm sure, that it offers an utterly enjoyable introduction to a few different varieties of language—notably the polite, even ceremonious speech of the bear (it's wacky, I told you!) and the written *de aru* style. There aren't too many kanji, and the grammar you'll learn is usefully basic in the sense that it will give you a good foundation to build upon as you go on and read the rest of the stories.

Appetizer

"Mukashi yūhi no kōen de" by Otsuichi

A glance at Otsuichi's photograph tells you that he's going to be confident and bold, and that's precisely what he is in this story. "Mukashi yūhi no kōen de" complements the charmingly desultory, warm-and-fuzzy atmosphere of "Kamisama" very nicely with its cool, dry, perfectly in-control but nonetheless gripping take on horror—if that's the word. Perhaps it isn't. There are no blood and guts, after all, just suspense. Impressively strong suspense that lasts right to the last line. The writing is sharp, simple, and focused; the kanji are quite manageable; and the vocabulary is everyday.

Fish Course

"Nikuya Ōmu" by Ishii Shinji

It seems a bit odd to have a story about a butcher for the fish course, but that's what we've got tonight—and I think you'll enjoy it. This piece, which echoes the playfulness of "Kamisama," is a good deal more plot-driven. A whole lot happens in its eleven pages. "Nikuya Ōmu" may be a little more demanding than "Kamisama," too: the author, Ishii Shinji, uses some not-so-common words, tosses in a few more new styles of speech for us to get used to, and spices up his text with a sprinkling of kanji that you may not have learned. I think you'll discover, though, that learning kanji by reading a story like this is a lot more fun than simply pouring over flashcards.

Meat Course

"Miira" by Yoshimoto Banana

Come to think of it, it's even odder—in fact it's beyond odd, it's even a tad gross—to have a story about a man who makes mummies for the meat course. But "Miira" has all the punch of a good steak. (Or perhaps, if you're a vegetarian, of a really, really good tomato.) Yoshimoto Banana's writing is harder than most experienced readers think, but it's worth making the effort to figure her sentences out. She uses Japanese in a way that few other writers do, skillfully melding the poetic and the colloquial, precise description and unspoken implication, the ordinary and the lovely and the painful and the profound, and doing it all in a way that looks (but isn't) almost unplanned. Her writing has its own, very particular flavor. Take your time with this story, savoring its challenges.

Cheese Course

"Hyakumonogatari" by Kitamura Kaoru

This story has something of the flavor of "Mukashi yūhi no kōen de": it's suspenseful and even a bit scary. The language is more challenging, though:

there are more kanji, the vocabulary is more advanced ("Mukashi yūhi no kōen de" is about an elementary school student, while the narrator of this story is in college), and you'll encounter a greater number of culturally specific references. "Hyakumonogatari" will also give you an opportunity to familiarize yourself with the different styles of speech that men and women often use in fiction—and, to an extent, depending on the age of the men and women in question, in real life. You'll find, too, that it illustrates beautifully what a good writer can do with a language that doesn't require that the subject of a sentence be explicitly stated.

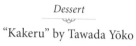

Dessert

"Kakeru" by Tawada Yōko

And finally—a delicious little taste, just a mouthful, of an incredibly rich, dizzyingly, dazzlingly mixed-up story. "Kakeru" is pure linguistic play. Perhaps you could compare it to a flourless chocolate cake, except that instead of omitting the flour, Tawada Yōko leaves out the plot. Completely. Wow. It might sound difficult, but it's not—this story was *made* for the language student. It was made for you.

THE STRUCTURE OF THE BOOK

If the stories have been arranged like a six-course dinner, the book as a whole has, more or less, the structure of a three-ring circus. In the main ring are the stories; in ring two, notes to the stories and a full-fledged dictionary containing every word that appears in the six texts, with the exception of certain particles and proper nouns; and in ring three, a recording of each of the stories, beautifully read by the actress Matsunaga Reiko.

As the title indicates, the whole idea behind *Read Real Japanese* is to give students of the language a chance to enjoy (yes, enjoy!) reading some real Japanese literature. So we've done everything we can to keep the stories as they were: not only are they presented in their full glory, unabridged and unedited—though Tawada Yōko kindly gave us permission to print a special, concentrated rewriting of "Kakeru" that she uses when she gives live readings—they have also been printed vertically, right to left, laid out just as they were in the Japanese books in which they were first collected.

The only changes that have been made are to number the paragraphs and to give the hiragana readings—the *furigana*—of every kanji word on its first appearance in each story.

The paragraph numbers will help you locate the tentative translations I offer, on the pages facing the texts, of potentially puzzling phrases; they will also guide you to the notes at the end of the book, which cover everything from grammatical patterns and the deep shades of meaning cast on sentences by seemingly insignificant particles, to the explanation of gestures and other bits of cultural background. I've done my best to keep the notes from becoming too mind-numbingly dry, and tried to strike a balance between reinforcement and repetitiveness. Most of the translations I give are for phrases rather than words, since you can look up individual words (using the convenient *furigana* readings!) in the dictionary at the end of the book, and because meaning is a product of context, and generally inheres in phrases and sentences, not words. You will notice, too, that the translations don't necessarily correspond in a "literal" one-to-one fashion to the Japanese phrases they translate, the way the English definitions in the dictionary correspond to the Japanese words they define. The translations are, ultimately, meant as samples: you will, I hope, come up with even better translations of your own.

On to the dictionary and the recordings. Like any dictionary, the one you have here comprises a list of words in dictionary form. In order to use it, you need to be able to derive this dictionary form from the conjugated form that appears in the text; when this seems likely to pose a problem, I give the game away in the notes. Generally speaking, I'd recommend that you limit your use of the dictionary—steer clear of becoming a dictionary addict. This book is called *Read Real Japanese*, after all, not *Look Up Real Japanese In the Dictionary*. The recordings, on the other hand, are something you will want to listen to repeatedly. Try listening to each story before you read it to see how much of it you can catch. The stories were read at a natural speed, so they will seem fast at first. Then, once you have taken your time reading through a given story, getting comfortable with it, go back and listen to the recording again, following along in the text with your finger—or, if you prefer, without your finger. If you can keep up, you're well on your way to becoming a fluent reader. Finally, listen to the recording once more and try to repeat after the narrator—shadowing her voice, as it were—doing your best to learn as much as you can from her pronunciation and enunciation. This is a good way to solidify your grasp on new words, and to train yourself to say new things, in a new accent and intonation.

I started out with a train ride and ended up talking about training. Either way, learning a new language is one of the most exciting intellectual and cultural activities a person can undertake, and the moment when she begins to read in that new language is one of the most thrilling in the whole long, frustrating, rewarding, mind-bending, eye-opening, and, of course, practically useful process. I hope this book helps you get wherever you're going with Japanese faster, and with a good deal more pleasure than you would have without it.

ACKNOWLEDGMENTS

I would like to extend my warmest thanks to the people who, in various ways, indirectly or directly, made this book possible: All my Japanese teachers, but especially Makino Seiichi, Mizumoto Terumi, and Uemiya Mariko; Itō Kiyo, the most wonderful host mother imaginable; and Michael Staley, whose editorial astuteness and savvy made this book not only possible but real and useful and, I hope you will agree, exciting.

To download the audio files, search for "Read Real Japanese Fiction" at kodansha.us.

川上弘美

Kawakami Hiromi

Some authors never let you down. In my experience, Kawakami Hiromi is one of these: I've enjoyed every one of her books, from her first collection of stories to her most recent novel.

As it happens, the story you are about to read, "Kamisama"—"God" would be a decent translation, though you might be able to come up with something better—is from that fantastic first collection, which was also titled *Kamisama*. Indeed, "Kamisama" was the first story Kawakami ever wrote. She submitted it to an online literary competition in 1994, took the prize, and had the pleasure of seeing it published in *GQ Japan*. When the collection finally came out from the publishing house Chūōkōron-Shinsha in 1998, it was awarded both the Murasaki Shikibu Prize and the Bunkamura Deux Magots Literary Prize. And Kawakami has only gotten better since she started. She won the prestigious Akutagawa Prize in 1996 for the story "Hebi o fumu" ("To Tread on a Snake") and the Tanizaki Jun'ichirō Prize for her novel *Sensei no kaban* (*The Teacher's Briefcase*). Either of these two works would be a good place to start reading more. If you're feeling ambitious, the 2006 novel *Manazuru* (the title is the name of a town about an hour from Tokyo by train) is a quiet, gorgeous masterpiece.

Kawakami was born in Tokyo on April Fool's Day, 1958. At the time of writing, then, she is likely to have eaten about 54,364 meals in her lifetime—give or take a few. Judging from her fiction, she has probably savored just about every one. Kawakami is an unmistakable "foodie," and her fiction includes dozens of the most mouthwatering descriptions of food I've ever come across. It's fitting, I suppose, that "Kamisama" is all about a picnic.

神様

川上弘美

くまにさそわれて散歩に出る。川原に行くのである。歩いて二十分ほどのところにある川原である。春先に、鴫を見るために、行ったことはあったが、暑い季節にこうして弁当まで持っていくのは初めてである。散歩というよりハイキングといったほうがいいかもしれない。

くまは、雄の成熟したくまで、だからとても大きい。三つ隣の305号室に、つい最近越してきた。ちかごろの引越しには珍しく、引越し蕎麦を同じ階の住人にふるまい、葉書を十枚ずつ渡してまわっていた。ずいぶんな気の遣いようだと思ったが、くまであるから、やはりいろいろとまわりに対する配慮が必要なのだろう。

ところでその蕎麦を受け取ったときの会話で、くまとわたしとは満更赤の他人というわけでもないことがわかったのである。

神様 God

1 くまにさそわれて散歩に出る having been invited by a bear, I set out on a walk ▪ 川原に行くのである we go to the riverbank ▪ 歩いて二十分ほどのところにある川原である it's a riverbank located about twenty minutes away on foot ▪ 春先に in early spring ▪ 鴫を見るために、行ったことはあったが I had gone to see the snipes, but ▪ 暑い季節に in the hot season ▪ こうして in this way ▪ 弁当まで持っていくのは taking along a lunch ▪ 初めてである it was the first time ▪ 散歩というよりハイキングといったほうがいい it would be more accurate to say we set out on a hike, rather than a walk ▪ かもしれない perhaps

2 くまは、雄の成熟したくまで、だからとても大きい the bear was a mature male bear, so he was very big ▪ 三つ隣の305号室に to room 305, which was three doors down ▪ つい最近 just a few days ago ▪ 越してきた had moved in ▪ ちかごろの引越しには珍しく following a custom that now seldom plays a part in a move ▪ 引越し蕎麦 (see note on p. 52 at back) ▪ …を同じ階の住人にふるまい distributed…to the people living on the same floor, and ▪ 葉書を十枚ずつ ten postcards each ▪ 渡してまわっていた went around passing out ▪ ずいぶんな気の遣いようだと思ったが it struck me as quite a display of solicitude, but ▪ くまであるから insofar as he was a bear ▪ やはり as you might expect ▪ いろいろと in various ways ▪ まわりに対する配慮が必要なのだろう it was necessary to show some consideration to the neighbors

3 ところで at any rate ▪ その蕎麦を受け取ったときの会話で as a result of the talk we had when I accepted my soba ▪ くまとわたしとは the bear and I ▪ 満更赤の他人というわけでもないこと that we were not exactly complete strangers ▪ わかったのである it became clear

表札を見たくまが、

「もしや某町のご出身では」

と訊ねる。確かに、と答えると、以前くまがたいへん世話になった某君の叔父という人が町の役場助役であったという。その助役の名字がわたしのものと同じであり、たどってみると、どうやら助役はわたしの父のまたいとこに当たるらしいのである。あるか無しかわからぬような繋がりであるが、くまはたいそう感慨深げに「縁」というような種類の言葉を駆使していろいろと述べた。どうも引越しの挨拶の仕方といい、この喋り方といい、昔気質のくまらしいのではあった。

そのくまと、散歩のようなハイキングのようなことをしている。動物には詳しくないので、ツキノワグマなのか、ヒグマなのか、はたまたマレーグマなのかは、わからない。面と向かって訊ねるのも失礼である気がする。名前もわからない。なんと呼びかければいいのかと質問してみたのであるが、近隣にくまが一匹もいないことを確認してから、

4 | 表札を見たくま noticing the nameplate on the door, the bear

5 | もしや...では you wouldn't, by any chance, happen to be...? ■ 某町のご出身 a native of such-and-such a town

6 | と訊ねる he asked ■ 確かに indeed I am ■ と答えると when I replied ■ 以前くまがたいへん世話になった某君の叔父という人 a person who was, evidently, the uncle of a certain someone who had given the bear a lot of assistance ■ 町の役場助役であったという had served at town hall as deputy mayor, he said ■ その助役の名字 this deputy mayor's family name ■ わたしのものと同じであり was the same as mine, and ■ たどってみると when you trace your way back ■ どうやら...らしい it would seem that... ■ またいとこ second cousin ■ ...に当たる be one and the same as... ■ あるか無しかわからぬような繋がりであるが it was an almost nonexistent relationship, and yet ■ たいそう considerably ■ 感慨深げに looking deeply moved ■「縁」というような種類の言葉を駆使して making liberal use of words of the "*enishi*" variety ■ いろいろと述べた went on ■ どうも...らしい judging from appearances, [the bear] seemed to be... ■ 引越しの挨拶の仕方といい、この喋り方といい the fashion in which he introduced himself to his new neighbors, the way in which he spoke... ■ 昔気質のくま an old-fashioned type of bear

7 | 散歩のようなハイキングのようなこと something between a walk and a hike ■ 動物には詳しくないので I don't know much about animals, so ■ ツキノワグマなのか、ヒグマなのか whether it was a Japanese white collar bear or a brown bear ■ はたまた or then again ■ マレーグマ a Malay bear ■ 面と向かって訊ねるのも asking him right to his face ■ 失礼である気がする I had a feeling it would be rude ■ なんと呼びかければいいのか how should I address him? ■ ...と質問してみたのであるが I tried asking...but ■ 近隣にくまが一匹もいないことを確認してから after verifying that there weren't any other bears in the area

「今のところ名はありませんし、僕しかくまがいないのなら今後も名をなのる必要がないわけですね。呼びかけの言葉としては、貴方、が好きですが、ええ、漢字の貴方です、口に出すときに、ひらがなではなく漢字を思い浮かべてくだされればいいんですが、まあ、どうぞご自由に何とでもお呼びください」

との答えである。どうもやはり少々大時代なくまである。大時代なうえに理屈を好む

とみた。

川原までの道は水田に沿っている。舗装された道で、時おり車が通る。どの車もわたしたちの手前でスピードを落とし、徐行しながら大きくよけていく。すれちがう人影はない。たいへん暑い。田で働く人も見えない。くまの足がアスファルトを踏む、かすかなしゃりしゃりという音だけが規則正しく響く。

暑くない？　と訊ねると、くまは、

「暑くないけれど長くアスファルトの道を歩くと少し疲れます」

8 | 今のところ for the time being ▪ 名はありませんし I have no name, and moreover ▪ 僕しかくまがいないのなら if I really am the only bear ▪ 今後も in the future, as well ▪ 名をなのる必要がないわけですね that means there's no need to introduce myself by name, doesn't it? ▪ 呼びかけの言葉としては、貴方、が好きです I like the word *anata* as a form of address ▪ ええ yes, that's right ▪ 漢字の貴方 *anata* written in kanji ▪ 口に出すときに when you say it ▪ ひらがなではなく漢字を思い浮かべてくだされればいいんですが it would be wonderful if you could have the kanji rather than the hiragana in mind, but ▪ まあ、どうぞご自由に何とでもお呼びください it's not a big deal, feel free to address me however you like

9 | との答えである was his answer ▪ どうもやはり it does indeed appear that ▪ 少々大時代なくまである he is a somewhat antiquated bear ▪ 大時代なうえに理屈を好む not only is he antiquated, he also has a taste for logic ▪ ...とみた I concluded that...

10 | 川原までの道は the road to the river ▪ 水田に沿っている ran along the edge of some rice paddies ▪ 舗装された道で the road was paved, and ▪ 時おり from time to time ▪ 車が通る a car would pass by ▪ どの車も every car (lit., "no matter which car it was") ▪ わたしたちの手前で a little before they reached us ▪ スピードを落とし would slow down and ▪ 徐行しながら moving slowly ▪ 大きくよけていく go by, swerving way out to avoid us ▪ すれちがう人影はない no one passed by, going in the other direction ▪ たいへん暑い it was sweltering ▪ 田で働く人も見えない there was no one to be seen working in the paddies, either ▪ くまの足がアスファルトを踏む、かすかなしゃりしゃりという音 the faint scrape of the bear's feet treading the asphalt ▪ 規則正しく響く sounded regularly

11 | 暑くない? aren't you hot?

12 | 長くアスファルトの道を歩くと when I walk on asphalt for a long time ▪ 少し疲れます I get a little tired

と答えた。

「川原まではそう遠くないから大丈夫、ご心配くださってありがとう」

続けて言う。さらには、

「もしあなたが暑いのなら国道に出てレストハウスにでも入りますか」

などと、細かく気を配ってくれる。わたしは帽子をかぶっていたし暑さには強いほうなので断ったが、もしかするとくま自身が一服したかったのかもしれない。しばらく無言で歩いた。

遠くに聞こえはじめた水の音がやがて高くなり、わたしたちは川原に到着した。たくさんの人が泳いだり釣りをしたりしている。荷物を下ろし、タオルで汗をぬぐった。くまは舌を出して少しあえいでいる。そうやって立っていると、男性二人子供一人の三人連れが、そばに寄ってきた。どれも海水着をつけている。男の片方はサングラスをかけ、もう片方はシュノーケルを首からぶらさげていた。

14 そう遠くないから、大丈夫 it's not that far, though, so I'll be okay ▪ ご心配くださってありがとう thank you for your concern

15 続けて言う he continued ▪ さらには then

16 もしあなたが暑いのなら if you should happen to feel hot ▪ 国道に出てレストハウスにでも入りますか we could head out to the highway and go to the rest stop or something, if you'd like

17 などと、細かく気を配ってくれる he said, among other things, showing me every consideration ▪ わたしは帽子をかぶっていたし I was wearing a hat, and furthermore ▪ 暑さには強いほうなので I bear up fairly well under the heat, so ▪ 断ったが I declined, though ▪ もしかすると...かもしれない it was possible that ▪ くま自身 the bear himself ▪ 一服したかった wanted to take a break ▪ しばらく無言で歩いた we walked on for a while without speaking

18 遠くに聞こえはじめた水の音 the sound of running water, which we came to hear in the distance ▪ やがて before long ▪ 高くなり grew louder, and ▪ わたしたちは川原に到着した we arrived at the riverbank ▪ 泳いだり釣りをしたりしている were swimming and fishing and so on ▪ 荷物を下ろし I set down my bags and ▪ タオルで汗をぬぐった wiped away my sweat with a towel ▪ 舌を出して少しあえいでいる was panting a little, his tongue hanging out ▪ そうやって立っていると as we were standing there like that ▪ 男性二人子供一人の三人連れ a group of three—two men and a child ▪ そばに寄ってきた came over ▪ どれも海水着をつけている they all had on bathing suits ▪ 男の片方は one of the men ▪ サングラスをかけ was wearing sunglasses, and ▪ もう片方は the other ▪ シュノーケルを首からぶらさげていた had a snorkel hanging from his neck

「お父さん、くまだよ」

子供が大きな声で言った。

「そうだ、よくわかったな」

シュノーケルが答える。

「くまだよ」

「そうだ、くまだ」

「ねえねえくまだよ」

何回かこれが繰り返された。シュノーケルはわたしの表情をちらりとうかがったが、くまの顔を正面から見ようとはしない。サングラスの方は何も言わずにただ立っている。子供はくまの毛を引っ張ったり、蹴りつけたりしていたが、最後に「パーンチ」と叫んでくまの腹のあたりにこぶしをぶつけてから、走って行ってしまった。男二人はぶらぶらと後を追う。

「いやはや」

19 | くまだよ it's a bear!

20 | 大きな声で in a loud voice

21 | よくわかったな you sure figured that out well!

22 | シュノーケルが答える replied the snorkel

25 | ねえねえくまだよ hey, hey, it's a bear!

26 | 何回か several times ■ これが this back-and-forth ■ 繰り返された was repeated ■ わたしの表情をちらりとうかがったが shot a glance my way, to see if he could read my expression, but ■ くまの顔を正面から見ようとはしない made no attempt to look at the bear's face straight on ■ サングラスの方は the one wearing the sunglasses ■ 何も言わずに without saying anything ■ ただ立っている just stood there ■ くまの毛を引っ張ったり、蹴りつけたりしていたが was pulling the bear's fur and kicking him and so on, but then ■ 最後に「パーンチ」と叫んで finally he yelled "Punch!" and ■ くまの腹のあたりに in the vicinity of the bear's stomach ■ こぶしをぶつけてから、走って行ってしまった after hitting him with his fist, he ran off ■ ぶらぶらと後を追う wandered lazily after him

27 | いやはや sheesh

しばらくしてからくまが言った。

「小さい人は邪気がないですなあ」

私は無言でいた。

「そりゃいろいろな人間がいますから。でも、子供さんはみんな無邪気ですよ」

そう言うと、わたしが答える前に急いで川のふちへ歩いていってしまった。

小さな細い魚がすいすい泳いでいる。水の冷気がほてった顔に心地よい。よく見ると魚は一定の幅の中で上流へ泳ぎまた下流へ泳ぐ。細長い四角の辺をたどっているように見える。その四角が魚の縄張りなのだろう。くまも、じっと水の中を見ている。何を見ているのか。くまの目にも水の中は人間と同じに見えているのであろうか。

突然水しぶきがあがり、くまが水の中にざぶざぶ入っていった。川の中ほどで立ち止まると右掌をさっと水にくぐらせ、魚を摑み上げた。岸辺を泳ぐ細長い魚の三倍はありそうなものだ。

「驚いたでしょう」

28 しばらくしてから after a while

29 小さい人は邪気がないですなあ ah, the little ones...they haven't a shred of ill will in them

30 私は無言でいた I remained silent

31 そりゃいろいろな人間がいますから sure, there are all kinds of people out there, it's true ■ 子供さんはみんな無邪気ですよ children never mean any harm

32 そう言うと with that ■ 急いで川のふちへ歩いていってしまった he hurried off toward the edge of the river

33 小さな細い魚 small, thin fish ■ すいすい泳いでいる were effortlessly swimming along ■ 水の冷気がほてった顔に心地よい the cool of the water felt good on my flushed face ■ よく見ると looking closely, I saw that ■ 一定の幅の中で within a certain fixed span ■ 上流へ泳ぎまた下流へ泳ぐ they swam upstream, then swam back downstream ■ 細長い四角の辺をたどっているように見える they seemed to be tracing the sides of a long, narrow rectangle ■ その四角が魚の縄張りなのだろう that rectangle must be the fishes' territory ■ じっと without moving ■ くまの目にも水の中は人間と同じに見えているのであろうか did things in the water look the same to the bear as they did to humans?

34 突然水しぶきがあがり there was a sudden splash, and ■ 水の中にざぶざぶ入っていった sloshed into the water ■ 川の中ほどで立ち止まると he stopped and stood in the middle of the river, whereupon ■ 右掌をさっと水にくぐらせ he quickly thrust his right hand into the water and ■ ...を摑み上げた snatched up... ■ 岸辺を泳ぐ細長い魚 the long, slender fish swimming along the bank ■ 三倍はありそうなものだ looked to be about three times bigger

35 驚いたでしょう I bet you're surprised

戻ってきたくまが言った。

「おことわりしてから行けばよかったのですが、つい足が先に出てしまいまして。大きい
でしょう」

くまは、魚をわたしの目の前にかざした。魚のひれが陽を受けてきらきら光る。釣りを
している人たちがこちらを指さして何か話している。くまはかなり得意そうだ。

「さしあげましょう。今日の記念に」

そう言うと、くまは担いできた袋の口を開けた。取り出した布の包みの中からは、小さ
なナイフとまな板が出てきた。くまは器用にナイフを使って魚を開くと、これもかねて用
意してあったらしい粗塩をぱっぱと振りかけ、広げた葉の上に魚を置いた。

「何回か引っくり返せば、帰る頃にはちょうどいい干物になっています」

何から何まで行き届いたくまである。

わたしたちは、草の上に座って川を見ながら弁当を食べた。くまは、フランスパンのと
ころどころに切れ目を入れてパテとラディッシュをはさんだもの、わたしは梅干し入りの

36 | 戻ってきたくま the bear, on his return

37 | おことわりしてから行けばよかったのですが I ought to have said something before I went, but ■ つい足が先に出てしまいまして my feet just started moving

38 | 魚をわたしの目の前にかざした held the fish out right in front of me ■ 魚のひれ the fish's fins ■ 陽を受けて in the sunlight ■ きらきら光る glittered ■ こちらを指さして何か話している were pointing in our direction, talking about something ■ くまはかなり得意そうだ the bear seemed quite proud of himself

39 | さしあげましょう this is for you ■ 今日の記念に as a memento of this day

40 | そう言うと so saying ■ 担いできた袋の口を開けた opened the top of the bag he'd brought with him ■ 取り出した布の包みの中からは from the cloth bundle he took out of it ■ 小さなナイフとまな板が出てきた a small knife and a chopping board emerged ■ 器用にナイフを使って making dexterous use of his knife ■ 魚を開くと when he had cut open the fish ■ これもかねて用意してあったらしい粗塩 fresh bay salt, which he had evidently also prepared in advance ■ …をぱっぱと振りかけ the bear sprinkled on…with a few shakes, and ■ 広げた葉の上に魚を置いた set it down on some leaves that he had spread out

41 | 何回か引っくり返せば if you flip it over a few times ■ 帰る頃にはちょうどいい干物になっています it will be just dry enough by the time we head home

42 | 何から何まで everything, from start to finish ■ 行き届いた attentive to detail

43 | 草の上に座って sat on the grass and ■ フランスパンのところどころに here and there in a loaf of French bread ■ 切れ目を入れてパテとラディッシュをはさんだもの with pâté and radishes tucked into incisions he had made ■ 梅干し入りのおむすび an *onigiri* (rice ball) with *umeboshi* (pickled plum) in it

29 　　神様

おむすび、食後には各自オレンジの皮を一個ずつ。ゆっくりと食べおわると、くまは、

「もしよろしければオレンジの皮をいただけますか」

と言い、受け取ると、わたしに背を向けて、いそいで皮を食べた。

少し離れたところに置いてある魚を引っくり返しに行き、ナイフとまな板とコップを流れで丁寧に洗い、それを拭き終えると、くまは袋から大きいタオルを取り出し、わたしに手渡した。

「昼寝をするときにお使いください。僕はそのへんをちょっと歩いてきます。もしよかったらその前に子守歌を歌ってさしあげましょうか」

真面目に訊く。

子守歌なしでも眠れそうだとわたしが答えると、くまはがっかりした表情になったが、すぐに上流の方へ歩み去った。

目を覚ますと、木の影が長くなっており、横にくまが寝ていた。タオルはかけていない。小さくいびきをかいている。川原には、もう数名の人しか残っていない。みな、釣りをす

■ 食後には各自オレンジを一個ずつ one orange each after our meal ■ ゆっくりと食べおわると after we had leisurely tucked away our meal

44 もしよろしければ if it's all right with you ■ オレンジの皮をいただけますか might I have the peel of your orange?

45 受け取ると when he had taken it ■ わたしに背を向けて he turned his back to me and

46 少し離れたところに置いてある魚 the fish, which he had set out a little distance away ■ …を引っくり返しに行き he went off to flip… ■ 流れで in the river ■ 丁寧に洗い carefully washed, and ■ それを拭き終えると when he had finished drying them ■ わたしに手渡した handed it to me

47 昼寝をするときに when you have your nap ■ お使いください please use this ■ 僕はそのへんをちょっと歩いてきます I'm going to take a little walk around ■ もしよかったら if you'd like ■ 子守歌を歌ってさしあげましょうか shall I sing you a lullaby?

48 真面目に訊く he asked earnestly

49 子守歌なしでも眠れそうだ I think I'll be able to sleep without a lullaby ■ がっかりした表情になったが looked disappointed, but ■ 上流の方へ歩み去った walked off upstream

50 目を覚ますと when I awoke ■ 木の影が長くなっており the shadows of the trees had lengthened, and ■ 横にくまが寝ていた the bear was sleeping beside me ■ タオルはかけていない he didn't have a towel over him ■ 小さくいびきをかいている he was snoring quietly ■ もう数名の人しか残っていない by now only a few people remained

る人である。くまにタオルをかけてから、干し魚を引っくり返しにいくと、魚は三匹に増えていた。

51 「いい散歩でした」
くまは305号室の前で、袋から鍵を取り出しながら言った。

52 「またこのような機会を持ちたいものですな」

53 わたしも頷いた。それから、干し魚やそのほかの礼を言うと、くまは大きく手を振って、

55 「とんでもない」
と答えるのだった。

57 「では」
と立ち去ろうとすると、くまが、

59 「あの」

■ 干し魚 dried fish ■ 魚は三匹に増えていた there were now three fish

52 | 鍵を取り出しながら while taking out the key

53 | またこのような機会を持ちたいものですな I certainly hope we'll have more occasions to do things together like this

54 | わたしも頷いた I nodded, agreeing ■ 干し魚やそのほかの礼を言うと when I thanked him for the dried fish and everything else ■ 大きく手を振って waving his hand energetically back and forth

55 | とんでもない not at all

57 | では well then...

58 | と立ち去ろうとすると I said, and was just making to leave when

59 | あの uhm...

と言う。次の言葉を待ってくまを見上げるが、もじもじして黙っている。ほんとうに大きなくまである。その大きなくまが、喉の奥で「ウルル」というような音をたてながら恥ずかしそうにしている。言葉を喋る時には人間と同じ発声法なのであるが、こうして言葉にならない声を出すときや笑うときは、やはりくま本来の発声なのである。

「抱擁を交わしていただけますか」

くまは言った。

「親しい人と別れるときの故郷の習慣なのです。もしお嫌ならもちろんいいのですが」

わたしは承知した。

くまは一歩前に出ると、両腕を大きく広げ、その腕をわたしの肩にまわし、頰をわたしの頰にこすりつけた。くまの匂いがする。反対の頰も同じようにこすりつけると、もう一度腕に力を入れてわたしの肩を抱いた。思ったよりもくまの体は冷たかった。

「今日はほんとうに楽しかったです。遠くへ旅行して帰ってきたような気持ちです。熊の神様のお恵みがあなたの上にも降り注ぎますように。それから干し魚はあまりもちません

60 次の言葉を待ってくまを見上げるが I looked up at the bear, waiting for him to go on, but ■ もじもじして黙っている he remained silent, fidgeting ■ 喉の奥で in the back of his throat ■ 「ウルル」というような音をたてながら making a sound along the lines of "ururu" ■ 恥ずかしそうにしている he was looking bashful ■ 言葉を喋る時には when he talked using words ■ 人間と同じ発声法なのであるが he used his voice the same way humans do, but ■ 言葉にならない声を出すときや笑うときは when he made noise that wasn't speech, and laughed, and so on ■ くま本来の発声 the vocalization proper to bears

61 抱擁を交わしていただけますか might you be so good as to hug me?

63 親しい人と別れるときの故郷の習慣なのです this is the custom in my hometown when two people who are close to each other say good-bye ■ もしお嫌ならもちろんいいのですが of course, it's quite all right if you don't want to

64 わたしは承知した I assented

65 くまは一歩前に出ると the bear took a step forward and ■ 両腕を大きく広げ spread his arms wide ■ その腕をわたしの肩にまわし wrapped those arms around my shoulders ■ 頬をわたしの頬にこすりつけた rubbed his cheek against mine ■ くまの匂いがする he smelled like a bear ■ 反対の頬 his other cheek ■ 同じように in the same way ■ もう一度 once again ■ 腕に力を入れてわたしの肩を抱いた he hugged my shoulders, putting a lot of strength into his arms ■ 思ったよりもくまの体は冷たかった the bear's body was colder than I expected

66 今日はほんとうに楽しかったです I really had a wonderful time today ■ 遠くへ旅行して帰ってきたような気持ちです I feel as if I've traveled somewhere very far, and then come back home again ■ 熊の神様のお恵みがあなたの上にも降り注ぎますように may the blessings of the bear god rain down upon you, too ■ あまりもちませんから doesn't keep very long, so

から、今夜のうちに召し上がるほうがいいと思います」

部屋に戻って魚を焼き、風呂に入り、眠る前に少し日記を書いた。熊の神とはどのようなものか、想像してみたが、見当がつかなかった。悪くない一日だった。

今夜のうちに tonight ◾ 召し上がるほうがいい it will be best if you eat them

67 | 部屋に戻って魚を焼き、風呂に入り、眠る前に少し日記を書いた I went back into my apartment and grilled the fish, had a bath, and wrote a bit in my diary before going to bed ◾ 熊の神とはどのようなものか、想像してみたが I tried to imagine what the bear god might be like, but ◾ 見当がつかなかった I hadn't the slightest idea ◾ 悪くない一日だった it wasn't a bad day

乙 一

Otsuichi

In 1996, when he was only seventeen and still in high school, Otsuichi was awarded the Jump Prize for Novels and Nonfiction for a work of horror, narrated from the perspective of a corpse, titled *Natsu to hanabi to watashi no shitai* (*Summer, Fireworks, and My Dead Body*). This was the start of a dazzling, genre-hopping career for Otsuichi, who devoted his energies early on to fiction in an illustrated, usually paperback genre known as "light novels" that tends to target fairly young readers, but soon began writing hardback books for adults. A number of his works have been turned into manga and movies.

Otsuichi was born in 1978 in Fukuoka Prefecture, which makes him the youngest writer in this book by a good twelve years. He's such a skilled storyteller, though, that he seems as if he ought to be a grandfather. If you enjoy the story I've included here—"Mukashi yūhi no kōen de" ("Long Ago, In the Park at Twilight"), which first appeared in book form in 2006 in *ZOO 2*—you might want to try reading some of the other stories in *ZOO 2*, or in *ZOO 1* (both volumes published by Shūeisha). Then maybe you could see the movie that was made of five of the stories in this series. For a very different sampling of his fiction, I'd recommend the 2003 collection *Ushinawareru monogatari* (*A Tale of Being Lost*), which pairs five stories from Otsuichi's "light novel" days with a few newer pieces. The title story, told from the point of view (so to speak) of a man left paralyzed and deprived of all five of his senses—except for the sense of touch, and that only on his right arm—is marvelous.

むかし夕日の公園で

乙一

1　小学生のとき、近所にこぢんまりとした公園があった。高い建物に囲まれており、夕方になると車の音や人のざわめきは消え去る。あとは静かな空間に、だれかの忘れた子供用の小さな靴がひとつころがっているだけになるような公園だった。

2　夕飯の時間になっていっしょに遊んでいた友達が家に帰っても、僕は両親が帰ってくるまで公園で時間をつぶしていなければいけなかった。

3　一人でブランコをこぐのにあきると、まるで何かから呼ばれたように僕は砂場で遊んだ。その公園の隅には砂場があった。しかし普段、子供たちはブランコや滑り台に夢中で、その一画はいつも忘れられていた。

4　建物と建物の間から差し込む太陽が音もなく世界を赤くにじませる夕方、話し相手もなく砂場で遊んだ。だれが置いていったのかわからないプラスチックの黄色いバケツがあっ

むかし夕日の公園で Long Ago, In the Park at Twilight

1　小学生のとき when I was in elementary school ▪ 近所に in the neighborhood ▪ こぢんまりとした公園 a little park ▪ 高い建物に囲まれており it was surrounded by tall buildings, and ▪ 夕方になると when evening fell ▪ 車の音や人のざわめき the noise of the cars and the sounds of people ▪ 消え去る vanished, leaving no trace ▪ あとは...になるような公園だった it was the sort of park that turns into...after that ▪ 静かな空間に a silent space in which... ▪ だれかの忘れた子供用の小さな靴 a small child's shoe that someone had forgotten ▪ ひとつころがっているだけ lay on its side on the ground

2　夕飯の時間になって when dinnertime rolled around ▪ いっしょに遊んでいた友達が家に帰っても even after the friends I'd been playing with went home ▪ 両親が帰ってくるまで until my parents came home ▪ 時間をつぶしていなければいけなかった I had to stay there killing time

3　一人でブランコをこぐのにあきると when I got tired of playing by myself on the swings ▪ まるで何かから呼ばれたように almost as though I had been summoned there by something ▪ 砂場で遊んだ I'd play in the sandbox ▪ その公園の隅には砂場があった in the corner of that park there was a sandbox ▪ 普段、子供たちはブランコや滑り台に夢中で ordinarily, the children were so engrossed with playing on the swings and the slide that ▪ その一画はいつも忘れられていた that corner was always forgotten

4　建物と建物の間から差し込む太陽 the sunlight shining down between the buildings ▪ 音もなく without a sound ▪ 世界を赤くにじませる夕方 evening, which makes the world run with red ▪ 話し相手もなく without anyone to talk to ▪ だれが置いていったのかわからない left behind by who knows who

た。靴を脱いで自分の足に砂をのせていく。砂はひやりとして、小さな粒が足の指の隙間に入り込んでいくのが心地よかった。

砂の中に深く手をつっこむという遊びもした。地中のどこまでが砂なのだろうかと、確かめたくなったのだ。

砂の中に腕を垂直に差し込むと、どこまでも深くもぐりこみ、最後には肩まで入るのではないか。このことを父に言ったとき、「砂場にも底はあるんだから、そんなはずがあるか」と信じてくれなかった。

父は間違っていると思った。現に、砂場の中に腕はどこまでも入るのだ。僕は何度も砂場の中に腕を差し込んでそれを確かめた。

それは何回目のことだったかすでに忘れてしまった。公園の隅に生えている木が夕日のために真っ黒な影絵のように見える時間、僕は右腕を砂の中に肩まで差し込んでいた。

指先に何かの当たる感触がした。砂の中に何かが埋まっているようだった。それはやわらかくて、冷たかった。僕はそれ

■ 靴を脱いで I took my shoes off and ■ 自分の足に砂をのせていく piled sand on my feet ■ 砂はひやりとして the sand felt cold, and ■ 小さな粒が足の指の隙間に入り込んでいくのが心地よかった it felt good having the tiny grains slip down between my toes

5 　砂の中に深く手をつっこむという遊びもした I amused myself, as well, by thrusting my hand deep down into the sand ■ 地中のどこまでが砂なのだろうかと how far down into the earth the sand went ■ 確かめたくなったのだ I had started wanting to check and see

6 　砂の中に腕を垂直に差し込むと when I stuck my arm straight down into the sand ■ どこまでも all the way ■ 深くもぐりこみ burrowed down deep ■ 最後には until finally ■ 肩まで入るのではないか darned if it didn't go in all the way to my shoulder ■ このこと what had happened ■「砂場にも底はあるんだから、そんなはずがあるか」"the sandbox has a bottom, you know—how could that be possible?" ■ と信じてくれなかった he said, and wouldn't believe me

7 　現に、砂場の中に腕はどこまでも入るのだ my arm really did go all the way into the sandbox ■ 何度も again and again ■ それを that [my arm went in all the way]

8 　それは the time when something happened ■ 何回目のことだったかすでに忘れてしまった I no longer recall how many times I had done it by then ■ 公園の隅に生えている木 the tree growing in the corner of the park ■ 夕日のために on account of the setting sun ■ 真っ黒な影絵のように見える時間 the time of day when it looked like a pitch-black shadow picture ■ 僕は右腕を砂の中に肩まで差し込んでいた I had my right arm thrust down in the sand up to my shoulder ■ 指先に何かの当たる感触がした I felt something brushing my fingers

9 　何かが埋まっているようだった something seemed to be buried

が何なのかを確かめようと、懸命に腕を砂場の奥底へ伸ばした。中指の先端がかろうじて触れるほど深いところに、ふっくらとして弾力のあるものがあった。つかんで引き上げたかったが、なかなか届かない。そのかわり、砂の中で指に何かが絡みつくのを感じた。砂

腕を引き抜いて確認すると、それは長い髪の毛だった。指に何本も絡みついていた。砂で汚れて傷んでいたが、それは女の子の髪の毛であるように思えた。

僕は再度、砂の中に腕を入れて、中に埋まっているものに触れようとした。しかし今度はいくら深く腕を入れても指先は何も見つけられない。僕は残念な気持ちになった。

赤い視界の中、公園のまわりを囲む高い建物は、どれも窓を閉め切っていて、巨大な壁のように僕とその砂場を切り取っていた。

不意に、砂の中へ入れていた右手に何かがつんと触れた気がした。魚がくちの先端でついたような、小さな感触だった。その直後に、手首をつかまれた。強い力だった。ぎりぎりと、手首がしめつけられる。腕を引き抜こうとしたが、右手は固定されたように動かなかった。周囲にはだれもおら

■ それが何なのかを確かめようと hoping to figure out what it was ■ 懸命に腕を砂場の奥底へ伸ばした I struggled to stretch my arm down to the very bottom of the sandbox ■ 中指の先端がかろうじて触れるほど深いところに down so deep that the tip of my middle finger could just barely brush against it ■ ふっくらとして弾力のあるもの something softly swollen and springy ■ つかんで引き上げたかったが I wanted to take hold of it and pull it up, but ■ なかなか届かない it was just out of reach ■ そのかわり instead ■ 指に何かが絡みつくのを感じた I felt something twining itself around my fingers

10 腕を引き抜いて確認すると when I pulled my arm out and looked it over ■ それは長い髪の毛だった it was long strands of human hair ■ 何本も several strands ■ 汚れて傷んでいたが they were dirty and damaged, but ■ それは女の子の髪の毛であるように思えた I had the impression that it was a girl's hair

11 再度 once again ■ 中に埋まっているものに触れようとした I tried to touch the thing that was buried in there ■ 今度は this time ■ いくら深く腕を入れても no matter how deep I thrust my arm in ■ 指先は何も見つけられない my fingers couldn't find anything ■ 僕は残念な気持ちになった I felt disappointed

12 赤い視界の中 within the red world before my eyes ■ 公園のまわりを囲む高い建物は the tall buildings enclosing the park ■ どれも窓を閉め切っていて every one had all its windows closed and ■ 巨大な壁のように僕とその砂場を切り取っていた cutting the sandbox and me off from the surroundings like an enormous wall

13 不意に all of a sudden ■ 砂の中へ入れていた右手 my right hand, which was down in the sand ■ …に何かがつんと触れた気がした I had the sense something had bumped up against… ■ 魚がくちの先端でつついたような、小さな感触だった it was just a small touch, as if a fish were pecking at me with the tip of its mouth

14 その直後に right after that ■ 手首をつかまれた something seized hold of my wrist ■ ぎりぎりと tightly ■ 手首がしめつけられる my wrist was squeezed ■ 腕を引き抜こうとしたが I tried to pull out my arm, but ■ 固定されたように動かなかった it felt as if it were fixed in place, and wouldn't move ■ 周囲にはだれもおらず there was no one around, so

ず、助けを呼んでも、声はただ建物に囲まれた公園に反響するだけだった。

15 砂の中で握り締めていた僕のこぶしが、何かの力で無理やり広げさせられた。手のひらに、小さなだれかの指先の感触がした。手のひらに、どうやら文字を書いているらしいと僕は気づいた。

16 17 の奥深くに差し込み、右手首をつかんでいるだれかの手の甲に指先で文字を書いた。砂の中にいるだれかは、僕の手のひらにそう書いた。僕は、地上にあった左腕を砂場

「ここからだして」

18 19 「だめ」

砂の中のだれかは残念そうに僕の右手首をはなした。僕は両腕を砂場から引き抜いて家に帰った。それ以来、砂場には近寄らなかった。公園が壊されてマンションになると き、砂場の様子を見に行ったが、中に何かが埋まるような深さはなかった。

■ 助けを呼んでも even when I called for help ■ 声はただ建物に囲まれた公園に反響するだけだった my voice simply echoed through the building-enclosed park

15 | 握り締めていた僕のこぶし my fist, which I had been clenching tightly ■ 無理やり広げさせられた was forcibly pried open ■ 手のひらに、小さなだれかの指先の感触がした I felt the touch of the small tips of someone's fingers on my palm ■ どうやら文字を書いているらしいと僕は気づいた I realized that she seemed to be writing something

16 | ここからだして get me out of here

17 | 砂の中にいるだれかは whoever was down there in the sand ■ そう書いた wrote those words ■ 地上にあった左腕 my left arm, which was above ground ■ ...の奥深くに down into the deepest reaches of... ■ 右手首をつかんでいるだれかの手の甲に on the back of whoever's hand was holding my right wrist

18 | だめ no

19 | 残念そうに僕の右手首をはなした released my hand, seeming disappointed ■ 両腕 both arms ■ それ以来 after that ■ 砂場には近寄らなかった I didn't go near the sandbox ■ 公園が壊されてマンションになるとき when [I heard] the park was to be wrecked and turned into an apartment building ■ 砂場の様子を見に行ったが I went to take a look at the sandbox, but ■ 中に何かが埋まるような深さはなかった it didn't look deep enough for anything to be buried within it

いしいしんじ

Ishii Shinji

In the early nineties, a small but conspicuous chorus line of thrillingly inventive writers started high-kicking their way into the limelight from backstage regions that seemed all but unrelated to the literary scene. Machida Kou and Nakahara Masaya, two of my own favorites, got their start as punk rockers. Kawakami Hiromi, whose story "Kamisama" appears in this volume, was a biology teacher. Abe Kazushige wandered into literature from film school.

Ishii Shinji is a half-member, I'd say, of this motley crew: as a young man he was determined to enroll in art school, and only ended up studying French literature at Kyoto University because this dream didn't pan out. He kept drawing, though: his first book, published in 1994 by a company that specializes in picture books—Ishii's all-hiragana name gives him the air of an author of children's books—is a funny, poignant, quirkily charming "illustrated travelogue" called *Amusuterudamu no inu* [*An Amsterdam Dog*]; his second, the irresistible novel *Buranko nori* [*A Kid on a Swing*], includes pictures, attributed to the narrator's younger brother, that Ishii himself drew at the age of four.

Ishii was born in Osaka in 1966 and raised in Kyoto. He has a distinctive, addictive prose style, a nose for evocative details, and is an incredibly good storyteller. He has authored or co-authored more than twenty books—novels, short story collections, books of essays, interviews—and, while some may grab you more than others, you can be sure that anything you pick up by him will be good. The story you're about to read, "Nikuya Ōmu" ("The Parrot Meat Market"), was first published in book form in *Shiro no tori to kuro no tori* [*White Birds and Black Birds*], which came out from Kadokawa Shoten in 2005. If you want to read more of Ishii Shinji's work, this collection is a great place to start. If you feel ready to lose yourself in a novel, *Buranko nori* is fantastic and short; *Pō no hanashi* [*Pō's Story*] is fantastic and long.

肉屋おうむ

いしいしんじ

1

「肉屋おうむ」は町はずれのほこりっぽい農道に建っていた。赤さびた鉄看板を真上に載せたコンクリートの平屋で、遠目には、路線バスの待合いか、空き瓶倉庫かなにかにみえた。けれど、だんだんと近づくにつれ、誰の耳にもきまちがえようのない、あの主人の声がきこえてくる。

2

「さあ、牛かい？　牛ならこうだ、ブオオオオッ！　な、いい響きだろう。じっさいこの肉は、いい声で鳴いたんだ。な、ブオオオオッ！　ブオオオオッ！」

肉屋は町にここ一軒しかなく、朝夕だいたいいつも、籠をさげた主婦たちの姿が店先にみられた。ぼくたちは通学の途中、かならず肉屋主人の口まねを耳にした（小学校も中学校も昔から農道の先にあった）。通りすがりに横目でのぞくと、小太りの主人が、声をあげながら目を真っ赤に染め、必死になって頬をふくらませていたりした。主婦たちは目

肉屋おうむ　50

肉屋おうむ The Parrot Meat Market

1 「肉屋おうむ」は "Parrot Meat Market" ■ 町はずれのほこりっぽい農道 a dusty farm road at the edge of town ■ …に建っていた stood along… ■ 赤さびた鉄看板を真上に載せた with a rusty iron sign perched right on top of it ■ コンクリートの平屋で it was a concrete one-story building ■ 遠目には seen from a distance ■ 路線バスの待合いか、空き瓶倉庫かなにかにみえた it looked like a bus station or a warehouse for empty bottles or something ■ だんだんと近づくにつれ as you gradually drew nearer ■ 誰の耳にもききまちがえようのない which no one could possibly mistake for any other ■ あの主人の声がきこえてくる that voice, belonging to the proprietor, becomes audible

2 さあ、牛かい? so, it's cow you want, is it? ■ 牛ならこうだ if it's a cow, it's like this ■ ブオオオオオッ! な、いい響きだろう buoooooh! How's that! Sounds great, doesn't it? ■ じっさいこの肉は、いい声で鳴いたんだ and as a matter of fact, this meat had a real nice moo

3 肉屋は町にここ一軒しかなく there was only this one meat market in town, and ■ 朝夕だいたいいつも…みられた morning and night… could almost always be seen ■ 籠をさげた主婦たちの姿 housewives holding baskets ■ 店先に in front of the store ■ ぼくたちは we ■ 通学の途中 on the way to school ■ かならず肉屋主人の口まねを耳にした would always hear the butcher doing his imitations ■ (小学校も中学校も (both the elementary school and the junior high school ■ 昔から since way back when ■ 農道の先に at the far end of the farm road ■ 通りすがりに as we passed by ■ 横目でのぞくと each time we shot him a sideways glance ■ 小太りの主人が、声をあげながら目を真っ赤に染め、必死になって頬をふくらませていたりした the plump butcher would be bellowing, his eyes bright red, frantically puffing up his cheeks ■ 目配せしあいながら while signaling to each other with their eyes

配せしあいながらにやにやと笑っていた。　肉を売るのと同じくらい、いや、ぼくたち子ども

もの目にはそれ以上の熱心さで、肉屋おうむの主人は、家畜の物まねに心血をそそいでい

るようにみえた。

彼の口まねは、ほんとうに見事だった。よそものが前を通ったなら、まちがいなく大農

場の家畜小屋と思いこんだことだろう。

牛に豚、羊に鶏。珍しく甲高いいななき声が店先から響いてくれば、農道をいく主婦た

ちには「ああ、馬肉がいったようだ」とわかるのだった。まいどあり、といって、空き缶にいれた

き缶と木箱で、ひづめの響きまで再現していた。肉屋の主人は、手にはめた空

おつりをじゃらじゃらと振った。

学校帰り、たまたまお客が誰もいなかったりすると、おうむの主人は物まねのこつを

こっそり披露してくれた。

「あのな、乳牛と肉牛じゃな、声のふるえがちがうんだよ」

喉の皮をひっぱって主人はつづける。

にやにやと笑っていた would be grinning ■ 肉を売るのと同じくらい just as much as selling meat ■ ぼくたち子どもの目には in the eyes of us kids ■ それ以上の熱心さで with even more enthusiasm than that (i.e., selling meat) ■ 家畜の物まねに心血をそそいでいるようにみえた it looked as though he was pouring his heart into his domestic animal imitations

4   ほんとうに見事だった was truly amazing ■ よそものが前を通ったなら if a stranger were to pass by ■ まちがいなく without any doubt ■ 大農場の家畜小屋と思いこんだことだろう he would have gotten the impression that the place was an animal shed belonging to some large farm

5   牛に豚、羊に鶏 cows and pigs, sheep and chickens ■ 珍しく甲高いいななき声が店先から響いてくれば on the rare occasion when a high-pitched whinny came bursting forth from the entrance to the store ■ 農道をいく主婦たち the housewives walking along the farm road ■ …には…とわかるのだった it would be clear to … ■ 馬肉がはいったようだ sounds like some horse meat has come in ■ 手にはめた空き缶と木箱で with empty cans and wooden boxes that he put on his hands ■ ひづめの響きまで再現していた he reproduced even the clip-clopping of their hooves ■ まいどあり thank you for your continued patronage ■ といって、空き缶にいれたおつりをじゃらじゃらと振った he'd say, giving the empty can into which he'd put the change a clattery shake

6   学校帰り on the way back from school ■ たまたまお客が誰もいなかったりすると if it happened that he had no customers ■ おうむの主人は物まねのこつをこっそり披露してくれた the proprietor of The Parrot would secretly let us in on the tricks of his mimicry

7   あのな (an exclamation that means something like "you see," "the thing is," "look," etc.) ■ 乳牛と肉牛じゃな、声のふるえがちがうんだよ milk cows and meat cows, they've got a different sort of tremolo in their voices

8   喉の皮をひっぱって主人はつづける the proprietor continues, pulling on the skin of his neck:

「乳牛は、どっちかといえば革袋から空気を押し出すような音だ。音色がやさしいんだ。角笛みたい

肉牛だと、ここんところに固い脂肪がたまってる。だからちょっぴり甲高い。

な、どことなくさびしい響きになる」

主人はもともとサーカス芸人だった。この世のどんな声、どんな音でもその場で再現し

てみせる「おうむ男」として世間に知られていた（ぼくはまだ生まれていなかった）。飛

行機のエンジン、ガラガラヘビのおどし、名女優のせりふ、よせくる波音。客席ではみ

な目をとじて、彼の喉から響くふしぎな物音にじっと耳をすませた。

おうむ男が肉屋に転身したのは、サーカスで死んだ馬を、市場へもっていったのがきっ

かけだったらしい。精肉商の親方が馬肉を買い取り、いっぽう、おうむ男は親方の娘に

ひと目ぼれした。弟子入りを決めた彼は、親方のもとでしばらく家畜のさばきかたや肉の

見分けかたを学んだ。ぼくたちの町に店をかまえたのは二十年も前のことになる。

奥さんが店先へ姿をみせることは滅多になかった。くしゃくしゃの髪をした、顔色の悪

い女で、たとえ三十年前だとしても、こんな女性にひと目ぼれしたなんて、ぼくたちに

9 どっちかといえば I suppose you could say ■ 革袋から空気を押し出すような音だ make a sound like air being squeezed out of a leather bag ■ 音色がやさしいんだ it's a gentle sound ■ 肉牛だと with meat cows ■ ここんところに right around here ■ 固い脂肪がたまってる there's a buildup of stiff fat ■ だからちょっぴり甲高い so they sound just the tiniest bit shrill ■ 角笛みたいな、どことなくさびしい響きになる they sound somehow lonely, like a hunting horn

10 主人はもともとサーカス芸人だった the butcher used to be in the circus ■ この世のどんな声、どんな音でも any kind of voice, any sort of sound in this world ■ その場で right on the spot ■ 再現してみせる「おうむ男」として世間に知られていた he was known to the community as the "Parrot Man," who could re-create ■ ぼくはまだ生まれていなかった I wasn't yet born then ■ 飛行機のエンジン、ガラガラヘビのおどし、名女優のせりふ、よせくる波音 the engine of an airplane, a rattlesnake's rattle, lines spoken by a famous actress, the rush of waves nearing the shore ■ 客席では out in the audience ■ みな目をとじて everyone would close their eyes and ■ 彼の喉から響くふしぎな物音にじっと耳をすませた listen, unmoving, to the amazing sounds that emerged from his throat

11 おうむ男が肉屋に転身したのは the Parrot Man's new life as a butcher ■ サーカスで死んだ馬を、市場へもっていったのがきっかけだったらしい seems to have gotten its start when he took a horse that had died in the circus to market ■ 精肉商の親方 the boss at the meat shop ■ 馬肉を買い取り bought the horse meat ■ いっぽう meanwhile ■ おうむ男は親方の娘にひと目ぼれした Parrot Man fell in love at first sight with the boss's daughter ■ 弟子入りを決めた彼は deciding to apprentice himself, he ■ 親方のもとで under the boss's tutelage ■ しばらく家畜のさばきかたや肉の見分けかたを学んだ spent a while learning how to butcher livestock and recognize quality meat ■ ぼくたちの町に店をかまえたのは二十年も前のことになる a good twenty years have passed since he set up shop in our town

12 奥さんが店先へ姿をみせることは滅多になかった his wife hardly ever appeared at the shop entrance ■ くしゃくしゃの髪をした、顔色の悪い女で she was a pallid woman with rumpled hair, and ■ たとえ三十年前だとしても even if it had been thirty years earlier ■ こんな女性にひと目ぼれしたなんて to think he'd fallen in love at first sight with a woman like her

はとてもほんとうだとは思えなかった。けれど主人はいつも陽気にふるまっていたし、自分で店を開いてから、奥さんとのあいだに息子までもうけていた。それがラーだ。ラーはぼくたちと同じ中学にかよっていたが、年は少なくとも五つは上だったと思う。

牛を立たせたような巨体だった。さまざまな声を自在に使いこなす父親とちがい、ラーはたったひとつのことばしか知らないようだった。授業中も、学校帰りも、町なかでいさつを送られても、彼はいつだって大口をひらき、こんなふうに叫ぶ。

「ラー！」

動物の鳴きまねが得意な主人、きわめて無口な奥さん、そして「ラー！」しかいえない巨体の一人息子。なんともかわった家族だったけれど、町に住む誰の目にも、肉屋おうむがうまくいっていることは明らかだった。ぼくたちはしょっちゅうラーを誘い、運河脇の草地でレスリングのまねごとをした。もちろん彼に勝てるものはいなかった。二人、三人でかかっても、フォールをとるのは無理だった。腰や腕にとりすがるぼくたちを、軽く片手で払いおとすと、彼は夏の太陽を背におおきく胸を張り、

■ ぼくたちにはとてもほんとうだとは思えなかった we just couldn't be-lieve it was true ■ けれど主人はいつも陽気にふるまっていたし but the butcher always had a very cheerful air, and ■ 自分で店を開いてから、奥さんとのあいだに息子までもうけていた after he opened his own store, he even had a son with his wife ■ それがラーだ "Laa" (or "Raa") was the boy's name ■ ラーはぼくたちと同じ中学にかよっていたが Laa went to the same junior high school as the rest of us, though ■ 年は少なくとも五つは上だったと思う he had to have been at least five years older than us

13 牛を立たせたような巨体だった he had an enormous build, like a cow someone had stood up on its hind legs ■ さまざまな声を自在に使いこなす父親とちがい unlike his father, who turned out all kinds of voices just as he wished ■ ラーはたったひとつのことばしか知らないようだった Laa appeared to know only one word ■ 授業中も、学校帰りも、町なかであいさつを送られても during class, on the way back from school, even when someone called out a greeting to him in town ■ いつだって always ■ 大口をひらき、こんなふうに叫ぶ he'd open his mouth wide and shout out, just like this:

15 動物の鳴きまねが得意な主人 a butcher good at imitating animal cries ■ きわめて無口な奥さん an extremely taciturn wife ■ そして「ラー!」しかいえない巨体の一人息子 and an enormous only-son unable to say anything but "Laa!" ■ なんともかわった家族 an indescribably pecu-liar family ■ 町に住む誰の目にも...明らかだった it was clear to all the town's residents ■ 肉屋おうむがうまくいっていることは that things were going well at the Parrot Meat Market ■ ぼくたちはしょっちゅうラーを誘い we often invited Laa to come out with us and ■ 運河脇の草地でレスリングのまねごとをした played at wrestling in the pasture along the canal ■ もちろん彼に勝てるものはいなかった of course, none of us could beat him ■ 二人、三人でかかっても、フォールをとるのは無理だった even if two or three of us went at him at once, it was impos-sible to score a pinfall ■ 腰や腕にとりすがるぼくたちを、軽く片手で払いおとすと having lightly brushed us aside with one hand as we clung to his waist or arm ■ 夏の太陽を背に with the summer sun at his back ■ おおきく胸を張り he'd stick out his broad chest and

「ラー」

と嬉しげにいったものだ。

ラーとのレスリングは愉快だったけれど、それよりいっそうぼくたちの心をとらえていたのは、土曜日の午後、農場で行われる「ばらし」、つまり牛や豚の解体作業だった。おうむの主人はなめし革の袋をさげ、古トラックででかけた。助手席にすわるのはラー、荷台にはぼくをふくめ、運のいい子どもが二、三人、膝を抱いて屈んでいる。ぼくはもちろん母から「ばらし」見学を禁じられていた。父はなにもいわなかった。祖父は小声で、柵へはいるんじゃないぞ、とだけいった。

農場の親方が、あれとあれ、それにあいつと放牧地を指ししめす。そばかす顔の農夫が動物たちに目隠しをし、首に綱をかけて、解体用の小屋へとみちびいていく。おうむの主人は革袋から刃物をだし（刃の大きさや角度はそのたびごとにちがう）、シャキン、シャキンと砥石でこすりあげる。動物たちは狭い柵のなかで吠えたりいなないたりしている。

17 | …と嬉しげにいったものだ gleefully cry out,…

18 | ラーとのレスリングは wrestling with Laa ▪ 愉快だったけれども was a lot of fun, but ▪ それよりいっそうぼくたちの心をとらえていたのは what captured our hearts even more than that ▪ 農場で行われる「ばらし」the "carving" that took place at the farm ▪ つまり in other words ▪ 牛や豚の解体作業 the work of dismembering the cows and pigs ▪ なめし革の袋をさげ carrying a tanned-hide bag ▪ 古トラックででかけた would set out in his old truck ▪ 助手席にすわるのはラー Laa would be the one to sit in the passenger seat ▪ 荷台にはぼくをふくめ、運のいい子どもが二、三人、膝を抱いて屈んでいる while in the bed of the truck, two or three lucky kids, including me, would be crouched, cradling their knees in their arms ▪ ぼくはもちろん母から「ばらし」見学を禁じられていた naturally, I had been forbidden by my mother to go watch the "carving" ▪ 父はなにもいわなかった my father didn't say anything ▪ 祖父は小声で、柵へはいるんじゃないぞ、とだけいった my grandfather simply told me in a low voice, Now don't you go inside the fence, you hear?

19 | 農場の親方が、あれとあれ、それにあいつと放牧地を指ししめす pointing out at the pasture, the head farmer would call out, That one and that one, and that guy over there ▪ そばかす顔の農夫 a freckled farmer ▪ 動物たちに目隠しをし would blindfold the animals ▪ 首に綱をかけて put a rope around their necks, and ▪ 解体用の小屋へとみちびいていく lead them on to the butchering hut ▪ 刃物をだし take out a knife and ▪ （刃の大きさや角度はそのたびごとにちがう）(the size and angle of the blade was different every time) ▪ シャキン、シャキンと砥石でこすりあげる hone it—*shakin, shakin!*—on the grindstone ▪ 狭い柵のなかで in the cramped pen ▪ 吠えたりいなないたりしている be lowing and braying and so on

主人は刃物をさげて動物に近づく。しゃがみこんで耳元に口をつけ、

「おまえさんらはむだ死にじゃないぞ」

やわらかいもので撫でるような、あたたかな声でいう。

「おまえさんは俺たちや、村のみんなの腹のなかにはいる。とてもいい栄養になるんだ。

おまえさんらのおかげで俺たちはもうしばらく生きていける。どうもありがとうよ」

おとなしくなった動物ののど元に、おうむの主人は一瞬の迷いもなく、刃物の切っ先を

突き刺す。農場の親方がほとばしる血をたらいで受ける。ラーは両手で動物のからだを支

え、ビニールの幕へと横たえる。小屋の外では犬たちが騒いでいる。けれど、どんなくず

肉も、おうむの親子、農場の親方たちはていねいに拾いあつめ、欠片ひとつ犬たちには残

さない。幕にこびりついた血のしずくは、ラーの携えてきた堅パンできれいさっぱりふき

取られる。仕事がおわるとラーはそれをちぎってぼくたちにくれた。帰りの荷台にすわ

り、厳かに黙ってぼくたちはパンをたべた。その風味をぼくの舌はまだはっきりとおぼえ

ている。赤黒い色のパンは、塩と脂と、まるで自分たちの指をかじっているような味がし

20 | 主人は刃物をさげて動物に近づく the butcher would approach the animal, the knife dangling from his hand ▪ しゃがみこんで耳元に口をつけ he would bend down and put his mouth to its ear

21 | おまえさんらはむだ死にじゃないぞ your deaths won't be wasted, hear?

22 | やわらかいもので撫でるような、あたたかな声でいう he'd say in a voice full of warmth, a voice like a caress with some soft object

23 | 俺たちや、村のみんなの腹のなかにはいる you're going to end up in my stomach, and the stomachs of everyone in the village ▪ とてもいい栄養になるんだ you'll be a very good source of nutrition ▪ おまえさんらのおかげで thanks to you all ▪ もうしばらく a bit longer ▪ 生きていける be able to keep living

24 | おとなしくなった動物ののど元に into the throat of the animal, now docile ▪ 一瞬の迷いもなく without a moment's hesitation ▪ 刃物の切っ先を突き刺す thrust the tip of the blade ▪ 農場の親方がほとばしる血をたらいで受ける the head farmer would catch the gushing blood in a tub ▪ 両手で動物のからだを支え supporting the animal's body with both hands ▪ ビニールの幕へと横たえる lay them down on a vinyl curtain ▪ 小屋の外では犬たちが騒いでいる the dogs would be raising a ruckus outside the hut ▪ どんなくず肉も even the slightest scrap of meat ▪ おうむの親子、農場の親方たちは the Parrot father and son, and the head farmer and the rest ▪ ていねいに拾いあつめ carefully pick up and gather…and ▪ 欠片ひとつ犬たちには残さない leave nothing, not even a single piece, for the dogs ▪ 幕にこびりついた血のしずくは、…きれいさっぱりふき取られる the drops of blood clinging to the curtain…would be completely wiped away ▪ ラーの携えてきた堅パンで with the stale bread Laa brought along ▪ 仕事がおわると when the work was done ▪ ラーはそれをちぎって Laa would tear it (i.e., the bread) up and ▪ 帰りの荷台にすわり sitting in the bed of the truck on the way back ▪ 厳かに黙って maintaining a solemn silence ▪ その風味をぼくの舌はまだはっきりとおぼえている even now, my tongue still remembers that taste very clearly ▪ 赤黒い色のパンは…ような味がした the red-black bread had a flavor like … ▪ 塩と脂と、まるで自分たちの指をかじっているような味がした salty and fatty, it tasted just as if we were chewing our own fingers

た。

夏休みがあけてすぐ、ひげの公証人が肉屋おうむに怒鳴り込んできた。おたくの息子（ラー）は、いま裏庭の樫に荒縄で縛りつけてある。まったくとんでもないことをしでかしてくれた。やつが今後二度とおもてを歩けんようとっくりと思いしらせてやる。

ただ、誘いをかけたのは娘のほうからだったと、ぼくたちにも町のみんなにもわかっていた。ラーは勝手にひとの寝床にもぐりこんだりしない。そもそも、遊び場で取り残されると泣き出すほどの臆病者なのだ。公証人の娘は脳しんとうをおこし、裸のまま、隣町の病院へ運ばれていた。家政婦によれば、ベッド際の壁には、ハンマーを打ち付けたみたいな、おおきなへこみが残っていた。娘が冗談半分に教えた「いけない遊び」は、たしかにレスリングに似ていなくもなかった。ただし、踏み割られたベッドの上は、あのラーとくんずほぐれつするには、運河脇の草地にくらべあまりにも狭すぎた。

おうむの主人はひら謝りに謝り、公証人はひげをしごきながら慰謝料の額をはじきだした。それはベッドや壁どころか、家をまるごと新築できそうな金額だったけれど、息子

25 | 夏休みがあけてすぐ soon after the end of summer vacation ▪ ひげの公証人 a mustachioed notary ▪ 肉屋おうむに怒鳴り込んできた came yelling into Parrot Meat Market ▪ おたくの息子 your son ▪ いま裏庭の樫に荒縄で縛りつけてある I've got him tied up with rope to the oak in our back garden ▪ まったくとんでもないことをしでかしてくれた he's gone and done something pretty damn unbelievable ▪ 今後二度とおもてを歩けんようとっくりと思いしらせてやる I'll give him one long, careful roasting such that he'll never be able to walk in public again

26 | ただ、誘いをかけたのは娘のほうからだったと、ぼくたちにも町のみんなにもわかっていた except that we and every one else in town knew that his daughter had been the one to put the moves on Laa ▪ ラーは勝手にひとの寝床にもぐりこんだりしない Laa wasn't the sort of guy to go around creeping into other people's beds uninvited ▪ そもそも to begin with ▪ 遊び場で取り残されると泣き出す he would burst out crying whenever he was left behind in the place where we had been playing ▪ ...ほどの臆病者なのだ he was such a coward that... ▪ 脳しんとうをおこし suffered a cerebral concussion and ▪ 裸のまま、隣町の病院へ運ばれていた had been brought to the hospital in the next town, still naked ▪ 家政婦によれば according to the maid ▪ ベッド際の壁には on the wall by the bed ▪ ハンマーを打ち付けたみたいな、おおきなへこみが残っていた a large dent had been left, as if someone had pounded it with a hammer ▪ 娘が冗談半分に教えた「いけない遊び」は the "forbidden game" that the young woman had taught him, half in jest ▪ たしかにレスリングに似ていなくもなかった was, after all, not entirely unlike wrestling ▪ ただし the only thing was ▪ 踏み割られたベッドの上は...運河脇の草地にくらべあまりにも狭すぎた the bed, now smashed by Laa's feet, was simply too narrow compared to the pasture along the canal ▪ あのラーとくんずほぐれつするには to engage in any sort of rough-and-tumble with Laa

27 | ひら謝りに謝り made a thousand apologies, and ▪ ひげをしごきながら stroking his moustache ▪ 慰謝料の額をはじきだした named his price ▪ それはベッドや壁どころか、家をまるごと新築できそうな金額だったけれど it was an amount high enough to rebuild not only the bed and the wall but the entire house, and yet

を五体満足でとりもどすため、あるいは本気で娘の心痛をおもって、主人は不平ひとつもらさずすぐさま支払い書に署名した。

ラーは顔面をかぼちゃのように腫らせ、しかし元気な足取りで肉屋へ帰ってきた。店先で待っていた主人はなにもいわず、少し背伸びをして、岩のようにそびえる肩をぽんぽんと叩いた。息子はうつむき、

「ラー」

とつぶやいた。

その冬、主人が命を落としたのは、長年患っていた肝臓のせいだという意見がある。きびしい寒さが最後の体力を奪った、というものもいた。いずれにせよ、倒れる日まで働きづめだったことはまちがいない。あらかじめ病気を知っていた彼は、まだ動けるうち慰謝料分を稼ぎ出そうとしたのかもしれない。勇敢なおうむの主人は、ふたつの点で見込みちがいをしていた。彼の死期は自分でおもっていたよりずいぶん早く来た。また、寒い戸外で連日無理をしたことが、彼の死期そのものを早めた。

■ 息子を五体満足でとりもどすため in order to get his son back in one piece ■ あるいは本気で娘の心痛をおもって or perhaps because he sincerely felt for the daughter in her pain ■ 不平ひとつもらさず without uttering a single complaint ■ すぐさま支払い書に署名した signed the payment slip right away

28 顔面をかぼちゃのように腫らせ his face puffed up like a pumpkin ■ しかし元気な足取りで but with a spring in his step ■ 肉屋へ帰ってきた came back to the meat store ■ なにもいわず without saying a word ■ 少し背伸びをして stood up a bit straighter and ■ 岩のようにそびえる肩をぽんぽんと叩いた patted his son's shoulders, which towered above him like a cliff ■ 息子はうつむき his son lowered his head

30 とつぶやいた he murmured

31 その冬 that winter ■ 主人が命を落としたのは...のせいだという意見がある some are of the opinion that...was responsible for the butcher's death ■ 長年患っていた肝臓 liver problems he'd had for many years ■ きびしい寒さが最後の体力を奪った the harsh winter robbed him of his last bit of strength ■ ...というものもいた others said that... ■ いずれにせよ whatever the case ■ 倒れる日まで働きづめだったことはまちがいない there was no doubt that he had been working like a machine until the day he collapsed ■ あらかじめ病気を知っていた彼は already aware that he was sick, he ■ まだ動けるうち while he could still work ■ 慰謝料分 enough to pay the amount he owed in compensation ■ ...を稼ぎ出そうとしたのかもしれない perhaps he had tried to earn... ■ 勇敢なおうむの主人は the brave proprietor of Parrot ■ ふたつの点で見込みちがいをしていた had miscalculated in two respects ■ 彼の死期は his last hour ■ 自分でおもっていたよりずいぶん早く来た came a good deal sooner than he expected ■ 寒い戸外で out in the cold ■ 連日無理をしたこと that he went overboard several days in a row ■ 彼の死期そのものを早めた actually hastened his death

以下は町医者が酒場で披露した話だ。

肉屋の主人は真っ青な顔で、寝床から妻と息子とを交互に見た。口の動きだけで（もう声を出せなかった）、彼はふたりに話しかけた。すまん、ほんとうにすまん、と彼はいっているようだった。奥さんは表情をかえなかったが、くちびるには堅くかんだ跡があった。息子はなにが起きているのかよくわかっていない様子で、ベッドの白い枠に指を滑らせていた。

主人のからだが、びくん、と橋のようにそりかえった。医者はあわてて注射薬を準備した。そのとき、息子のラーが、白目をむく父親の耳にそっと口を寄せた。そして、たどしい口調で口まねをはじめた。

「おまえさん、むだじに、じゃないぞ」

父親はまた、びくんとふるえた。

「おれたち、いきていける。おまえさん、むだじに、じゃないぞ」

同じことばをラーは何度も何度もくりかえしささやいた。だんだんと彼の口調は父親

32 以下は what follows ▪ 町医者が酒場で披露した話だ is a story the town doctor told at the bar

33 真っ青な顔で his face deathly pale ▪ 寝床から from his bed ▪ 妻と息子とを交互に見た looked back and forth from his wife to his son ▪ 口の動きだけで with only the movement of his mouth ▪ （もう声を出せなかった）(by then he could no longer speak) ▪ 彼はふたりに話しかけた he addressed the two of them ▪ すまん、ほんとにすまん、と彼はいっているようだった he seemed to be saying, I'm sorry, I really am sorry ▪ 奥さんは表情をかえなかったが his wife didn't change her expression, but ▪ くちびるには堅くかんだ跡があった there were marks on her lips where she had bitten them hard ▪ なにが起きているのかよくわかっていない様子で didn't appear to have much understanding of what was going on, and ▪ ベッドの白い枠に along the white frame of the bed ▪ 指を滑らせていた was sliding his fingers

34 からだが、びくん、と橋のようにそりかえった his body suddenly arched like a bridge ▪ あわてて hurriedly ▪ 注射薬を準備した got the injection ready ▪ 白目をむく父親 his father, whose eyes were rolled back in their sockets ▪ ...の耳にそっと口を寄せた softly pressed his mouth to the ear of... ▪ たどたどしい口調で in a halting tone

36 びくんとふるえた a tremor ran through his body

38 何度も何度もくりかえしささやいた whispered over and over again

そっくりに響きだした。それと同時に、父親の寝息は次第に安らかになっていった。肉屋の息子として、幼いころから耳になじんだせりふを、ラーは一心に、おだやかな口調で、父の息が絶えるまでささやきつづけた。

それからラーが慰謝料を払いきるまで一年とかからなかった。昼間は肉屋、夜は河岸の補修工事にと、ラーのからだはまったく疲れを知らず動きまわった。冬のあいだに、公証人の娘の腹はぷっくりとふくれていた。ぼくたち家族はその年末、遠い東の都会へと引っ越しをした。なので、ぼくが自分の目で見たのはここまでということになる。

友人の手紙によれば、ラーと娘の子どもは死産だった。しかし翌年、またもや公証人の娘はラーの子種を身ごもることになった。二番目の子どもは元気に産声をあげ、公証人は渋々とながら、ふたりの結婚を認めた。

肉屋おうむは、おそらくまだあの同じ町はずれに建っているだろう。年老いた母親はあいかわらず店の奥にこもり、陽に焼けた若い妻は両手を打ちならし、お客へぞんざいに声

父親そっくりに響きだした began to sound just like his father ■ それと同時に and at the same time ■ 父親の寝息は his father's breathing, as he slept ■ 次第に安らかになっていった gradually grew easier, less labored ■ 肉屋の息子として、幼いころから耳になじんだせりふ words that, as the son of a butcher, he had been accustomed to hearing ever since he was small ■ 一心に with all his heart ■ おだやかな口調で in a mild tone ■ 父の息が絶えるまで until his father stopped breathing ■ ささやきつづけた continued whispering

39 払いきる to pay off completely ■ 一年とかからなかった it didn't even take a year ■ 昼間は肉屋、夜は河岸の補修工事にと by day he was at the butcher; by night he did maintenance work on the riverbank ■ まったく疲れを知らず without feeling the slightest bit tired ■ 動きまわった moved around ■ 公証人の娘の腹はぷっくりとふくれていた the notary's daughter's stomach was bulging ■ ぼくたち家族はその年末 toward the end of that year, my family ■ 遠い東の都会へと to a city far off in the east ■ 引っ越しをした moved ■ 自分の目で見たのはここまでということになる this is as much as I saw with my own eyes

40 友人の手紙によれば according to a letter from a friend ■ 死産 a stillbirth ■ 翌年 the following year ■ またもや yet again! ■ ラーの子種を身ごもることになった became pregnant with Laa's child ■ 二番目の子どもは元気に産声をあげ the second child cried out vigorously when it was born, and ■ 渋々とながら grudgingly ■ ふたりの結婚を認めた allowed the two to marry

41 おそらくまだあの同じ町はずれに建っているだろう probably still stands there, on the outskirts of that same town ■ 年老いた母親は [Laa's] elderly mother ■ あいかわらず as always ■ 店の奥にこもり holed up in the back of the shop ■ 陽に焼けた suntanned ■ 若い妻 his young wife ■ 両手を打ちならし claps her hands together and ■ お客へぞんざいに声をかける calls out brusquely to the customers

をかける。

店先で、うまれたばかりの赤ん坊を抱いているのは若き父親のラーだ。

「ラー！　ラー！　ラー！」

彼の深い声は、赤ん坊をあやすのにちょうどぴったりに響く。　広いてのひらの上で身をよじる幼いからだは、いまは亡き祖父が切り取った新鮮な肉のように、黄色い陽ざしを浴び、ぴかぴかと輝いている。　幼子はときおり父をみあげ、らあ、らあ、とたどたどしく口まねをする。　そしてきっと、もうしばらく経つうちに、この世のあちこちで響く、もっとさまざまな物音を、その小さな口でまねるようになる。

42 | うまれたばかりの赤ん坊を抱いているのは the one dawdling the newborn infant ▪ 若き父親のラーだ is the young father, Laa

44 | 彼の深い声は his deep voice ▪ 赤ん坊をあやすのにちょうどぴったりに響く has just the right tone for soothing a baby ▪ 広いてのひらの上で on his broad palms ▪ 身をよじる幼いからだは the tiny body twisting and turning ▪ いまは亡き祖父 his now deceased father ▪ 切り取った新鮮な肉のように like fresh meat just cut from the animal ▪ 黄色い陽ざしを浴び awash in yellow rays of sun ▪ ぴかぴかと輝いている shines brightly ▪ 幼子は the infant ▪ ときおり every so often ▪ 父をみあげ looks up at his father ▪ とたどたどしく uncertainly ▪ そしてきっと and no doubt ▪ もうしばらく経つうちに after a little time has passed ▪ この世の in this world ▪ あちこち here and there ▪ もっとさまざまな物音 lots of other different sounds ▪ まねるようになる will start mimicking

よしもとばなな[*]

Yoshimoto Banana

[*] She changed her name from 吉本ばなな to よしもとばなな in August 2002.

hances are, seeing as you're reading this book, that you've come across the name Banana Yoshimoto—perhaps even in Japanese, as Yoshimoto Banana—before. She is one of very few Japanese authors who have been lucky enough to gain access, through translation, to a wide and avid international following. Or rather, she is one of very few authors whose works international audiences are fortunate enough to have available in translation. Her first book, *Kitchin* (*Kitchen*), sold almost two million copies in Japan when it was published in 1987, became a runaway bestseller in Italy in 1991, and went on to be translated into twenty-eight other languages. It's English translation blipped onto the *New York Times* bestseller list in 1993, and Yoshimoto has had devoted fans ever since.

Yoshimoto, who was born in Tokyo in 1964, has received too many prizes to enumerate, including three in Italy—most notably the prestigious Maschera d'Argento, which she was awarded in 1999. She has published more than thirty works of fiction and over twenty collections of essays, and while her essays (though very good) may not need to be penciled in at the top of your reading list, her fiction is perfect for beginning readers of Japanese: Yoshimoto tends to prefer everyday language and doesn't use many kanji, but she dances

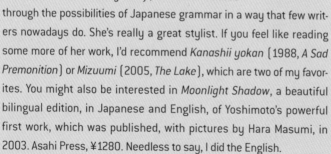

through the possibilities of Japanese grammar in a way that few writers nowadays do. She's really a great stylist. If you feel like reading some more of her work, I'd recommend *Kanashii yokan* (1988, *A Sad Premonition*) or *Mizuumi* (2005, *The Lake*), which are two of my favorites. You might also be interested in *Moonlight Shadow*, a beautiful bilingual edition, in Japanese and English, of Yoshimoto's powerful first work, which was published, with pictures by Hara Masumi, in 2003. Asahi Press, ¥1280. Needless to say, I did the English.

The story I've included here, "Miira" ("Mummy"), was first published in the short-story collection *Karada wa zenbu shitte iru* (*The Body Knows Everything*), issued by Bungei Shunjū in 2000.

ミイラ

吉本ばなな

二十代になる直前の娘というものはたいてい生意気盛りで、世の中を自分の小さな頭の中にすっかりとおさめているつもりになっているものだが、私ももちろんそうだった。

そしてたいていは何かわけもわからずむしゃくしゃしたりいらいらしているものだ。多分、ホルモンの問題なのだろう。しかしそのホルモンの乱れが異常に鋭敏な感性を生むことがある。それは空にほんのいっときだけ鮮やかに虹がかかるように、とても短い期間の輝きだ。その上、その匂いをかぎとることができる存在というのも稀にはいる。

薬学部に通っていた私は、六月だというのにすでに大学に退屈していた。冴えない気持ちで歩いていたその夕方、学校の帰りに公園を通りながら、私は空の高いところにうっすらと輝く消えかけた虹を見つけた。そして、しばらくはこんなふうに空を見あげないかもしれないな、とふと思ったのだった。

ミイラ Mummy

1 | 二十代になる直前の娘というものは a young woman just about to enter her twenties ■ たいてい generally ■ 生意気盛りで is as cheeky as she'll ever be and ■ 世の中を自分の小さな頭の中にすっかりとおさめているつもりになっているものだが thinks she's got the whole world neatly tucked away in her little head ■ 私ももちろんそうだった needless to say, that's how I was, too ■ たいていは in most cases ■ 何かわけもわからず without knowing why ■ むしゃくしゃしたりいらいらしているものだ [such a woman] goes around in a bad mood, feeling annoyed ■ 多分、ホルモンの問題なのだろう it's probably a hormone thing ■ そのホルモンの乱れが異常に鋭敏な感性を生む this hormonal irregularity gives rise to an extraordinarily fine sensibility ■ …ことがある it sometimes happens that … ■ 空にほんのいっときだけ鮮やかに虹がかかるように like a brilliant rainbow stretched across the sky for just the briefest moment ■ とても短い期間の輝きだ a glow that lasts only a very short time ■ その上 and what's more ■ その匂いをかぎとることができる存在というのも稀にはいる there are, if only very rarely, beings able to catch the scent of people in that state

2 | 薬学部に通っていた I was taking classes at a college of pharmaceutics ■ 六月だというのに even though it was only June ■ すでに大学に退屈していた I was already bored with school ■ 冴えない気持ちで feeling dull ■ その夕方 one evening ■ 学校の帰りに on the way home from school ■ 公園を通りながら as I was passing through the park ■ 空の高いところに way up high in the sky ■ うっすらと輝く消えかけた虹を見つけた I noticed a partially vanished rainbow, glowing ever so faintly ■ しばらくは for quite a while ■ こんなふうに like this ■ 空を見あげないかもしれないな、とふと思ったのだった it struck me suddenly that I might not look up at the sky

予感は当たっていた。私はその日、公園で出会った、近所に住む顔見知りの青年に連れ去られるようにして軟禁され、しばらく家には帰れなかったのである。

4 私は田島というその青年を、大学院生だということと、遺跡の発掘の手伝いのバイトをしていて年に半分はエジプトに行っている人だということしか知らなかった。よく日に焼けていて、めがねをかけたやさ男で、ちょっともてそうな家庭教師のお兄さんタイプの青年だった。目が好きだな、とは昔から思っていて、道で会うと必ずあいさつくらいはした。

5 「こんばんは。」

6 私は無邪気に声をかけて、頭を軽く下げた。彼は少し笑って、今論文を書いていたが気分転換に散歩に出たんだ、と言った。

7 「先月ここで殺人があったんだよ。」

8 と彼は言った。

3 | 予感は当たっていた that premonition was right ▪ 私はその日…青年に連れ去られるようにして軟禁され that very day, I…was sort of led off by a young man and kept in a state of confinement ▪ 公園で出会った、近所に住む顔見知りの青年 a young man I knew by sight, who lived nearby, and whom I ran into in the park ▪ しばらく家には帰れなかったのである I was unable to return home for some time

4 | 私は田島というその青年を…しか知らなかった all I knew about that young man, whose last name was Tajima, was… ▪ 大学院生だということと that he was a graduate student and ▪ 遺跡の発掘の手伝いのバイトをしていて年に半分はエジプトに行っている人だということ that he was a guy who had a part-time job helping excavate ancient ruins, and spent half of every year in Egypt ▪ よく日に焼けていて he had a deep tan and ▪ めがねをかけたやさ男で was a delicately featured man who wore glasses ▪ ちょっともてそうな家庭教師のお兄さんタイプの青年 a young man of the nice-young-man-who-works-as-a-home-tutor-and-looks-like-he'd-be-pretty-popular-with-the-girls type ▪ 目が好きだな、とは昔から思っていて I'd always thought he had gorgeous eyes and ▪ 道で会うと必ずあいさつくらいはした I always said hi when we passed on the street

6 | 私は無邪気に声をかけて I called out casually to him and ▪ 頭を軽く下げた lightly bowed my head ▪ 今論文を書いていたが気分転換に散歩に出たんだ、と言った I'm writing a paper right now, and I came out for a walk, to give myself a break, he said

7 | 先月ここで殺人があったんだよ there was a murder here last month, you know

「あぶないからひとりで歩かないほうがいいよ。送ってあげようか?」

あんたがあぶなくないという保証がどこにある、と私は思ったが口には出さなかった。

「犯人はまだつかまってないんですか?」

私は言った。

「うん、うちの大学にも聞き込みがあったよ。僕達はよく夜中に研究室にいるからな。人をばらばらにできそうな道具もあるし。」

彼は言った。

「ばらばらになったの? 死んだ人は。」

「そうらしいよ。 首だけ見つからないって。」

「首……。」

これから起こることに関するほとんどの情報は実は前もって知らされているものだ。その時、私が首に手をやった時の彼の目の中に、私は数時間後の自分の運命を、ほんとうは読み取っていた。

9 あぶないからひとりで歩かないほうがいいよ you shouldn't be walking alone, it's dangerous ■ 送ってあげようか? want me to walk you home?

10 あんたがあぶなくないという保証がどこにある who's to say you're not dangerous yourself ■ 口には出さなかった I didn't speak these words

11 犯人はまだつかまってないんですか? the culprit hasn't been caught yet?

13 うん yeah ■ うちの大学に to my university ■ 聞き込みがあったよ they came and questioned people (lit., "there were inquiries") ■ 僕達はよく夜中に研究室にいるからな because we're often in the lab at night ■ 人をばらばらにできそうな道具もあるし and we have tools that look like they could be used to cut people up

15 ばらばらになったの? it was cut up? ■ 死んだ人は the body, I mean?

16 そうらしいよ apparently so ■ 首だけ見つからないって I heard they've found everything but the head

18 これから起こることに関するほとんどの情報は almost all the information about what is going to happen in the future ■ 実は in fact ■ 前もって in advance ■ 知らされているものだ we tend to know (lit., "it tends to be known") ■ その時、私が首に手をやった時 just then, when I raised my hand to my neck ■ 彼の目の中に、私は数時間後の自分の運命を、ほんとうは読み取っていた the truth is I had already read, in his eyes, the fate that awaited me just a few hours later

しかし、夕闇のせまる公園で、殺人犯と顔見知りという安直な比べ方をして、闇にひ

そんでいるかもしれない殺人犯に一瞬おびえ、理性的な判断をしたつもりになった。私

は彼を選び彼と並んで歩きだしたのである。人間には発情期はない、年中　瞬間的に欲

情できるというのもついていった理由のひとつだ。私は多分、その目の光に何か自分をひ

きつけるものをかぎとったのだろう。もしも私が野生生物だったら、とっくに逃げ去って

いただろう。　生命の危険を読み取って。　しかし単なる鈍い人間の女であった私は、発情

をよしとした。　逃げるチャンスはその瞬間だけだったのに。

しかし遅かった。　その時にはもう、暗い木々のシルエットの中で私達はもっと真っ暗

なふたりだけの世界に向けて降りて行く途中だったのだ。

家の近くで彼は突然言い出した。

「僕達はこのまま別れちゃいけないと思うんだ。」

目が真剣だった。　私は言った。

19 | 夕闇のせまる公園で in the park, upon which dusk was descending
■ 殺人犯と顔見知りという安直な比べ方をして I made the too-simple
comparison of murderer and acquaintance, and ■ 闇にひそんでいる
かもしれない殺人犯 the murderer who could be lurking in the dark ■
…に一瞬おびえ seized momentarily with fear of... ■ 理性的な判断
をしたつもりになった I came to believe I had made a rational decision
■ 私は彼を選び彼と並んで歩きだしたのである I chose him, and started
walking alongside him ■ 人間には発情期はない、年中瞬間的に欲情で
きるというのもついていった理由のひとつだ the fact that we humans
have no mating season and can feel desire right away, at any time of
the year, also explains why I went with him ■ その目の光に in the way
his eyes glittered ■ 何か自分をひきつけるもの something that attracted
me ■ …をかぎとったのだろう I must have sensed... ■ もしも私が野
生生物だったら if I had been a wild animal ■ とっくに逃げ去っていた
だろう I'm sure I would have been long gone by then ■ 生命の危険を
読み取って sensing that my life was in danger ■ 単なる鈍い人間の女
であった私は as a simple, dull, human female, I ■ 発情をよしとした
chose the desire to breed ■ 逃げるチャンスはその瞬間だけだったのに
even though that moment offered the only chance I had to get away

20 | しかし遅かった but it was too late ■ その時には by then ■ 暗い木々
のシルエットの中で among the trees' dark silhouettes ■ もっと真っ暗な
ふたりだけの世界 an even darker world that belonged only to us ■
…に向けて降りて行く途中だったのだ I was descending into...

21 | 家の近くで彼は突然言い出した all of a sudden, when we got near my
house, he spoke

22 | このまま別れちゃいけないと思うんだ I don't think we can just say good-
bye like this

23 | 目が真剣だった the look in his eyes was dead serious

「また会う約束をするとか？　そういうこと？」

彼は私の好きなタイプでは全然なかった。話も全然合わなかったし、興味の対象も違った。ただ、並んでいる時の、何かに包み込まれるような感じ……それだけだった。興味のある点は。ふたりが駅前かどこかの喫茶店で待ち合わせている光景なんて全く浮かばなかったし、ばかばかしく思えて、私は立ち去ろうとした。

「待って、見てほしいものがあるんだ。」

彼はそう言って、人気のない夕方の路地で私を抱きすくめた。古いセーターみたいな枯れた匂いがした。ついていかなかったら、いずれはつけまわされて殺される、いずれにしても長くなってしまう、早くすませてしまおう。私はそう思った。いや、単についていきたかったのかもしれない。その時私はどうしても彼と体の一部を触れあわせていたかった。情熱が伝わってきた。その情熱は今まで感じたことのない気持ちが悪い熱だったが、何か私の魂に触れるものがあった。

彼の部屋は倉庫のように広く、実際大家さんの家にあった蔵を改装した部屋だという

24 また会う約束をするとか？ そういうこと？ we should agree to meet again, in other words? Is that what you mean?

25 彼は私の好きなタイプでは全然なかった he wasn't my type at all ∎ 話も全然合わなかったし、興味の対象も違った we had nothing to talk about, and we were interested in different things ∎ ただ it was just ∎ 並んでいる時の、何かに包み込まれるような感じ the feeling I had when we were standing beside each other, as if I were enveloped in something ∎ それだけだった。興味のある点は that's all it was. The only thing about him that interested me ∎ ふたりが駅前かどこかの喫茶店で待ち合わせている光景なんて the image of the two of us meeting up at a café, in front of the train station or somewhere ∎ 全く浮かばなかったし、ばかばかしく思えて just wasn't coming to me at all, and it seemed so ridiculous that ∎ 私は立ち去ろうとした I made to leave

26 待って、見てほしいものがあるんだ wait, I've got something I want you to see

27 人気のない夕方の路地で there in the deserted, dusky alley ∎ 私を抱きすくめた he hugged me to him ∎ 古いセーターみたいな枯れた匂いがした I noticed a withered smell, like an old sweater ∎ ついていかなかったら if I don't go with him ∎ いずれはつけまわされて殺される I'll end up being stalked and killed eventually ∎ いずれにしても長くなってしまう this will just drag on anyway ∎ 早くすませてしまおう I'd better just hurry up and get it over with ∎ いや no, come to think of it ∎ 単についていきたかったのかもしれない maybe I just wanted to go with him ∎ どうしても no matter what ∎ 彼と体の一部を触れあわせていたかった I wanted to have part of my body in contact with his ∎ 情熱が伝わってきた I could feel his passion ∎ 今まで感じたことのない気持ちが悪い熱 a repulsive heat, unlike anything I had ever felt until now (lit., "the likes of which, up until now, I had never felt") ∎ 何か私の魂に触れるもの something that touched my soul

28 彼の部屋は倉庫のように広く his apartment was as spacious as a storehouse ∎ 実際大家さんの家にあった蔵を改装した部屋だということだった he said it actually was a remodeled storehouse that used to stand on the landlord's property

ことだった。天井が高く、はしごがあってロフトがついていた。私はその中にぽつんと座っていた。彼はコーヒーをいれた。お湯で窓が曇るのをじっと見ていた。部屋の中には気味の悪い置き物がたくさんあった。エジプトの古代のお墓から出てきたようなもの……。つぼや、矢尻のようなものや、ワニの頭の石像や、土器のかけらのようなもの。

「見せたいものって。」

私は言った。どうせお互いにやることしか考えてないのに、くだらない質問だ、と我ながら思った。

「後にしよう。」

私の内心を見抜いたかのように、彼は私をたたみの上に押し倒した。

私は彼の体つきも、している時の顔も、ビデオで勉強したようなしつこいセックスの仕方も、なにひとつ好きではなかった。彼の欲望は挿入よりも何よりも見る、ということにつきていて、私を楽しませようという考えはあまりないようだった。あまりのしつこ

■ 天井が高く、はしごがあってロフトがついていた the ceiling was high, and there was a ladder and a loft ■ 私はその中にぽつんと座っていた I was sitting all alone there in the apartment ■ 彼はコーヒーをいれた he made coffee ■ お湯で窓が曇るのをじっと見ていた I watched, motionless, as the windows grew foggy from the hot water ■ 気味の悪い置き物 creepy objects ■ エジプトの古代のお墓から出てきたようなもの things that seemed to have come out of an ancient Egyptian tomb ■ つぼや、矢尻のようなものや、ワニの頭の石像や、土器のかけらのようなもの urns, things that looked like arrowheads, a stone statue of a crocodile head, and what appeared to be fragments of earthenware pots

29 | 見せたいものって what is it you wanted to show me?

30 | どうせ anyway ■ お互いにやることしか考えてないのに even though neither one of us has anything in mind but getting it on ■ くだらない質問だ what a stupid question to ask ■ 我ながら if I say so myself

31 | 後にしよう let's save that for later

32 | 私の内心を見抜いたかのように as if he had seen into my heart ■ 彼は私をたたみの上に押し倒した he pushed me down onto the tatami

33 | 彼の体つき his build ■ している時の顔 his expression while we were doing it ■ ビデオで勉強したようなしつこいセックスの仕方 the insistent way he had sex, as if he had learned from watching videos ■ なにひとつ...なかった there wasn't a single thing ■ 彼の欲望は挿入よりも何よりも見る、ということにつきていて above all else, more than entering me or anything else, his desire was focused on *looking*, and ■ 私を楽しませようという考えはあまりないようだった he didn't seem particularly intent on giving me pleasure

さに思わず何回も絶頂に達したが、それは普通のセックスで普通に気持ちいいというものではなくて、何か歪んだよろこびだった。しかし、なんと言えばいいのだろう。

その腕の妙に細いことも、背骨が浮いていることも、すごく毛深いところも、めがねを取ったらまつ毛が長かったことも、くっきりと日焼けしていることも、いやならいやなほどよかった。終始無言なところも私をひきつけた。

それはちょうど、幼い頃に海に行って、波打ち際に寝転んだ時の感触に似ていた。やわらかく水を含んだ砂が体の下で揺れるよう。その感触はとてもうっとりと快いが、水着の中にどんどん砂が入ってきて、後で面倒臭いということがわかっているのに、もうどうでもよくなって水際に寝ていた時のあの気持ち。一度身をひたすまでは嫌悪があるのに、ひとたびあの柔らかい砂の力につかまったらだらだらとそこにいたくなる。

一回目が終わると私達はロフトのはしごを裸であがった。私は親に連絡も取らせてもらえず、一晩中彼の好きなようにされた。

私は幼いなりに、自分で恋愛の基準を持っていた。それは、その人がいやらしい想像の

■ あまりのしつこさに思わず何回も絶頂に達した he was so persistent that I found myself climaxing, time after time ■ それは that [pleasure] ■ 普通のセックスで普通に気持ちいいというものではなくて wasn't the ordinary pleasure of ordinary sex ■ 何か歪んだよろこびだった it was, somehow, a twisted joy ■ しかし、なんと言えばいいのだろう and yet, how can I explain it?

34 その腕の妙に細いこと the unnatural thinness of his arms ■ 背骨が浮いていること the way his spinal cord rose out of his back ■ すごく毛深いところ the fact that he was so hairy ■ めがねを取ったらまつ毛が長かったこと the length of his eyelashes when he took off his glasses ■ くっきりと日焼けしていること the clear lines of his suntan ■ いやならいやなほどよかった if he was nasty—and he was—he was so nasty it was terrific ■ 終始無言なところも私をひきつけた the fact that he didn't say a word throughout attracted me, too

35 それはちょうど...に似ていた it was just like... ■ 幼い頃に海に行って、波打ち際に寝転んだ時の感覚 how I felt when I was little, when we went to the beach and I lay down where the waves hit the shore ■ やわらかく水を含んだ砂が体の下で揺れるようす the way the soft, water-logged sand swept back and forth under my body ■ その感触 that sensation ■ うっとりと快い was mind-numbingly pleasant ■ 水着の中にどんどん砂が入ってきて more and more sand kept pouring into my bathing suit ■ 後で面倒臭いということがわかっているのに I knew it was going be a pain later, and yet ■ もうどうでもよくなって by then I no longer cared ■ 水際に寝ていた時のあの気持ち that feeling I felt lying at the water's edge ■ 一度身をひたすまでは until I actually steeped myself in the water ■ 嫌悪がある I loathed the thought ■ ひとたびあの柔らかい砂の力につかまったら once I had been seized by the power of that soft sand ■ だらだらとそこにいたくなる I started wanting to stay there, doing nothing

36 一回目が終わると when our first encounter was over ■ ロフトのはしご the ladder to the loft ■ ...を裸であがった we climbed up...naked ■ 私は親に連絡も取らせてもらえず not even allowed to contact my parents ■ 一晩中彼の好きなようにされた he had his way with me all night

37 私は幼いなりに childish as I was ■ 自分で恋愛の基準を持っていた I had my own standard when it came to love ■ その人 the person in question

中で自分をどんなふうに扱っても許せるか否か、だった。それがいやならどんなに仲がよくてもお友達だ。そして、これまではそれが許せる人としか恋愛をしてこなかったつもりだった。しかし、許せるも何もなく、こんなふうにただセックスするためにしか存在しない関係なんて、考えたこともなかった。世の中にはまだまだいろいろな新しいことがあるんだな、と私は思った。私達はしゃべることもなく、なごむこともなく、ひたすらやり続けた。ひとつだけ聞いた。「最後にセックスしたのはいつ?」彼のスタミナにおそれをなしての質問だった。「高校生の時、一度だけ。」と彼は答えた。そういうことか、と私は納得した。

時間が知りたくても彼は時計をかくしてしまったし、窓には部屋を暗室にする時のための重い真っ黒なカーテンがついていた。一回眠って目が覚めてしまうと私はもうどうでもよくなり、水ばかり飲んでいた。もちろんトイレにもプライバシーはなかった。しばられたままもらしたりしたこともあった。親兄弟の前でできないことをほとんど見知らぬ他人の前でならできるとは、セックスとは全く不思議なものだ。時間が経過して行くにつれ

■ いやらしい想像の中で in his lewd fantasies ■ 自分をどんなふうに
扱っても許せるか否か whether or not I could tolerate the things he
did with me, no matter what they were ■ それがいやなら if I didn't
like it ■ どんなに仲がよくてもお友達だ however well we got along, we
were simply friends ■ これまでは until this point ■ それが許せる人
としか恋愛をしてこなかったつもりだった I had done my best to get
involved only with people I could allow to do those things ■ 許せる
も何もなく it wasn't a question of being able to forgive him ■ こんな
ふうにただセックスするためにしか存在しない関係なんて a relationship
like this one, whose only reason for existing was sex ■ 考えたこともな
かった I had never even considered the possibility ■ 世の中にはまだ
まだいろいろな新しいことがあるんだな I guess there are still all kinds
of new things out there ■ しゃべることもなく、なごむこともなく without talking, without becoming intimate ■ ひたすらやり続けた we just
kept having sex, again and again ■ ひとつだけ聞いた I asked him just
one question ■「最後にセックスしたのはいつ?」 "when was the last
time you had sex?" ■ 彼のスタミナにおそれをなしての質問だった I asked
because I was so overwhelmed by the level of his stamina ■「高校生
の時、一度だけ」 "when I was in high school, just once" ■ そういうこ
とか that explains it ■ 私は納得した I felt like I understood

38 時間が知りたくても even if I wanted to know what time it was ■ 彼は
時計をかくしてしまった he had hidden the clock ■ 部屋を暗室にする
時のための重い真っ黒なカーテンがついていた heavy, pitch-black cur-
tains used to turn a room into a darkroom hung [over the windows]
■ 一回眠って目が覚めてしまうと when I woke, after falling asleep once
■ 私はもうどうでもよくなり I no longer cared at all ■ 水ばかり飲んでい
た I did nothing but drink water ■ もちろんトイレにもプライバシーは
なかった needless to say, I had no privacy in the bathroom, either ■
しばられたまま still tied up ■ もらしたりしたこともあった I sometimes
wet myself ■ 親兄弟の前でできないこと things you couldn't do in front
of parents or siblings ■ ...をほとんど見知らぬ他人の前でならできると
は the fact that you can do...if you're in front of someone you hardly
know ■ セックスとは全く不思議なものだ sex really is an amazing thing
■ 時間が経過して行くにつれて as time passed

て、ずっとこういうふうに暮らしていたような錯覚をした。

「見せたかったものがあるのは嘘じゃないんだ。」

親が警察に電話する前に家に電話しないと、と十二回目くらいに私が言うと、突然彼はそう言い、きちんと資料が並んでいる棚の奥の方から、細長い箱を出してきた。ふたを開けると、そこには小さくひからびた猫のミイラがあった。

「うわあ。」

私は言った。

「自分でつくったんですか？」

彼はうなずいた。私はびっくりした。半分冗談で言ったのだから。

「ほんとうにかわいがっていた猫で、十八年生きたんだ。それで、エジプトのミイラと同じように、自分で内臓を出して、匂いのいい薬草をつめて、作ったんだ。作り方は長くなるからはぶくけど、かなり根気と勇気がいった。実際にミイラは自分で作れるのか？

ミイラ　90

■ ずっとこういうふうに暮らしていたような錯覚をした I succumbed to the illusion that we had been living together like this all along

39 | 見せたかったものがあるのは嘘じゃないんだ I wasn't lying when I said I had something I wanted to show you

40 | 親が警察に電話する前に家に電話しないと、と十二回目くらいに私が言うと after I had told him for about the twentieth time that I'd better call home before my parents called the police ■ 突然彼はそう言い he blurted out abruptly and ■ きちんと資料が並んでいる棚 a shelf neatly lined with research materials ■ …の奥の方から from the back of... ■ 細長い箱を出してきた pulled out a long, thin box ■ ふたを開けると when he took the top off ■ そこには小さくひからびた猫のミイラがあった there was a small, shriveled mummy of a cat inside

41 | うわあ Oooo!

44 | 彼はうなずいた he nodded ■ 私はびっくりした I recoiled ■ 半分冗談で言ったのだから because I had been half joking when I asked him that

45 | ほんとうにかわいがっていた猫で I adored that cat, I really did ■ 十八年生きたんだ it lived for eighteen years ■ それで so ■ エジプトのミイラと同じように just like they did with mummies in Egypt ■ 内蔵を出して I took out the organs ■ 匂いのいい薬草をつめて packed in some nice-smelling medicinal herbs and ■ 作り方は長くなるからはぶくけど I'll omit the details about how you make a mummy because it would take too long ■ かなり根気と勇気がいった it took a whole lot of perseverance and bravery ■ 実際にミイラは自分で作れるのか？ という好奇心もあったけれど curiosity about whether or not I could actually make a mummy myself certainly played a part in it, but...

という好奇心もあったけれど、それだけではあんなこわいことはできない。」

「つらい作業だったでしょうね。」

「ほんとうにつらかったよ。君は僕が楽しんで作ったと思うかもしれないけど、ほんとうに淋しくて、悲しくて、つらい作業だった。思い出したくもない。自分が殺したのでもないのに、自分が殺したのと同じ重みの思い出ができてしまった。」

「そうでしょうね。」

「でもどうしても残したかったんだ。姿を。」

「技術を知っていれば、他にもそうしたい人はいると思うわ。はくせいにしたり、毛でセーターを作る人とあまり変わらない気持ちなんじゃない？」

私は言った。　間をおいて彼は言った。

「もう会ってくれないのはわかってる、でももう一日だけいっしょにいてくれないか。

今、家に電話していいから。」

「むりよ。」

■ それだけでは...できない that's not enough to be able to do ■ あんなこわいこと such a frightening thing

46 | つらい作業 painful work

47 | 君は僕が楽しんで作ったと思うかもしれないけど you probably imagine I enjoyed making it, but ■ ほんとうに淋しくて、悲しくて so lonely, and so sad ■ 思い出したくもない I don't even want to think about it ■ 自分が殺したのでもないのに it wasn't as though I had killed it myself, and yet ■ 自分が殺したのと同じ重みの思い出ができてしまった I ended up saddled with a memory as heavy as if I'd actually killed it myself

49 | でもどうしても残したかったんだ。姿を but I wanted, no matter what, to preserve it. The form

50 | 技術を知っていれば if they knew the technique ■ 他にもそうしたい人はいると思うわ I think there are other people besides you who would want to do that ■ はくせいにしたり、毛でセーターを作る人とあまり変わらない気持ちなんじゃない？ I bet the feelings behind what you did weren't all that different from what people feel when they have an animal stuffed or make a sweater from its hair or something, don't you think?

51 | 間をおいて after a brief pause

52 | もう会ってくれないのはわかってる I know you won't see me again ■ もう一日だけ just one more day ■ いっしょにいてくれないか won't you please stay with me? ■ 今、家に電話していいから I'll let you call home now, all right?

53 | むりよ I can't do that

私は言った。猫のミイラがそっと、きれいな布にくるまってそこに置いてあった。彼の優しさを、彼の人格を見てしまったら、もうさっきまでのように獣にはなれない。情という不純物が心に押し寄せてきていた。

よく親に怒られたが、子供の頃から私にはそういういやに冷たい面があった。たとえば、デパートに行って、接客もできないし気も回らなくて物をすすめるのも下手な店員がいて、そのせいで母が買い物をそこでするのをやめたりすることがあると「あの店員、虫以下ね。」などと言ってしまい、そういうことを思うんじゃない、とたいそうしかられたりした。人を見下しているからだ、と言われた。しかし私には人を見下すほどの誇らしい点は何もない。ただ、私にはその時、その店員がほんとうにそう見えたのだ。目的がわからず闇雲に箱の中をうろうろする虫みたいに。この時もそうだった。それは率直な気持ちだった。私はつきあっていく気もない人に対して優しい気持ちになりたくなかったから、去ろうとしたのだ。

「家に電話する。」

54 猫のミイラがそっと…そこに置いてあった the mummified cat still lay where he had, ever so gently, set it down ▪ きれいな布にくるまって wrapped up in a clean cloth ▪ 彼の優しさを、彼の人格を見てしまったら now that I had seen his gentleness, his personality ▪ もうさっきまでのように獣にはなれない I could no longer make myself an animal, as I had been until just a moment ago ▪ 情という不純物 the impurity we call feelings ▪ 心に押し寄せてきていた had surged into my heart

55 よく親に怒られたが I used to get chewed out by my parents [for this] ▪ 私にはそういういやに冷たい面があった I had this awfully cold side to me ▪ たとえば、デパートに行って for instance, say we'd go to a department store, and ▪ 接客もできないし気も回らなくて物をすすめるのも下手な店員がいて there was some clerk who didn't know how to interact with customers and wasn't attentive and did a bad job trying to get you interested in things, and ▪ そのせいで because of her ▪ 母が買い物をそこでするのをやめたりすることがあると if my mother decided not to do her shopping there or something ▪ 「あの店員、虫以下ね。」などと言ってしまい I might say something like "God, that clerk is lower than an insect," and then ▪ そういうことを思うんじゃない I don't want you thinking thoughts like that! ▪ …とたいそうしかられたりした I would get a good scolding to the effect of… ▪ 人を見下しているからだ、と言われた it's because you look down on people [—that's why you say such terrible things], I was told ▪ 私には人を見下すほどの誇らしい点は何もない there is nothing so splendid about me that I could feel justified in looking down on others ▪ ただ it's just that ▪ 私にはその時、その店員がほんとうにそう見えたのだ at that moment, the clerk honestly had seemed that way to me ▪ 目的がわからず闇雲に箱の中をうろうろする虫みたいに like a bug bumbling around blindly in a box, with no idea where it was trying to go ▪ この時もそうだった that's how it was now, too ▪ それは率直な気持ちだった that, in all candor, was how I felt ▪ つきあっていく気もない人に対して toward a person I had no intention of dating ▪ 優しい気持ちになりたくなかった I didn't want to start feeling tender ▪ 去ろうとしたのだ I made to leave

56 家に電話する I'm going to call home

と私が自分のバッグから携帯電話を取り出そうとすると、彼はそれを取り上げ、踏みつぶした。

「何するのよ！」

と言って立ち上がってドアに向かった私を、彼は突き飛ばして押し倒し、またもや犯そうとした。私は耐えられず、そのへんにあった長細い像を握って、彼の顔にうちおろした。土でできたその像はぐしゃりと割れ、彼の顔が血まみれになった。

それを見た時、私の中に眠っていた愛情という概念の全てが沸点に達した。これまでに愛した人々、これからの人生で愛する人々、その人たちとの通じあえない思い、たまらなさ、切なさ、全てを表すものがその瞬間私を一杯に満たした。

「ごめんなさい、何ていうことを！」

私の目からは涙があふれ、「両手は彼を抱き締めた。

「いいんだ、悪いのは僕だ。」

彼は言った。

57 | 私が自分のバッグから携帯電話を取り出そうとすると as I tried to take my cell phone from my bag ▪ 彼はそれを取り上げ、踏みつぶした he took it from me and stomped on it, crushing it

58 | 何するのよ！ what the hell are you doing!

59 | 立ち上がってドアに向かった私を、彼は突き飛ばして押し倒し I had just gotten up and was heading for the door when he gave me violent shove, pushed me down with his body, and ▪ またもや犯そうとした tried yet again to have his way with me ▪ 私は耐えられず unable to take it anymore ▪ そのへんにあった長細い像を握って I grabbed hold of a tall, narrow statue that happened to be standing nearby and ▪ 彼の顔にうちおろした brought it down hard on his face ▪ 土でできたその像 the statue, which was made of clay ▪ ぐしゃりと割れ crumbled, and ▪ 彼の顔が血まみれになった his face was soon covered in blood

60 | 私の中に眠っていた愛情という概念の全てが沸点に達した all those things I conceived of as love, feelings that had been slumbering inside me, reached the boiling point ▪ これまでに愛した人々 all the people I had loved in the past ▪ これからの人生で愛する人々 all the people I would love in the future ▪ その人たちとの通じあえない思い all the feelings that they and I could never communicate to each other ▪ たまらなさ、切なさ、全てを表すものがその瞬間私を一杯に満たした the unbearable agonies, the heart-wrenching pain—something that expressed all of that—filled me, in an instant, to the brim

61 | ごめんなさい、何ていうことを！ I'm sorry, I can't believe I did that!

62 | 私の目からは涙があふれ tears spilled from my eyes and ▪ 両手は彼を抱き締めた my hands embraced him tightly

63 | いいんだ、悪いのは僕だ that's okay, it's my fault

私は彼の傷を消毒し、親に電話をして、思うところがあるので二、三日旅に出ます。

と言ってがしゃりと切った。

そして、今度は一段階恋愛に近い状態でまた彼のロフトのふとんに入った。

傷に当たらないように気にしながら抱き合った。

にしても、もう別れの時は近づいていた。お互いにそれがわかっていた。

夜中に目を覚ましたら、細く街灯の光が入っている中で、彼が起き上がっていた。そして私のむきだしのお腹をじっと見ていた。じっと。内臓まで見ているかのように。私は思った。私をミイラにしたいんだ……不思議とこわくはなかった。そしてまた眠ってしまった。

また目が覚めたら今度は大雨が降っている音がした。雨がやんだら帰る、と私は言い、彼はうなずいた。顔の傷の血もすっかり固まっていた。雷の音が大きく鳴り響く中で、最

後の時間を過ごした。

65 | 私は彼の傷を消毒し I sterilized his wound and ■ 思うところがあるので二、三日旅に出ます there's something I want to do, so I'm going on a trip for two or three days ■ がしゃりと切った I banged the receiver down

66 | 今度は this time ■ 一段階恋愛に近い状態で in a state one step closer to love

67 | 傷に当たらないように気にしながら being careful not to touch his cuts ■ 抱き合った we embraced each other

68 | にしても even so ■ もう別れの時は近づいていた the time for us to part was drawing near ■ お互いに both of us

69 | 夜中に目を覚ましたら waking up in the middle of the night ■ 細く街灯の光が入っている中で illuminated by the thin beam of light that streamed in from the streetlamp outside ■ 彼が起き上がっていた he had gotten out of bed ■ 私のむきだしのお腹をじっと見ていた he was staring fixedly at my exposed stomach ■ じっと without moving ■ 内臓まで見ているかのように as if he could see straight through to my guts ■ 私をミイラにしたいんだ he wants to turn me into a mummy ■ 不思議とこわくはなかった I was oddly unafraid

70 | また目が覚めたら when I awoke again ■ 大雨が降っている音がした there was the sound of heavy rainfall ■ 雨がやんだら帰る as soon as the rain stops, I'm going home ■ 顔の傷の血もすっかり固まっていた the blood from the cut on his face had completely hardened ■ 雷の音が大きく鳴り響く中で、最後の時間を過ごした we passed our final moments together amidst the loud boom and crackle of thunder

親にどのくらい怒られたかは、思い出したくもない。彼が殺人犯だったら面白いおちが

ついたのだが、そんなことはなく、殺人犯はまもなくつかまった。変質者のおじさんが、

愛人を殺してばらばらにしたのだった。

　その後、道で田島さんに会うことはなかった。うわさでは、外国でマラリアにかかっ

て、その後帰国してからはノイローゼになって入院とか通院とか、そういう話だった。

私は大学を卒業して、薬剤師になって町を出た。

　さらに数年後、彼はエジプトを舞台にした推理小説でデビューし、ちょっと有名になっ

て雑誌に出たりするようになった。これもまた、なんとベタなおちだろう、と私は思っ

た。賢くて、考古学が好きで、異常な感性を持っているからって、そのまんまの職業に

つくなんて、大した人じゃなかったんだ、と私はまたも親に怒られそうな傲慢な意見を抱

いた。

　彼は結婚したらしく、グラビアには奥さんも出ていた。服の上からでもわかるくらい

に、奥さんの体つきが私の体に似ているのを見た時、私の胸の奥のほうがかすかに痛ん

71 | 親にどのくらい怒られたかは、思い出したくもない I don't even want to remember how much my parents bawled me out ■ 彼が殺人犯だったら if he ended up being the murderer ■ 面白いおちがついたのだが the story would have had a good punch line, but ■ そんなことはなく that wasn't the case, for ■ 殺人犯はまもなくつかまった the murderer was caught soon after ■ 変質者のおじさんが、愛人を殺してばらばらにしたのだった it turned out to be a middle-aged sicko who had killed his lover, then cut her into pieces

72 | その後 after that ■ 道で田島さんに会うことはなかった I never bumped into Tajima on the street again ■ うわさでは rumor had it that ■ 外国でマラリアにかかって he had succumbed to malaria in some foreign country and then ■ その後帰国してからは after that, when he returned to Japan ■ ノイローゼになって入院とか通院とか、そういう話だった he'd had a breakdown and been institutionalized, or at least started seeing a doctor—it was some sort of story like that ■ 私は大学を卒業して、薬剤師になって町を出た I graduated from college, became a pharmacist, and left my hometown behind

73 | さらに数年後 the story continues a few years later ■ 彼はエジプトを舞台にした推理小説でデビューし he made his authorial debut with a mystery set in Egypt and ■ ちょっと有名になって雑誌に出たりするようになった got a bit famous and started turning up in magazines and so on ■ これもまた、なんとベタなおちだろう、と私は思った once again, I thought, matters take the most perfectly clichéd turn ■ 賢くて、考古学が好きで、異常な感性を持っているからって、そのまんまの職業につくなんて、大した人じゃなかったんだ he's clever, he's into archaeology, and he's got an abnormal sensibility, and sure enough, he ends up doing exactly the kind of work you'd predict—I guess he wasn't such an impressive person, after all ■ と私はまたも親に怒られそうな傲慢な意見を抱いた I thought, once again taking an arrogant perspective of the sort my parents would have scolded me for

74 | 彼は結婚したらしく、グラビアには奥さんも出ていた evidently he got married—his wife was in the magazines photos, too ■ 服の上からでもわかる it was obvious even through her clothes ■ ...くらいに、奥さんの体つきが私の体に似ているのを見た時 when I saw that her physique was so like mine that... ■ 私の胸の奥のほうがかすかに痛んだ I felt a faint flicker of pain deep in my heart

だ。

私は普通の恋愛をしていて、恋人とデートしたり、話をしたり、おしゃれして会ったり、セックスしたりしている。もう二度と、夜道で出会った誰かに欲情することはないだろう。あれは若い日の異様に拡大した感受性が、ファンタジーを現実にしてしまった瞬間だった。ものごとはふつう、いろいろな角度から成り立っている。しかしもしも全てを取り払って、ただひとつの世界を見つめたらなんでも可能になる。あの夕方、ふたりはたまたま出会い、私の異様な内面世界に彼が全く同じ力で反応し、化学変化のようなことが起こり、ふたりともが現実とは違う位相に飛び込んでしまったのだ。お互いがとまどうほど強烈な力が働いたのだろう。

時々思う。しかし今の、いろんなことを多様に含んだこの生活のほうが、絶対に、正しくて幸せなのだろうか?

あの夜、目を開けたまま抱き合ってふとんの中で聞いた雷の音の美しさ。もしかしたら、私は、あのままあの世界から出ることができなくなっていたかもしれない。

75 私は普通の恋愛をしていて I'm having an ordinary love affair ■ 恋人とデートしたり、話をしたり、おしゃれして会ったり、セックスしたりしている my boyfriend and I go on dates, we talk, we dress up when we get together, we have sex ■ もう二度と…ことはないだろう I will probably never again… ■ 夜道で出会った誰かに欲情する feel desire for some random person I meet on the street at night ■ あれは…瞬間だった that was an instant when… ■ 若い日の異様に拡大した感受性が、ファンタジーを現実にしてしまった youth's unusually heightened sensibilities turned fantasy into reality ■ ものごとはふつう、いろいろな角度から成り立っている ordinarily, things are made up of all sorts of different angles ■ もしも全てを取り払って、ただひとつの世界を見つめたらなんでも可能になる if one were to take all that away and stare out into a world that is single, unified—then anything becomes possible ■ あの夕方、ふたりはたまたま出会い that evening, the two of us just happened to run into each other and ■ 私の異様な内面世界に彼が全く同じ力で反応し he responded with precisely the same force to the weirdness of my internal world ■ 化学変化のようなことが起こり something like a chemical reaction took place and ■ ふたりとも both of us ■ 現実とは違う位相に飛び込んでしまったのだ plunged into a dimension different from reality ■ お互いがとまどうほど強烈な力が働いたのだろう I guess some force, so intense that we were both thrown for a loop, must have acted on us

76 時々思う sometimes I find myself wondering ■ いろんなことを多様に含んだこの生活のほうが、絶対に、正しくて幸せなのだろうか？ is it unequivocally true that this life, with all its variety, is the correct and happy one?

77 あの夜、目を開けたまま抱き合ってふとんの中で聞いた雷の音の美しさ the beauty of the peals of thunder I heard that night as I lay embracing him in his futon, my eyes wide open ■ もしかしたら it could be that ■ 私は、あのままあの世界から出ることができなくなっていたかもしれない I might have stayed there, just as I was, unable to leave that world

想像する。例えばあの猫のように、ミイラにされてしまった異次元の私を。例えば私の、息ができなくなるほどの愛情に打ち壊されて頭を割られて死んでしまった彼を。それはそんなに悪いことにはどうしても思えなかった。

78 | 想像する I let my imagination wander ■ あの猫のように、ミイラにされてしまった異次元の私を me in some other dimension, made into a mummy like that cat ■ 私の、息ができなくなるほどの愛情に打ち壊されて頭を割られて死んでしまった彼を him dead, his head crushed in by a love so strong it suffocated me

79 | それはそんなに悪いことにはどうしても思えなかった somehow, I simply couldn't convince myself that that would have been such an awful thing

北村　薫

Kitamura Kaoru

When he made his debut as an author in 1989 with *Sora-tobu uma* (*The Flying Horse*), Kitamura Kaoru kept his identity, including his age and sex, completely hidden—he was what is known in Japanese as a "masked writer." The fact that the narrator of his first two works was a female college student inspired rumors that he, too, was a woman of the same age. (His gender-neutral pen name helped here.) Needless to say, Kitamura was not then a college-age woman, and in fact he had never been one. The rumors were, no doubt, a testimony to the persuasiveness of his narrative voice.

Kitamura was born in Saitama Prefecture in 1949. Like Tawada Yōko, who is also represented in this collection, he graduated from the literature department at Waseda University. He has been nominated for the prestigious Naoki Prize five times, won the Mystery Writers of Japan Award in 1991 for *Yoru no semi* (*Night Cicadas*), and received the Honkaku Mystery Prize in 2006 for his tour de force *Nippon kōka no nazo* (*The Japanese Nickel Mystery*), a marvelously wacky pastiche, complete with footnotes, that purports—as its subtitle, "Ellery Queen's Last Case," suggests—to be a translation  of the unpublished final work, set in Japan, of the celebrated pseudonymous mystery author and detective, Ellery Queen. This work was also given the Bakamisu Prize, which might be translated as the "Are You Kidding Me!? Mystery Prize," awarded annually to mysteries with the most mind-boggling, flabbergasting, or ridiculous plots or endings.

"Hyakumonogatari" ("One Hundred Stories") was included, along with twenty-two other very short stories, in the collection *1950 nen no bakkutosu* (*1950 Back Toss*), which was published by Shinchōsha in 2007. If you feel inclined to dig deeper into Kitamura's fictional world after you read this story, this book is a good place to start.

百物語

北村 薫

1

「わたし、寝たくないの」

駄々っ子のように嫌々をしながら、美都子がいう。これは、文字通り《眠りたくない》という意味である。あるいは恐れているのかもしれない、──横になってしまったら、おかしなことをされるのではないかと。

安西も男だから、若い娘と朝まで過ごすことになって、甘い気分にならないわけではない。しかし、条件が悪すぎる。美都子は、ついさっきまで周期的な吐き気に襲われていた。足元がふらついていた。安西も、そんな娘に襲いかかれるほどの人でなしではない。ましてや、先輩から《おい、お前、送ってやれや》と命令されたのである。その手前もあ

2 　駄々っ子のように like a spoiled child ▪ 嫌々をしながら shaking her head back and forth ▪ これは、文字通り...という意味である the literal meaning of this was... ▪《眠りたくない》"I don't want to go to sleep" ▪ あるいは or then again ▪ 恐れているのかもしれない maybe she is afraid ▪ 横になってしまったら、おかしなことをされるのではないかと afraid that if she lies down, she may end up on the receiving end of some unseemly act

3 　安西も男だから Anzai is a guy like any other, so ▪ 若い娘と朝まで過ごすことになって when circumstance dictates that he stay up until morning with a girl ▪ 甘い気分にならないわけではない he does, of course, start feeling a bit romantic ▪ 条件が悪すぎる the conditions are simply too bad ▪ ついさっきまで until just a moment ago ▪ 周期的な吐き気に by regular bouts of nausea ▪ 襲われていた kept being seized ▪ 足元がふらついていた she was shaky on her legs ▪ 安西も、そんな娘に襲いかかるほどの人でなしではない Anzai isn't the sort of inhuman brute who would try and have his way with a girl in that state ▪ ましてや and what's more ▪ 先輩から...と命令された he had been ordered by a senior classmate... ▪《おい、おお前、送ってやれや》"hey, Anzai...see her home, will you?" ▪ その手前もある he had his relationship with that classmate to consider, too

る。

順当なら、今頃はとっくに布団に入って高いびきだ。それが雷のおかげで面倒なことになった。

帰り道が途中まで一緒なのと、いわゆる人畜無害な人柄ゆえに、酔い潰れた一年生を預けられた安西なのだ。しかし地下鉄のアナウンスは、落雷のため、ある路線が不通で復旧の見込みがたっていないと繰り返した。美都子のアパートに向かう線だった。

美都子は、調子の定まらない声で笑い、次いで、胸を押さえ、切れ切れに、

「先輩の、とこで、休ませて、ください」

当たり前ならタクシーを使うところだが、まだ学生の安西には、そういう気がまわらなかった。金がないわけでもない。安西はいわゆる《お坊ちゃま》なのだ。それだけに小回りのきかないところもある。ただ、いたって真面目に、後輩を助けようと思った。そして、交通至便の自分のワンルームマンションに美都子を連れ込んだのである。

安西はいった。

4 | 順当なら ordinarily ▪ 今頃は by now ▪ とっくに ages ago ▪ 布団に入って under the covers ▪ 高いびきだ be snoring loudly ▪ それが雷のおかげで面倒なことになった but the thunder had complicated matters (lit., "but it had become a hassle thanks to the thunder")

5 | 帰り道が途中まで一緒なのと they took the same route part of the way home and ▪ いわゆる人畜無害な人柄ゆえに because he was the sort of guy who "wouldn't hurt a fly," as people say ▪ 酔い潰れた一年生 a dead-drunk freshman ▪ …を預けられた安西なのだ Anzai had found himself put in charge of… ▪ 地下鉄のアナウンス an announcement on the subway ▪ 落雷のため as a result of being struck by lightning ▪ ある路線が不通で復旧の見込みがたっていない a certain track was impassable, and it was unclear when service would be resumed ▪ …と繰り返した kept repeating that… ▪ 美都子のアパートに向かう線 the line that went in the direction of Mitsuko's apartment

6 | 調子の定まらない声で笑い had laughed, an uncertain waver in her voice ▪ 次いで then ▪ 胸を押さえ pressing a hand to her chest ▪ 切れ切れに speaking in fragments

7 | 先輩の、とこで、休ませて、ください please…let me…rest at…your place

8 | 当たり前ならタクシーを使うところだが if he were used to this kind of thing, he would have gotten a taxi, but ▪ まだ学生の安西には、そういう気がまわらなかった Anzai, who was still a student, hadn't thought of that ▪ 金がないわけでもない it wasn't that he didn't have the money ▪ いわゆる《お坊ちゃま》what people call a "rich boy" ▪ それだけに being that type ▪ 小回りのきかないところもある he tended to be somewhat less adaptable ▪ ただ simply ▪ いたって真面目に in as earnest a manner as possible ▪ 後輩を助けようと思った he wanted to help this underclasswoman out ▪ そして and so ▪ 交通至便の自分のワンルームマンションに to his studio apartment, which was conveniently located near the station ▪ 美都子を連れ込んだのである he had brought Mitsuko back

9 | 安西はいった Anzai had said:

「頼むから、静かにしててくれよ」

美都子は黙ったまま、部屋に入り、床に膝を抱いて座ったかと思うと、そのまま眠りそうになった。

頭が一回揺れた。それだけで、すぐに引き起こすように首を上げ、ぐるりを見渡し、

「どうしたんですか、あたし?」

不思議なことに、酔いは一気に醒めたようだ。その声は裏返って、普段の美都子のものではなかった。あからさまな恐怖が、そこにあった。

安西は半分感情を害し、半分奇妙な興奮を覚えた。美都子は夏らしくノースリーブのミニワンピース、色は黒である。白のレースのオーバーブラウスを、お洒落にはおっている。浜辺に寄せる波の泡立ちのようなレース模様が、その波の下のきっぱりした黒と、柔らかな女の肌の色を引き立たせていた。

心理学のサークルの中でも、安西達のところは女性が特に少ない。顔立ちの整っている美都子は、お姫様のような扱いを受けていた。しかし、酒の席には殆ど顔を見せなかっ

10 頼むから、静かにしててくれよ please, you've got to keep quiet, okay?

11 美都子は黙ったまま、部屋に入り Mitsuko had entered the room without saying a word, and ■ 床に膝を抱いて座ったかと思うと no sooner had she sat down on the floor, hugging her knees, than ■ そのまま眠りそうになった she started looking as if she might fall asleep on the spot

12 頭が一回揺れた her head bobbed once ■ それだけで that was as far as she went ■ すぐに引き起こすように首を上げ she soon raised her head, practically hoisting it up ■ ぐるりを見渡し surveyed her surroundings and

13 どうしたんですか、あたし？ what happened to me?

14 不思議なことに oddly ■ 酔いは...醒めたようだ she seemed to have sobered up ■ 一気に all at once ■ その声は裏返って、普段の美都子のものではなかった her voice had gone into falsetto—it wasn't her ordinary voice ■ あからさまな恐怖が、そこにあった there was, in her tone, an undisguised sense of fear

15 半分感情を害し、半分奇妙な興奮を覚えた felt half hurt, half oddly excited ■ 夏らしくノースリーブのミニワンピース、色は黒である a suitably summery minidress, black in color ■ 白のレースのオーバーブラウスを、お洒落にはおっている she had on a white lace blouse over the dress—a nicely chic combination ■ 浜辺に寄せる波の泡立ちのようなレース模様 the pattern of the lace, which was like a crest of foam on a wave rushing up the shore ■ その波の下のきっぱりした黒と、柔らかな女の肌の色を引き立たせていた showed to advantage the crisp black beneath the wave, and the tones of her soft, feminine skin

16 心理学のサークルの中でも even compared to the other psychology clubs on campus ■ 安西達のところは女性が特に少ない the group Anzai belonged to had particularly few women ■ 顔立ちの整っている美都子は Mitsuko, with her regular features ■ お姫様のような扱いを受けていた was treated like a princess ■ 酒の席には殆ど顔を見せなかった she hardly ever came to drinking parties

た。それが、どういう風の吹き回しか、新しい洋服を買って参加した今回は、最後まで付き合ってしまったのだ。

コーヒーをいれてやる。美都子は始発の時間を聞いた。気分は大分よくなったらしい。

2

17 「一番で帰るの？」

18 大きな目で、にらむようにして繰り返す。

19 「わたし、それまで起きていたいんです」

20 「一番で帰るの？」

21 「はい」

22 「かえって目立つよ」

23 「それはいいんです」

24 「うちの人が電話かけてくるのか」

■ それが、どういう風の吹き回しか and yet, blown by who knew what fickle wind ■ 新しい洋服を買って参加した今回は this time, having joined the group in a new outfit ■ 最後まで付き合ってしまったのだ she had ended up staying to the very end

17 | コーヒーをいれてやる he made her some coffee ■ 始発の時間 the hour of the first train ■ 気分は大分よくなったらしい she seemed to be feeling much better

18 | わたし、それまで起きていたいんです I want to stay up until then

19 | 大きな目で、にらむようにして繰り返す she kept repeating, glaring at him with her large eyes

20 | 一番で帰るの？ you're going to go back on the first train?

22 | かえって目立つよ you'll only end up attracting more attention, you know

23 | それはいいんです that doesn't bother me

24 | うちの人が電話かけてくるのか what, are your parents going to call?

「それは……分かりませんけど」

「アリバイ、ちゃんと考えてから受けた方がいいよ」

美都子は黙って頷く。

とにかく、始発で帰る、朝まで寝ないと決めている。安西は、おもりをする気になり、

《そうか。それじゃあ……》と、当てもなくいいかけ、そこで、何かで読んだ言葉がひらめいた。

「――百物語でもやるか」

「え?」

「聞いたことない?　百本、蠟燭つけといてね、お化けの話、するんだよ。一つ話すたびに、一本消す。最後の話が終わって真っ暗になった時、本物のお化けが出て来るんだって」

「……」

「女の子って、恐い話が好きだろう」

26 | アリバイ、ちゃんと考えてから受けた方がいいよ make sure you think up a good alibi before you answer (lit., "you'd better take the call [only] after you do a good job thinking")

27 | 黙って頷く nodded without speaking

28 | とにかく、始発で帰る、朝まで寝ないと決めている at any rate, she would go home on the first train, and she had made up her mind not to sleep until morning ■ 安西は、おもりをする気になり Anzai, feeling like a babysitter ■《そうか。それじゃあ》…… "I see. Well, in that case..." ■ 当てもなくいいかけ he began, without having anything in mind to say ■ そこで、何かで読んだ言葉がひらめいた when a word he'd read somewhere flashed into his mind

29 | 百物語でもやるか why don't we do a hundred stories?

30 | え? huh?

31 | 聞いたことない? you've never heard of it? ■ 百本、蝋燭つけといてね、お化けの話、するんだよ you light a hundred candles, you know, and then you tell scary stories ■ 一つ話すたびに、一本消す with each story you tell, you extinguish one candle ■ 最後の話が終わって真っ暗になった時 when the last story is over and the room is totally dark ■ 本物のお化けが出て来るんだって a real monster is supposed to show up

33 | 女の子って、恐い話が好きだろう girls are supposed to like scary stories

「真っ暗に……」美都子は、つぶやいた。それから、我に返ったように、「でも百本の蠟燭なんてあるんですか」

「そりゃあないさ。第一、百だとしたら、二人で話して五十ずつ。大変過ぎる。もっと簡単にやろう」

安西はもう寝るのをあきらめている。いかに退屈しないで朝まで過ごすかが問題なのだ。美都子はいぶかしげに、

「どうするんです」

「この部屋もトイレも風呂も、とにかく明かりのあるところは全部点けるのさ。そして、片方が一つ恐い話をしたら、一つ明かりを消す。そういうわけさ」

美都子は、なるほどと頷く。そして、青白い顔で注文をつけた。

「カーテンを……」

「そうか。閉め切らないと、最後に暗くならないからね」

完全主義者だなと、いささか面倒に思いつつ、安西は立ち上がってカーテンに手をのば

34 | つぶやいた murmured ▪ 我に返ったように as if she had just awoken from a daze ▪ でも百本の蠟燭なんてあるんですか but you don't have a hundred candles, do you?

35 | そりゃあないさ　hardly ▪ 第一、百だとしたら、二人で話して五十ずつ besides, if we did it with a hundred, with the two of us talking, we'd each have fifty ▪ 大変過ぎる it'd be too much ▪ もっと簡単にやろう let's do it more simply

36 | 安西はもう寝るのをあきらめている by now, Anzai had given up on sleeping ▪ いかに退屈しないで朝まで過ごすかが問題なのだ the problem was how to make it to morning without getting bored ▪ いぶかしげに looking suspicious

37 | どうするんです then what will we do?

38 | この部屋もトイレも風呂も in this room, and in the WC, and in the bathroom ▪ とにかく明かりのあるところは全部点けるのさ we'll turn on every light, in every place that's got one ▪ 片方が一つ恐い話をしたら when one or the other of us has told a scary story ▪ 一つ明かりを消す we'll turn out a light ▪ そういうわけさ that's how we'll do it

39 | なるほどと頷く nodded, indicating that she understood ▪ そして、青白い顔で注文をつけた then, her face pale, she made one request

40 | カーテンを…… the curtain needs to be...

41 | そうか good point ▪ 閉め切らないと、最後に暗くならないからね because if we don't shut the curtain nice and tight, it won't get dark at the end, will it?

42 | 完全主義者だなと、いささか面倒に思いつつ、安西は立ち上がって she's quite a perfectionist, Anzai thought, and, though he found it a bit of a bother, he stood up and ▪ ……に手をのばした reached for...

した。　街路灯の光が見えた。　それがするりと視界から隠れた。　密閉された空間に二人は入った。

安西は机の上のスタンドから懐中電灯にいたるまで、総ての明かりを点けた。　部屋は明るい箱になった。

「さて、いい出したのは僕の方だから、こっちから始めよう」

安西は、本で読んだ化け猫の話をして、風呂場を暗くした。

演技なのか、それとも酒のせいか、美都子は眉を寄せると、子供の時に聞いたらしい山姥の昔話をした。　そして、ゆらりと立ち上がり、部屋の明かりを消した。

3

次第に闇は深さを増していく。

美都子は、思いのほか巧みな語り手だった。

■ 街路灯の光が見えた he could see the light from the streetlamps ■ それがするりと視界から隠れた in a flash, they vanished from sight ■ 密閉された空間に二人は入った the two were now in a completely closed-in space

43 机の上のスタンドから懐中電灯にいたるまで from the lamp on his desk to his flashlight ■ 総ての明かりを点けた he turned on every single light ■ 部屋は明るい箱になった the room became a bright box

44 さて well then ■ いい出したのは僕の方だから I'm the one who suggested this, so ■ こっちから始めよう why don't I start

45 安西は、本で読んだ化け猫の話をして Anzai told a story about a demonic cat, and ■ 風呂場を暗くした darkened the bathroom

46 演技なのか、それとも酒のせいか、美都子は眉を寄せると Mitsuko furrowed her brow—she was either acting or under the influence of the alcohol, it wasn't clear which—and then ■ 子供の時に聞いたらしい山姥の昔話をした told a folk tale, evidently one she had been told as a child, about an old mountain witch ■ ゆらりと立ち上がり she rose slowly to her feet and ■ 部屋の明かりを消した turned off the overhead light

47 次第に闇は深さを増していく gradually the darkness deepened

48 美都子は、思いのほか巧みな語り手だった Mitsuko was a surprisingly skillful storyteller

「……でも、雨戸を開けてみたら、誰もいなかったそうです」

いくつめかの物語を終えた後、視線をさまよわせている。安西がいった。

「もう、そこしかないだろう」

懐中電灯を別にすれば、開いたトイレのドアからこぼれてくる光だけが、残ったよう

だった。しかし、美都子はいった。

「ビデオ……」

見ると確かに、そこに時刻表示の文字が浮かんでいる。

「そいつも、切るの」

安西は、相手の細かさに辟易しながら、仕方なく立ち上がってコンセントを抜いた。自

分のいい出したことだから文句もいえない。

友達に聞いた高速道路の怪談をして、仕返しのように冷蔵庫のコードを抜いた。そこに

も通電表示の小さな灯がともっていたのだ。しかし、美都子はにこりともしなかった。

学校の机の因縁話をすると、立ち上がってトイレの明かりを消した。ぐんと、頭から押

49 ……でも、雨戸を開けてみたら、誰もいなかったそうです but they say that when he opened the rain door, there was no one there

50 いくつめかの物語を終えた後、視線をさまよわせている having finished her story—it wasn't clear how many they had told by then—she let her eyes wander around the room

51 もう、そこしかないだろう that's the only one left, right?

52 懐中電灯を別にすれば other than the flashlight ■ 開いたトイレのドアからこぼれてくる光だけが、残ったようだった the glow spilling from the open door of the WC seemed to be all that was left

54 見ると確かに glancing over, he saw that she was right: ■ そこに時刻表示の文字が浮かんでいる the numbers marking the time hovered there [in the darkness]

55 そいつも、切るの you want to turn that off, too?

56 相手の細かさに辟易しながら though he felt a bit irked by his partner's attention to detail ■ 仕方なく立ち上がってコンセントを抜いた he had no choice but to stand up and pull the plug ■ 自分のいい出したことだから文句もいえない he had suggested playing the game, so he couldn't complain

57 友達に聞いた高速道路の怪談をして after telling a scary story, set on a highway, that he had heard from a friend ■ 仕返しのように as if in retaliation ■ 冷蔵庫のコードを抜いた he pulled the plug on the refrigerator ■ そこにも通電表示の小さな灯がともっていたのだ there had been a little light burning on it, as well, showing that it was getting electricity ■ にこりともしなかった didn't even grin ■ 学校の机の因縁話をすると after telling a story about the bad karma of a school desk ■ ぐんと、頭から押し付けられるように暗くなった it became so dark that it was like being shoved down from above [by the darkness]

し付けられるように暗くなった。

安西は、美都子の足元に懐中電灯の黄色い光を向けながら、

「もう、こいつだけだね」

美都子は、ぼんやりとしてよく見えない顔を横に振り、

「……電話があります」

それは嫌な気がした。

だが、どうして、それが嫌なのか安西にも、よく分からない。

「なるほど」

格段に闇が深くなったせいで、小さな光も目立つ。確かに美都子のいう通り、電話機の

ところに、苺シロップのような色の光が見えた。

安西は、ほとんど意地になって、早口に小話めいた怪談をして、電話機のコンセントを

抜いた。そして、懐中電灯を振り、

「さあ。これでこいつだけだぞ」

58 | 美都子の足元に懐中電灯の黄色い光を向けながら　while aiming the flashlight's yellow beam at Mitsuko's feet

59 | もう、こいつだけだね it's just this now, huh?

60 | ぼんやりとしてよく見えない顔 her face, which looked blurred and indistinct ▪ …を横に振り she shook…and (said…)

61 | ……電話があります there's the phone

62 | それは嫌な気がした this gave him an unpleasant feeling

63 | だが、どうして、それが嫌なのか安西にも、よく分からない and yet Anzai himself didn't know where that unpleasant feeling came from

64 | なるほど you're right

65 | 格段に闇が深くなったせいで since the darkness had grown considerably deeper ▪ 小さな光も目立つ even a little light caught the eye ▪ 確かに美都子のいう通り it was just as Mitsuko said ▪ 電話機のところに、苺シロップのような色の光が見えた he could make out a light the color of strawberry syrup over where the phone was

66 | ほとんど意地になって almost obstinately ▪ 早口に小話めいた怪談をして told a scary story that seemed more like an ordinary anecdote, speaking very rapidly ▪ 電話機のコンセントを抜いた unplugged the phone ▪ 懐中電灯を振り waving the flashlight back and forth

67 | さあ。これでこいつだけだぞ all right. Now it's really just this

美都子は、ふうっと首をめぐらし、そうですね、と満足そうにいい、座った。安西は、

その手に最後の光を渡した。

4

いろいろと話が出ましたけれど、本当に恐いのは、わけの分からないもの。見えるものよりは見えないもの。そうですよね。とすれば、自分て恐くありません？

額や顎、うなじや頭の上なんて、自分では絶対に見えませんよね。それって、凄く、恐くありませんか。一番近いのに、決して見ることができない。

それどころじゃない。眠ると自分が消えますね。何をしているのかどころか、どうなっているのかも分からない。仮にですよ、寝ている間は魚になっていたって、自分には分からない。角が生えて牛になっていたって。いえ、もっとわけの分からない、何かになっていたって。

68 ふうっと首をめぐらし slowly swiveled her head around and ■ そうで
すね、と満足そうにいい、座った remarked with evident satisfaction
that he was right, then sat down ■ その手に最後の光を渡した passed
her the last light

69 いろいろと話が出ましたけれど we've heard all kinds of different stories, but ■ 本当に恐いのは the truly frightening ones ■ わけの分か
らないもの are those you can't even understand ■ 見えるものよりは見
えないもの more than the visible, it's the invisible ■ そうですよね I
mean, wouldn't you agree? ■ とすれば、自分て恐くありません? and if
that's the case, wouldn't you say that we ourselves are frightening?

70 額や顎、うなじや頭の上なんて things like your forehead and chin, the
back of your neck and the top of your head ■ 自分では絶対に見えま
せんよね there's absolutely no way you can see them by yourself, is
there? ■ それって、凄く、恐くありませんか now that's *really* frightening, don't you think? ■ 一番近いのに、決して見ることができない you
can never see them, even though they're closer to you than anything

71 それどころじゃない and it's much worse than that ■ 眠ると自分が消
えますね you disappear when you go to sleep, right? ■ 何をしている
のかどころか、どうなっているのかも分からない not only do you have
no idea what you're doing, you don't even know what's happening to
you ■ 仮にですよ suppose, just for the moment ■ 寝ている間は魚に
なっていたって suppose you were a fish the whole time you were
sleeping—even then ■ 自分には分からない you wouldn't know ■ 角
が生えて牛になっていたって even if you grew horns and turned into a
cow ■ いえ or one might go further ■ もっとわけの分からない、何か
になっていたって even if you turned into something else, something
more bizarre

そうでしょう？

そういう娘の話です。小さいうちは何でもなかった。別に変なことは感じなかった。で

もある時から、一人で寝るようにいわれたのです。

泊まりがけの修学旅行も行かせてはもらえなかった。合宿のある部活動はいけないと

いわれました。とにかく、よそに泊まるのは駄目だといわれたのです。ええ、父親にで

す。

納得できないでしょう？　初めはしつけがきびしいだけだと思っていましたから、反発

しました。

高校の時に、文化祭の準備で遅くなった。そうしたら、父親が学校まで来ました。屈

辱ですよね。友達にあわす顔がない。自分の部屋に閉じこもったきり、出て来ない日が続

いた。そうしたら、父親が頬をスプーンですくったように痩せた顔になって、総てを話す

といいました。

その家には、特別ないい伝えがあるというのです。夜に熟睡すると、体があるものに

73 | そういう娘の話です this is a story about a girl like that ▪ 小さいうちは何でもなかった there was nothing wrong when she was little ▪ 別に変なことは感じなかった she didn't notice anything particularly odd ▪ でもある時から but after a certain point ▪ 一人で寝るようにいわれたのです she was told she had to sleep by herself

74 | 泊まりがけの修学旅行も行かせてはもらえなかった she wasn't allowed to go on any overnight field trips, either ▪ 合宿のある部活動はいけないといわれました she was told not to join any clubs that involved overnight training sessions ▪ とにかく、よそに泊まるのは駄目だといわれたのです no matter what the reason, she was not to spend the night anywhere else, she was told ▪ ええ、父親にです yes, that's right—by her father

75 | 納得できないでしょう? how could you accept that? ▪ 初めはしつけがきびしいだけだと思っていましたから、反発しました at first she thought her parents were simply trying to bring her up very strictly, so she rebelled

76 | 高校の時に、文化祭の準備で遅くなった in high school, preparations for Culture Festival kept her at school until late at night ▪ そうしたら、父親が学校まで来ました and so her father came all the way to school to get her ▪ 屈辱ですよね it's humiliating, isn't it? ▪ 友達にあわす顔がない she can't look her friends in the eyes ▪ 自分の部屋に閉じこもったきり she holed up in her room and stayed there ▪ 出て来ない日が続いた several days passed without her coming out ▪ 父親が頬をスプーンですくったように痩せた顔になって her father's face grew so emaciated it was as if his cheeks had been scooped out with a spoon, and ▪ 総てを話すといいました he said he would tell her everything

77 | その家には、特別ないい伝えがあるというのです he tells her there is a special legend that has been passed down in her family ▪ 夜に熟睡すると、体があるものに変ずるというのです he tells her that at night when she is fast asleep, her body changes into a certain thing

変ずるというのです。

娘は呆れ返って、そんな馬鹿な話のために、今までわたしの外泊を禁じていたのかと、なじりました。大体、《何》になるのだ、と聞きました。ところが父親は、《あるもの》としか分からない。自分も《それ》が動く音を壁越しに聞いただけだというのです。

それが、もし、わたしのことなら――と、娘はいいました。わたしのことなら、子供の頃、母の実家にいったことがあるではないかと。

父親は答えました。それは、この家の娘が一人前になってから起こることなのだ。男にはそういうことはない。父の代、祖父の代と男ばかりが続いたから問題はなかったのだ、と。そして、さらに恐ろしいことをいいました。父自身、そんないい伝えなど馬鹿げたものだと思っていたそうです。しかし娘が、子供でなくなったと知った時に、背筋に氷の針を通されたような感じがしたそうです。これはいけない、と思った。母に部屋を別にしろといったそうです。子供の自立心を養うということだけで説得すればよかったのに、気がせいて、いい伝えの話をしたそうです。母は一笑にふし、そして、――その夜から、正気

78 娘は呆れ返って the young woman is astounded, and ▪ そんな馬鹿な話のために、今までわたしの外泊を禁じていたのかと、なじりました blasts her father, asking, Did you seriously forbid me to sleep away from home all this time, all on account of some stupid story like that? ▪ 大体、《何》になるのだ、と聞きました and anyway, *what* is it that I become? she asked ▪ ところが父親は、《あるもの》としか分からない but "a certain thing" is as much as her father knows ▪ 自分も《それ》が動く音を壁越しに聞いただけだというのです he himself has only heard the sound of "it" moving, he says, from the other side of the wall

79 それが、もし、わたしのことなら——と、娘はいいました if this is actually supposed to happen to me, the young woman says ▪ わたしのことなら、子供の頃、母の実家にいったことがあるではないかと if this is actually me you're talking about, well, I sometimes stayed at mom's parents' house when I was a child, didn't I?

80 それは、この家の娘が一人前になってから起こることなのだ it's something that occurs when the girls in our family reach adulthood ▪ 男にはそういうことはない it doesn't happen with the men ▪ 父の代、祖父の代と男ばかりが続いたから問題はなかったのだ、と there was never any problem in my father's generation, or in my grandfather's generation, because only boys were born, he told her ▪ そして、さらに恐ろしいことをいいました and then he said something even more frightening ▪ 父自身 her father himself ▪ そんないい伝えなど馬鹿げたものだと思っていたそうです used to believe, it seems, that this was just a ridiculous old legend ▪ しかし娘が、子供でなくなったと知った時に and yet the moment he realized his daughter was no longer a child ▪ 背筋に氷の針を通されたような感じがした he felt as if a needle of ice had been run through his spine ▪ これはいけない、と思った things can't go on as they have been, he thought ▪ 母に部屋を別にしろといったそうです he told her mother to move her into a separate room ▪ 子供の自立心を養うということだけで説得すればよかったのに he should have persuaded her simply by saying it was necessary to encourage the child's sense of independence, but ▪ 気がせいて、いい伝えの話をしたそうです it seems he was too agitated, and so he told her about the legend ▪ 母は一笑にふし、そして her mother laughed it off, and then ▪ その夜から、正気を失ったそうです *that very night*, it seems, she lost her mind

を失ったそうです。

だからなのだ、と父は苦渋に満ちた顔でいいます。信じられる話ではありません。それでは深夜、自分はメデューサになるというのか。いえ、蛇の髪は忌まわしいとはいえ、その姿が知れています。知られぬ恐怖の底無しに比べれば、それも甘いものに思えます。娘はことの真偽を知れるものなら、何を捨ててもいいとまで思いました。

そう、今はビデオがあります。娘は自分の部屋にカメラを仕掛け、明るいままで寝てみました。しかし駄目です。驚いたことに浅い眠りに入ったところで、娘は立ち上がりカメラのスイッチを切ってしまうのです。何度やってもそうでした。自己保存の本能というのは強いものです。そういう行動が無意識に出るということに、娘は震えました。父の言葉を信じる気になりました。

先祖の女達はどうして来たのか。夫に寝姿を見せぬようにして来たのでしょう。戦前はその地方の名のある家だったといいますから、そういういい伝えを知っても来る婿があったのでしょう。

81 | だからなのだ、と父は苦渋に満ちた顔でいいます that's the reason for all this, her father said, his expression full of torment ■ 信じられる話ではありません you can't believe a story like that ■ それでは深夜、自分はメデューサになるというのか so are they saying that late at night I turn into a Medusa, is that it? ■ 蛇の髪は忌まわしいとはいえ having snakes for hair would certainly be loathsome, it's true, but ■ その姿が知れています that form is well within the realm of our understanding ■ 知られぬ恐怖の底無しに比べれば compared to the bottomless depths of an unknown terror ■ それも甘いものに思えます even that seems too mild ■ 娘はことの真偽を知れるものなら、何を捨ててもいいとまで思いました the young woman reached the point where she would be willing to give up anything, if only this would allow her to discover the truth of the matter

82 | そう、今はビデオがあります and yes, we have video recorders now ■ カメラを仕掛け set up a camera ■ 明るいままで寝てみました tried going to sleep with the lights on ■ 駄目です it didn't work ■ 驚いたことに astonishingly ■ 浅い眠りに入ったところで no sooner had she fallen into a light sleep than ■ 娘は立ち上がり the young woman would stand up and ■ カメラのスイッチを切ってしまうのです turn off the camera ■ 何度やってもそうでした no matter how many times she tried, the result was the same ■ 自己保存の本能というのは強いものです the instinct for self-preservation is a mighty thing ■ そういう行動が無意識に出るということに、娘は震えました the fact that she embarked on this action, unconsciously, set the young woman trembling ■ 父の言葉を信じる気になりました she became inclined to believe her father's words

83 | 先祖の女達はどうして来たのか how had her female ancestors dealt with this? ■ 夫に寝姿を見せぬようにして来たのでしょう they must have kept their husbands from seeing them asleep ■ 戦前はその地方の名のある家だったといいますから they say that before the war, her family had been well-known in the region, so ■ そういういい伝えを知っても来る婿があったのでしょう there must have been men willing to marry into the family even knowing the legend

しかし、娘は今の世の人間です。これからの人生をどう過ごせばよいのでしょう。普段は何でもない、ただの女です。しかし内には、得体の知れぬ怪物を隠しているのです。そ

れを思うと、娘は毎夜の眠りが恐くてならないのです。

5

語り終えて、美都子は懐中電灯の灯を消した。

面白い話だなと、安西は思った。この物語の、何が何の譬えなのか、心理学的には、ご

く簡単に解けそうな気がする。

誰の目も届かぬ漆黒の闇にくるまれて、美都子は、ほっと息をついたようだった。話し

かけようとしたが、奇妙に口が動かずにいる内に、すうすうという寝息が聞こえ出した。

体が、その一息ごとに強ばるのを、安西は感じた。美都子のいる辺りの闇が濃くなるよう

な気がした。

84 | 娘は今の世の人間です the young woman is a being of this world ▪ こ
れからの人生をどう過ごせばよいのでしょう how should she live the
rest of her life? ▪ 普段は何でもない、ただの女です most of the time
she's just an unremarkable, ordinary woman ▪ しかし内には、得体の
知れぬ怪物を隠しているのです and yet she conceals within her an unknown beast ▪ それを思うと、娘は毎夜の眠りが恐くてならないのです
when she thinks of that, she becomes helplessly afraid of going to sleep
each night

85 | 語り終えて having finished her story ▪ 懐中電灯の灯を消した switched
off the flashlight

86 | 面白い話だなと wow, that was a good story ▪ この物語の、何が何の
譬えなのか、心理学的には、ごく簡単に解けそうな気がする he had the
sense that it would be a very simple matter to figure out, from a
psychological perspective, what in this tale served as a metaphor for
what

87 | 誰の目も届かぬ漆黒の闇にくるまれて shrouded in the perfect dark-
ness, where no eyes could reach her ▪ ほっと息をついたようだった
seemed to have given a little sigh of relief ▪ 話しかけようとしたが he
was about to say something to her, but ▪ 奇妙に口が動かずにいる内
に while he was sitting there, unable for some odd reason to make his
mouth move ▪ すうすうという寝息が聞こえ出した he began to hear
the deep, regular breathing of a person fast asleep ▪ 体が、その一息ご
とに強ばるのを、安西は感じた Anzai sensed his body growing stiffer
with each successive breath [he heard] ▪ 美都子のいる辺りの闇が濃
くなるような気がした he had the impression that the darkness where
Mitsuko was sitting was growing deeper

安西は動こうとしたが動けぬ自分を感じた。馬鹿なと笑おうとしたが、頬がひきつった

だけだった。

美都子のいたところで、──何かが動いた。

夜明けまで、まだ間がありそうだった。

88 動こうとしたが動けぬ自分を感じた tried to move, only to find himself immobile ■ 馬鹿なと笑おうとしたが this is ridiculous, he thought, and tried to laugh, but ■ 頰がひきつっただけだった his cheeks just stiffened

89 美都子のいたところで、――何かが動いた where Mitsuko had been ... something moved

90 夜明けまで、まだ間がありそうだった daybreak was, it seemed, still a while away

多和田葉子

Tawada Yōko

I've long wondered whether something of Tawada Yōko's unique character as an author could be traced back to her name. The "yō" in her given name is written, after all, with the character meaning "leaf" that appears in *kotoba* 言葉, the Japanese word for "word." And few writers derive as much creative nourishment from words as she does: she is less a literary lion, racing through the tundra on the tail of a fast-moving plot, than a literary rabbit who sits for a while in a peaceful field, nibbling a clump of those "leaves" we call "words," then darts off in a flash of brown fur in some unexpected direction. You'll see what I mean, I think, when you read this story, "Kakeru," whose title could easily be translated in a dozen ways—the most appropriate of which, perhaps, is "To Pun."

Tawada, who was born in Tokyo in 1960, studied Russian literature at Waseda University. She moved to Germany in 1982, and has been based there—first in Hamburg, now in Berlin—ever since. Her first book, a bilingual collection of poems and stories in German and Japanese called *Nur da wo du bist, da ist nichts* (*Only There Where You Are, There Is Nothing*) was published in Germany in 1987; since then, she has authored more than two dozen books in one language or the other, or both.

Tawada has received more well-deserved awards than there are pockets in a fisherman's vest. By the time this book lands in your hands, she'll probably have garnered a few more.

"Kakeru" was first published in book form in *Kitsune tsuki* (*Fox-moonlighting* is the best I can do with this punning title), which was issued by Shinshokan in 1998. The text you're about to read is a greatly condensed version of this long, wacky story that Tawada sometimes performs at readings.

かける

多和田葉子

枕にカヴァーをかけ、ブラウスにアイロンをかけ、掃除機をかけ、洗濯機をかける主婦の仕事にはあまり縁のないわたしでも、朝食のトマトには塩をかけ、原稿を書くためにめがねをかけ、椅子に腰をかける。昼になれば鍋を火にかけてカレーを暖め、それを御飯にかけて食べ、満腹すると眠くなって、書ける！　と思っていた原稿の続きが書けなくなって、意識の扉に鍵をかけ、ラジオをかけたまま、ふとんをかけて寝てしまう。このまま静かにしていれば誰の邪魔にもならないけれど、本当はもっと他人に迷惑をかける方がいいのかもしれない、という気がしてくる。迷惑だって人にかける橋なのだから自閉的になるよりはまし。従順な人を罠にかけたい、博識を鼻にかけたい、賭け事がしたい、そういう悪いことばかりして、縄をかけられ、道徳という裁判にかけられ、そうなったら尻に帆かけて逃げる。日が暮れかけた頃に目が醒めて、かけそばを食べる。どんなに保険を

かける To Pun

1 枕にカヴァーをかけ put the covers on the pillows ▪ ブラウスにアイロンをかけ iron blouses ▪ 掃除機をかけ run the vacuum cleaner ▪ 洗濯機をかける run the laundry machine ▪ 主婦の仕事にはあまり縁のないわたしでも even I, who have very little to do with the work of housewives ▪ 朝食のトマトには on my morning tomato ▪ 塩をかけ sprinkle salt ▪ 原稿を書くために in order to write a manuscript ▪ めがねをかけ put on my glasses ▪ 椅子に腰をかける sit down on a chair ▪ 昼になれば when noon rolls around ▪ 鍋を火にかけて set a pot on the stove ▪ カレーを暖め heat up some curry ▪ それを御飯にかけて食べ pour it over rice and eat it ▪ 満腹すると when I get full ▪ 書ける！と思っていた原稿の続きが書けなくなって I'm no longer able to write the continuation of the manuscript I felt so sure I could write, and ▪ 意識の扉に鍵をかけ turn the key in the door of my consciousness ▪ ラジオをかけたまま with the radio still on ▪ ふとんをかけて寝てしまう pull the covers over me and fall asleep ▪ このまま静かにしていれば if I stay here like this, nice and quiet ▪ 誰の邪魔にもならない I won't get in anyone's way ▪ 本当は actually ▪ もっと他人に迷惑をかける方がいいのかもしれない it might well be better if I did inconvenience people more ▪ ...という気がしてくる I start to feel that... ▪ 迷惑だって人にかける橋なのだから even inconvenience is a bridge reaching out to another person, so ▪ 自閉的になるよりはまし it's better than withdrawing into oneself ▪ 従順な人を罠にかけたい wanting to set a trap for obedient people ▪ 博識を鼻にかけたい wanting to show off one's prodigious knowledge ▪ 賭け事がしたい wanting to gamble ▪ そういう悪いことばかりして do nothing but bad things like that and ▪ 縄をかけられ get tied up with ropes ▪ 道徳という裁判にかけられ be put on trial in the court of morality ▪ そうなったら if that were to happen ▪ 尻に帆かけて逃げる I would take to my heels (lit., "put a sail on my butt") and flee ▪ 日が暮れかけた頃に around the time when the sun begins to set ▪ 目が醒めて、かけそばを食べる I awake and have a bowl of *kakesoba* ▪ どんなに保険をかけても no matter how big an insurance policy you take out

かけても、いつかは死んでしまうのだから、面白いことは今のうちにやっておこう。たとえば、文学。言葉に磨きをかけ、人に声をかけ、謎をかけ、催眠術をかける。鳥が巣をかけるように、わたしの中に巣食った掛け言葉の習慣が、話の筋を勝手に決めてしまう。それよりも、猫と犬をかけあわせて混血文化を促進し、楽天主義にエンジンをかけ、時間をかけて物語という布地にミシンをかけた方がいい。七に七をかけて三で割る夢の中ではいつも橋を渡りかけてやめる。川の向こう岸には売店がある。その売店で、言いかけてやめた言葉を駄菓子といっしょに売っている。日が暮れかけると、空から馬のようなものが駆けてくる。月が欠ける。その月をかじった歯が欠ける。茶碗の縁が欠けるように。ひとり欠けるともう一人芝居はできない。

■ いつかは死んでしまうのだから you're going to die eventually, so ■ 面白いことは今のうちにやっておこう let's do the fun stuff now, while we still can ■ たとえば、文学 for instance: literature ■ 言葉に磨きをかけ polish your writing ■ 人に声をかけ talk to someone ■ 謎をかけ set her a riddle ■ 催眠術をかける put her in a state of hypnosis ■ 鳥が巣をかけるように the way a bird builds its nest ■ わたしの中に巣食った掛け言葉の習慣 the habit of punning that roosts within me ■ 話の筋を勝手に決めてしまう determines, all on its own, the story's plot ■ 声を掛け合っても犯罪は防げない talking to each other won't prevent crime ■ それよりも … 方がいい better than that is to … ■ 猫と犬をかけあわせて mix dogs and cats ■ 混血文化を促進し promote a mongrel culture ■ 楽天主義にエンジンをかけ start the engines of optimism ■ 時間をかけて take your time ■ 物語という布地にミシンをかけた方がいい had better stitch the fabric of a tale on a sewing machine ■ 七に七をかけて三で割る夢の中では in a dream of multiplying seven and seven and dividing by three ■ 橋を渡りかけてやめる I start to cross a bridge, then stop ■ 川の向こう岸には売店がある there is a store on the river's far shore ■ 言いかけてやめた言葉 words people started to say, then didn't ■ 駄菓子といっしょに along with candy ■ 日が暮れかけると as the sun begins to set ■ 空から馬のようなものが駆けてくる something like a horse gallops down from the sky ■ 月が欠ける the moon wanes ■ その月をかじった歯が欠ける the tooth that bit the moon gets chipped ■ 茶碗の縁が欠けるように the way the edge of a teacup chips ■ ひとり欠けるともう一人芝居はできない when you're short one person, you can no longer stage a one-man play

Japanese-English Dictionary

Fiction

あ

ああ oh, ah

あい【愛】 love, affection ―愛する to love, to care for

あいかわらず【相変わらず】 still; (as...) as ever; always

あいさつ【挨拶】 greeting ―あいさつ(を)する to greet ―あいさつを送る to greet

あいじょう【愛情】 love, affection

あいじん【愛人】 lover

あいだ【間】 ―...の間 while ―AとBの間 between [among] A and B

あいつ [third-person pronoun; informal] he, she; it (that one)

あいて【相手】 the other person

アイロン iron ―...にアイロンをかける to iron, to press

あう¹【会う】 to see, to meet

あう²【合う】 ➤ はなし(話)

あえぐ【喘ぐ】 to pant, to breathe hard, to gasp for air

あおじろい【青白い】 pale

あかい【赤い】 red ―赤く red

あかぐろい【赤黒い】 dark red

あかさび【赤錆び】 red rust ―赤さびる to get rusty ―赤さびた rusty

あかのたにん【赤の他人】 complete [total] stranger

あからさま(な) plain, clear

あかり【明かり・灯り】 light

あがる【上がる】 to go up, to climb; to rise ➤ みずしぶき(水飛沫)

あかるい【明るい】 bright ―明るいままで with the light(s) on

あかんぼう【赤ん坊】 baby

あきかん【空き缶】 empty can

あきびん【空き瓶】 empty bottle

あきらか(な)【明らか(な)】 clear, obvious ―明らかに clearly, obviously

あきらめる【諦める】 to give up

あきる【飽きる】 to get tired of

あきれかえる【呆れ返る】 to be shocked [disgusted]

あける【開ける】 to open; to take off (a lid) ―開けた open

あげる【上げる】 to raise ➤ こえ(声), うぶごえ(産声)

-あげる ―...してあげる [added to verbs to show that the subject acts to benefit the object]

あご【顎】 jaw

あさ【朝】 morning

あさい【浅い】 light (describing sleep)

あざやか(な)【鮮やか(な)】 bright, colorful ―鮮やかに colorfully

あさゆう【朝夕】 morning and evening

あし【足】 foot; leg

あじ【味】 taste, flavor ―味がする to taste, to have a flavor

あしどり【足取り】 one's step, one's pace

あしもと【足元】 one's step ➤ ふらつく

あずける【預ける】 to leave, to entrust ―AをBに預ける to leave A with B

アスファルト asphalt

あせ【汗】 sweat

あそび【遊び】 play, game

あそびば【遊び場】 playground

あそぶ【遊ぶ】 to play

あたし [same as わたし but more informal; used mostly by women] I; me

あたたかい【暖かい・温かい】 warm, kind

あたたかな【暖かな・温かな】 ➤ あたたかい(暖かい・温かい)

あたためる【暖める・温める】 to warm (up), to heat (up)

あたま【頭】 ① head ② mind ―頭を下げる to bow one's head

あたらしい【新しい】 new

あ

か

さ

た

な

は

ま

や

ら

わ

あたり【辺り】—…の辺りに[の] around …, in the neighborhood of…

あたりまえ(の)【当たり前(の)】natural —当たり前なら under ordinary circumstances

あたる【当たる】①to hit; to touch ② to prove right ③to be… (indicating relation)

あちこち here and there

あつい【暑い】hot (describing weather)

あつかい【扱い】treatment —(…な)扱いを受ける to get (special, VIP, etc) treatment

あつかう【扱う】to treat

あつさ【暑さ】heat, hot weather

あて【当て】—当てもなく aimlessly

あと¹【後】back —…の後(は) after —…後に・後で later —後を追う to go after, to follow

あと²【跡】mark, trace

アナウンス announcement (over a PA system)

あなた【貴方】—あなたは・あなたが you —あなたの your —あなたに・あなたを you

あの ①that ②er, uh, um

アパート apartment

あびる【浴びる】to bathe —日差しを浴びて in the sunlight

あぶない【危ない】dangerous

あぶら【脂】fat, oil, grease

あふれる【溢れる】to be filled with; to run over

あまい【甘い】①romantic ②all too easy

あまど【雨戸】(sliding) shutter

あまり【余り】—あまり…ない not very…, not…much

あまりに(も)【余りに(も)】too, overly

あまりの【余りの】excess; too…

あめ【雨】rain

あやす to cradle

あやまる【謝る】to apologize

あゆみさる【歩み去る】to walk off [away]

あらう【洗う】to wash

あらかじめ【予め】beforehand, in advance

あらじお【粗塩】coarse salt

あらなわ【荒縄】thick straw rope

あらわす【表す】to express

ありがとう【有難う】Thank you.

アリバイ alibi

ある¹【有る】to be, to exist; there is [are] …; to have

ある²【或る】a certain…; one

あるいは【或いは】①or ②maybe, possibly

あるきだす【歩き出す】to start [begin] to walk

あるく【歩く】to walk, to go on foot —歩いて on foot

あれ that

あわす【合わす】—…に合わす顔がない to be ashamed to show one's face to…

あわだち【泡立ち】foaming, frothing

あわてる【慌てる】to hurry, to rush —あわてて in a hurry [flurry], hurriedly

あんしつ【暗室】darkroom

あんた [casual form of あなた] you

あんちょく(な)【安直(な)】easy, simple

あんな such, that (sort)

い

いい [different form of よい] nice, good; okay

いいかける【言いかける】to start to say, to begin

6

いいだす【言い出す】 to propose, to suggest, to bring up

いいつたえ【言い伝え】 legend, tradition

いう【言う】 to say, to tell ➤れい（礼） ―…に…するよう言う to tell…to do

いえ¹【家】 ① house; (one's) home ② one's family ―家に (at) home

いえ² [same as いいえ] no

いか【以下】 the following ―…以下（の）below, under, less than

いかに【如何に】 how

いき【息】 breath ―息をする to breathe ―息が絶える to breathe one's last, to pass away ―息をつく to draw one's breath

いきる【生きる】 to live

いく【行く】 ① to go, to come; to visit ② to go away, to leave ―…しに行く to go (and) do, to go to do

いくつか（の）【幾つか（の）】 some, several

いくら【幾ら】 ―いくら…しても no matter how…, however…

いけない bad; ugly ―…してはいけない must not do; should not do ―…しなければいけない must do, have to do

いけん【意見】 opinion

いささか a little; rather

いじ【意地】 ―意地になる to be obstinate, to be stubborn

いしき【意識】 consciousness

いじげん【異次元】 different dimension

いしゃ【医者】 doctor

いしゃりょう【慰謝料】 compensation

-いじょう【以上】 more than…

いじょう（な）【異常（な）】 extraordinary, unusual ―異常に extraordinarily, unusually

いす【椅子】 chair

いずれ（は）【何れ（は）】 eventually, some day, sooner or later ―いずれにしても・いずれにせよ anyway, anyhow, in any case

いせき【遺跡】 ruins, remains

いぜん【以前】 before, once, formerly

いそう【位相】 phase

いそぐ【急ぐ】 to hurry, to rush ―急いで hurriedly, in a hurry

いだく【抱く】 to have, to hold

いただく【頂く】 [humble expression] to be given, to receive ―…していただく [polite way of saying that one receives a favor from someone of higher status]

いたって【至って】 very

いたむ¹【痛む】 to hurt, to ache

いたむ²【傷む】 to damage ―傷んでいる damaged

いたる【至る】 ―AからBにいたるまで from A (down) to B

いち【一】 one

いちご【苺】 strawberry

いちど【一度】 once, one time

いちにち【一日】 a [one] day

いちにんまえ【一人前】 ―一人前になる to mature

いちねん【一年】 a [one] year

いちねんせい【一年生】 freshman

いちば【市場】 market

いちばん【一番】 most; the first

いちぶ【一部】 a [one] part

いつ【何時】 when

いつか【何時か】 someday, one day

いっかい【一回】 once, one time ―一回目 the first time; the first round

いっかく【一画】 lot

いつかは【何時は】 eventually

いっき（に）【一気（に）】 at a breath; all

at once, immediately

いっけん【一軒】 a [one] house [building]

いっしゅん【一瞬】 (for) a moment, momentarily

いっしょ（に）【一緒（に）】 together, with… ―一緒の the same…

いっしょう【一笑】 ―一笑に付す to laugh off, to brush aside with a laugh

いっしん（に）【一心（に）】 wholeheartedly, intently

いっそう【一層】 even (more), still (more); all the more

いつだって ➢いつも

いつつ【五つ】 five (years)

いってい（の）【一定（の）】 a fixed…

いっとき【一時】 a moment; a while

いっぱい（の）【一杯（の）】 full ―一杯にする to fill

いっぴき【一匹】 one… ➢-ひき・びき・ぴき（匹）

いっぷく【一服】 rest, break ―一服する to have a rest, to take a break

いっぽ【一歩】 a [one] step

いっぽう【一方】 meanwhile

いつも【何時も】 always, all the time

いな【否】 not, no ➢-か

いななき（ごえ）【いななき（声）】 neigh, whinny

いななく to neigh, to whinny

いぬ【犬】 dog

いのち【命】 life ―命を落とす to lose one's life

いびき【鼾】 snoring; snore ―いびきをかく to snore

いぶかしげに【訝しげに】 quizzically

いま【今】 ① now; at the moment ② today ―今の present; current, today's ―今のところ at the moment, at present ―今のうちに now; before it is too late

―今の世 the world today

いまごろ【今頃】 by this time, by now

いままで【今迄】 till [until, up to] now ―今まで…したことがない to have never done

いまわしい【忌まわしい】 detestable

いみ【意味】 meaning ―…という意味である to mean that…

いや【否】 no

いやいや【嫌々】 ―嫌々をする to shake one's head no

いや（な）【嫌（な）】 ① unpleasant, disgusting ② ominous ―（…するのが）嫌である to be reluctant (to do), do not want (to do); to dislike, to hate ―嫌な気がする to have a bad feeling (about)

いやに【嫌に】 awfully, terribly

いやはや Oh dear!; Dear me!

いやらしい lewd, lascivious

いよう（な）【異様（な）】 strange, odd, queer ―異様に unusually

-いらい【-以来】 since ―それ以来 since then

いらいら ―いらいらする to get irritated

-いり【-入り】 with…

いる¹【居る】 ① to be, to exist; there is [are]… ② to stay

いる²【要る】 to need (patience); to take (nerve)

いれる【入れる】 ① to put…in [into] ② ➢きれめ（切れ目）、コーヒー、ちから（力）―（…の中に）入れておく to keep (something) in…

いろ【色】 color ―…色の -colored

いろいろ（な）【色々（な）】 various, many ―いろいろ（と） in various ways

いろんな ➢いろいろ（な）（色々（な））

いわ【岩】 rock

いわゆる【所謂】 so-called, what is called

いんねん【因縁】karma; fate ―因縁 話
a tale describing a person's or object's
previous existence

う

うえ【上】top ―その上 besides ―…
の上の[に, を] on, upon; over ―…
は上である to be older (by X number
of years)

うかがう【窺う】to take a look

うかぶ【浮かぶ】① to occur to one, to
cross one's mind ② to shine brightly

うく【浮く】to stand out

うけとる【受け取る】to receive, to get,
to take

うける【受ける】to catch, to receive, to
get ➤ ひ²(陽), あつかい(扱い), でんわ
(電話)

うごき【動き】movement, motion

うごきまわる【動き回る】to go [move]
around

うごく【動く】to move

うし【牛】cow, ox; cattle

うしなう【失う】to lose ➤ しょうき(正気)

うそ【嘘】lie

うたう【歌う】to sing

うち【内】① inside ② ➤いま(今) ―う
ちの our ―…のうち(に) in…, within… ―…するうち(に) while doing

うちおろす【打ち下ろす】to bring…down
(on…)

うちこわす【打ち壊す】to break down,
to destroy

うちつける【打ち付ける】to bang, to strike

うちならす【打ち鳴らす】to clap (one's
hands) loudly

うちのひと【うちの人】one's family member

うつくしさ【美しさ】beauty; purity

うっすら(と) faintly

うっとり(と) fascinatingly

うつむく【俯く】to hang one's head

うで【腕】arm

うなじ nape of one's neck

うなずく【頷く】to nod

うばう【奪う】to take (away)

うぶごえ【産声】the first cry (of a newborn baby) ―産声をあげる to give
one's first cry

うま【馬】horse

うまく【上手く】well, fine ―うまくいく
to go (along) well

うまる【埋まる】to be buried

うまれる【生まれる】to be born ―生ま
れたばかりの newborn

うみ【海】sea

うむ【生む】to produce, to cause

うめぼし【梅干し】pickled *ume* [plum]

うらがえる【裏返る】to go (into) falsetto

うらにわ【裏庭】backyard

うる【売る】to sell

ウルル [growl of a bear] grr

うれしい【嬉しい】happy, delightful
―嬉しげに happily; delightfully, with
delight

うろうろ ―うろうろする to wander about

うわあ Oh my God!

うわさ【噂】rumor

うん¹ [casual affirmative reply] yes,
yeah; uh-huh

うん²【運】luck, fortune ―運のいい
lucky

うんが【運河】canal

うんめい【運命】fate; the future course
of events

え

えいびん(な)【鋭敏(な)】keen, sharp

えいよう【栄養】nutrition 　―栄養のある nutritious

ええ　[form of affirmative reply] yes, that's right

えきまえ（の）【駅前（の）】in front of a station

エジプト　Egypt

えたい【得体】　―得体の知れぬ strange, mysterious

えにし【縁】karma; (turn of) fate, destiny

えらぶ【選ぶ】to choose

えんぎ【演技】performance

エンジン　engine 　―エンジンをかける to start an engine

お

お-【御-】[prefix added for politeness or to show respect]

おい　Hey!

おう【追う】to go after

おうむ【オウム・鸚鵡】parrot

おえる【終える】to finish

-おえる【-終える】― …し終える to finish doing

おおあめ【大雨】heavy rain 　―大雨が降る It rains hard [heavily].

おおきい・おおきな【大きい・大きな】big, large; great; loud 　―大きく largely, greatly; wide; loud(ly)

おおきさ【大きさ】size

おおぐち【大口】a wide-open mouth ―大口を開く to open one's mouth wide ―大口を開いて with one's mouth wide open

おおじだい（な）【大時代（な）】old-fashioned, antiquated

オーバーブラウス　overblouse

おおや【大家】landlord

おかげ【お陰】―…のおかげで thanks to …, because of…

おかしな　improper

おかす【犯す】to rape

おきあがる【起き上がる】to get up, to sit up (in bed)

おきもの【置き物】ornament

おきゃく【お客】➢きゃく（客）

おきる【起きる】①to wake up ②to happen, to go on 　―起きている to be awake; to sit [stay] up (late)

おく¹【奥】the back, the depths; the bottom (of one's heart)

おく²【置く】to put, to place, to lay, to set ➢ま（間）　―置いていく to leave… behind

おくさん【奥さん】one's wife

おくそこ【奥底】the bottom, the depths

おくびょうもの【臆病者】coward, chicken

おくふかい【奥深い】deep 　―奥深く deeply

おくる【送る】①to see (a person) home ②➢あいさつ（挨拶）

おこす【起こす】➢のうしんとう（脳震盪）

おごそか（な）【厳か（な）】solemn 　―厳かに solemnly

おことわり【お断り】➢ことわり（断り）

おこなう【行う】to do, to carry out

おこる¹【起こる】to occur, to happen

おこる²【怒る】to scold

おさえる【押さえる】to hold, to press

おさない【幼い】①young, small ②childish

おさなご【幼子】young child

おさめる【納める・収める】to master, to understand

おじ【叔父】uncle

おしえる【教える】to teach

おじさん【小父さん】middle-aged man

おしたおす【押し倒す】to push...down [over]

おしだす【押し出す】to push out

おしつける【押し付ける】to press

おしゃれ【お洒落】fashionability, stylishness　—おしゃれな fashionable, stylish　—おしゃれに fashionably, stylishly　—おしゃれ（を）する to get dressed up, to dress smartly

おしよせる【押し寄せる】to surge, to rush (like a flood)

おす【雄】male　—雄の　male

おそい【遅い】(too) late　—遅くなる to be late

おそいかかる【襲いかかる】to assault

おそらく【恐らく】probably

おそれ【恐れ】awe　—恐れをなす to stand in awe (of...)

おそれる【恐れる】to be afraid

おそろしい【恐ろしい】horrible

おそわれる【襲われる】➤はきけ（吐き気）

おたがい【お互い】➤たがい（互い）

おたく【お宅】—おたくの　your

おだやか（な）【穏やか（な）】calm, gentle, quiet

おち【落ち】the end; the twist (at the end of a story), unexpected ending　—落ちがつく to have an unexpected ending

おっと【夫】one's husband

おつり【お釣り】change

おと【音】sound, noise　—音もなく quietly, silently　—音を立てる to make a noise [sound]

おとうさん【お父さん】dad, father

おとこ【男】man

おどし【脅し】threat, scare

おとす【落とす】① to lower (speed) ②➤いのち（命）

おとなしい【大人しい】quiet

おどろく【驚く】to be surprised　—驚いたことに to one's surprise

おなか【お腹】stomach, belly

おなじ【同じ】[irregular adjective of neither the -i nor -na type] the same　—同じように in the same way　—...と同じくらい as much as...

おにいさん【お兄さん】young man

おばけ【お化け】ghost

おびえる【怯える】to be scared [frightened]

おひめさま【お姫様】princess

おぼえる【覚える】① to remember　② to feel

おぼっちゃま【お坊ちゃま】[also お坊ちゃん] well-bred young man (with a connotation of not being streetwise)

おまえ【お前】[second-person pronoun; used when addressing a friend or person of lower status] you

おまえさん【お前さん】➤おまえ（お前）

おむすび rice ball

おもい¹【重い】heavy

おもい²【思い】feeling, thought

おもいうかべる【思い浮かべる】to have a picture [image] (of...), to be reminded (of...)

おもいこむ【思い込む】to assume, to believe

おもいしらせる【思い知らせる】to show; to make (a person) sorry

おもいだす【思い出す】to remember, to recall

おもいで【思い出】memory

おもいのほか【思いの外】unexpectedly

おもう【思う】to think; to feel; to imagine; to guess　—思うところがある to have something to think about　—しようと

思う to intend to do

おもえる【思える】to seem, to appear; it seems (that)…

おもしろい【面白い】① interesting; fun ② funny, amusing

おもて【表】outside, the outdoors

おもみ【重み】importance, significance

おもり【お守り】babysitting　―お守りをする to look after; to sit with

おもわず【思わず】in spite of oneself; involuntarily

おや【親】one's parent(s)　―親兄弟 one's family

おやかた【親方】one's boss

おやこ【親子】father and son; parent and child

およぐ【泳ぐ】to swim

おりる【降りる】to go [come] down, to descend

おる【居る】[a written form of いる] to be, to exist

おれ【俺】[first-person pronoun used by men; somewhat brusque, rough] I

オレンジ　orange

おろす【下ろす】to put [set] down

おわる【終わる】to finish, to end; to be over

おんな【女】woman; girl

おんなのこ【女の子】girl

か

-か　(either)…or…; whether…(or not)　―…か否か whether…or not

-が　but; and

カーテン　curtain

かい【階】floor

-かい【-回】[counter for the number of times]

がいこく【外国】foreign country

かいすいぎ【海水着】swimsuit, (swimming) trunks

がいする【害する】➤かんじょう（感情）

かいそう【改装】refurbishment　―改装する to refurbish, to remodel

かいたい【解体】slaughter (and dressing of meat animals)　―解体する to slaughter (animals)

かいだん【怪談】ghost story

かいちゅうでんとう【懐中電灯】flashlight

がいとう【街灯】streetlamp

かいとる【買い取る】to buy (up)

がいねん【概念】idea, concept

がいはく【外泊】staying overnight somewhere other than at home

かいぶつ【怪物】monster

かいもの【買い物・買物】shopping　―買い物（を）する to shop; to buy

がいろとう【街路灯】streetlight

かいわ【会話】conversation

かう【買う】to buy

カヴァー　pillowcase; cover (in general)

かえって【却って】all the more

かえり【帰り】return　―…の帰りに on the [one's] way (home) from…

かえりみち【帰り道】one's way home

かえる¹【帰る】to go [come] home, to go [come] back, to return

かえる²【変える】to change

かえる³【返る】➤われ（我）

かお【顔】① face ② look, expression　―顔を見せる to appear　―顔を横に振る to shake one's head

かおいろ【顔色】color, complexion　―顔色の悪い pale

かおだち【顔立ち】features　―顔立ちの整った good-looking; having regular features

かおみしり【顔見知り】acquaintance

かがく【化学】chemistry ―化学の chemical ―化学変化 chemical reaction

かがむ【屈む】to crouch, to squat

かがやき【輝き】radiance, brilliance

かがやく【輝く】to shine

かかる¹【掛かる】① to take on, to challenge (a person) ② to take (time)

かかる²【架かる】to hang, to span ―虹がかかる A rainbow appears [forms].

かかる³【罹る】to contract (an illness), to become infected (with…)

かがん【河岸】riverbank

かぎ【鍵】key; lock ―鍵をかける to lock

かぎとる【嗅ぎ取る】to smell; to detect, to sense

かく¹【書く】to write

かく² ➤いびき（鼾）

がく【額】price; sum (of money)

かくじ【各自】each…

かくす【隠す】to hide

がくせい【学生】college [university] student

かくだい【拡大】expansion, extension ―拡大する to expand, to escalate ―拡大した expanded, escalated

かくだん（に）【格段（に）】remarkably

かくど【角度】angle

かくにん【確認】check, confirmation ―確認する to check, to see; to make sure

かくれる【隠れる】to hide; to disappear

かげ【影】shadow

かけあう【掛け合う】➤こえ（声）

かけあわせる【掛け合わせる】to cross (one breed) with another

かげえ【影絵】shadow picture; silhouette

かけごと【賭け事】gambling ―賭け事をする to gamble

かけことば【掛け言葉】a pun, a play on words; a pivot word

かけそば【掛け蕎麦】*soba* (noodles) in hot broth

かけら【欠片】(broken) piece, fragment

かける¹【掛ける】① to put on, to cover, to put…over [around] ② to have (glasses) on, to wear ③ to turn on ④ to multiply ⑤ to start (an engine) ⑥ ➤ こえ（声）, さいばん（裁判）, さいみんじゅつ（催眠術）, さそい（誘い）, じかん（時間）, す（巣）, でんわ（電話）, なぞ（謎）, なわ（縄）, はし（橋）, はな（鼻）, ほ（帆）, ほけん（保険）, みがき（磨き）, ミシン, わな（罠）

かける²【書ける】to be able to write, can write

かける³【駆ける】to run, to gallop

かける⁴【欠ける】① to wane ② to chip ③ to be short of, to lack

−かける ―…しかける to be about to do; to begin [start] to do

かこむ【囲む】to surround

かざす【翳す】to hold up (over one's head)

かし【樫】oak

かしこい【賢い】smart, intelligent

がしゃり bang; slam ―がしゃりと切る to slam (the phone) down

かじる【齧る】to bite

かすか（な）【微か（な）】faint, slight ―かすかに faintly, slightly

かぜ【風】wind ―どういう風の吹き回しか for some reason or other

かせいふ【家政婦】housekeeper

かせぐ【稼ぐ】to earn

かぞく【家族】family

13

かた【肩】shoulder

-かた【-方】way [method] of doing, how to do…

かたい【固い・堅い】hard, solid; firm　—堅く firmly, hard

かたて【片手】one hand

かたパン【堅パン】[generally means "hardtack" or "biscuit"] stale bread

かたほう【片方】one (of two people)

かたまる【固まる】to coagulate, to congeal

かたりおえる【語り終える】to finish talking, to finish one's story

かたりて【語り手】(story)teller

かちく【家畜】livestock; cattle　—家畜小屋 livestock shed

かつ【勝つ】to beat, to defeat

がっかり　—っかりする to be disappointed　—っかりした disappointed

かつぐ【担ぐ】to carry … on one's shoulder(s)

がっこう【学校】school

がっしゅく【合宿】training camp

かって(に)【勝手(に)】1 without permission　2 arbitrarily; automatically

かていきょうし【家庭教師】tutor, private teacher

かてる【勝てる】≻かつ（勝つ）

かなしい【悲しい・哀しい】sad, sorrowful, unhappy

かならず【必ず】without fail; always

かなり　pretty, quite, fairly

かね【金】money

かねて　previously, in advance

かのう(な)【可能(な)】possible

かぶる【被る】to put (a hat) on　—かぶっている to wear, to have (a hat) on

かべ【壁】wall　—壁越しに through the wall

かぼちゃ【カボチャ・南瓜】pumpkin

かまえる【構える】to set up (a shop)

かみ¹【神】god

かみ²【髪】hair

かみさま【神様】God

かみなり【雷】thunder, lightning

かみのけ【髪の毛】hair

かむ【嚙む】to bite

カメラ　camera; video camera

-かもしれない　maybe, perhaps; it might be that…

かよう【通う】to attend, to go to…

-から　1 from, out of　2 after; from, since　3 because, as, since　4 so (that)

がらがらへび【がらがら蛇・ガラガラヘビ】rattlesnake

からだ【体】body

からだつき【体つき】one's figure, one's build

からみつく【絡みつく】to tangle [twist] around…

かりに【仮に】suppose (that)…

かりゅう【下流】downstream, the lower reaches (of a river)

かるい【軽い】easy; light, slight　—軽く easily; lightly, slightly

かれ【彼】　—彼は・彼が he　—彼の his　—彼を・彼に him

カレー　curry

かれる【枯れる】to wither, to die　—枯れた withered, dead

かろうじて【辛うじて】barely

かわ¹【川】river

かわ²【皮】skin; peel

かわいがる【可愛がる】to love, to take good care of

かわす【交わす】to exchange ≻ほうよう（抱擁）

かわった【変わった】strange, odd

かわぶくろ【革袋】leather bag

かわら【川原】the shore of a river, river-bank

かわる【変わる】to be different, to differ

かんがいぶかい【感慨深い】to be deeply moved; to be filled with deep emotion

かんがえ【考え】thought, idea

かんがえる【考える】to think (of)

かんかく【感覚】feeling, sense

かんけい【関係】relations, relationship

かんじ¹【感じ】feeling, impression

かんじ²【漢字】kanji

かんじゅせい【感受性】sensitivity, sensibility

かんじょう【感情】feeling(s) —感情を害する to be offended, to feel hurt

かんしょく【感触】(the sense of) touch, feel

かんじる【感じる】to feel, to sense

かんする【関する】—...に関する about, on, concerning

かんせい【感性】sensitivity

かんぜんしゅぎ【完全主義】perfectionism —完全主義者 perfectionist

かんぞう【肝臓】liver

かんだかい【甲高い】high-pitched

かんたん(な)【簡単(な)】easy, simple —簡単に easily, simply

かんばん【看板】signboard

がんめん【顔面】face

き

き¹【気】① mind, feelings ② intention, will —気がする to feel (like...), to have a feeling that... —気が回る to be attentive to others, to be considerate —...する気がある to feel like doing; to want to do —...する気になる to be brought to do —気がせく to get upset

—気にする to care about, to have...on one's mind —気を遣う to care about, to pay attention to (others) —気を配る to show consideration, to care about

き²【木】tree

きいろい【黄色い】yellow

きえさる【消え去る】to vanish

きえる【消える】to disappear —消えかけた almost gone, about to disappear

きかい【機会】opportunity, chance, occasion

きかん【期間】period

きぎ【木々】trees

ききこみ【聞き込み】gathering information by inquiries, questioning

ききまちがえる【聞き間違える】to mishear, to hear...wrongly

きく¹【聞く】① to hear, to listen to... ② to ask

きく²【訊く】to ask

きく³【利く】➤こまわり(小回り)

きけん【危険】danger —危険な dangerous

きこえる【聞こえる】to hear, to be heard

きこく【帰国】—帰国する to return [come back] to one's country

きしべ【岸辺】bank (of a river)

ぎじゅつ【技術】skill, technique

きじゅん【基準】standard; criterion

きず【傷】wound

きせつ【季節】season

きそくただしい【規則正しい】regular; orderly —規則正しく regularly

きちんと neatly, orderly

きっかけ beginning, occasion

きづく【気付く】to notice, to realize

きっさき【切っ先】knifepoint

きっさてん【喫茶店】café, coffee shop, tearoom

きっと　surely, certainly

きっぱり　ーきっぱりした　clear, definite

きねん【記念】souvenir

きばこ【木箱】wooden box

きびしい【厳しい】harsh, severe; strict

きぶん【気分】feeling; physical condition　ー（...な）気分になる　to feel...

きぶんてんかん【気分転換】change of mood　ー気分転換に　for a change; to clear one's mind

きみ¹【君】[casual form of あなた] you

きみ²【気味】ー気味（の）悪い weird; creepy

きみょう（な）【奇妙（な）】strange　ー奇妙に　strangely

きめる【決める】to decide, to determine, to make up one's mind

きもち【気持ち・気持】feeling, mood　ー気持ち（が）悪い unpleasant, uncomfortable　ー気持ちいい to feel good　ー（...な）気持ちになる to feel...

きゃく【客】customer

きゃくせき【客席】seats (for spectators)

きよう（に）【器用（に）】skillfully, dexterously

きょう【今日】today

きょうし【教師】➣かてい（家庭）

きょうだい【兄弟】one's sibling(s), one's brothers and sisters

きょうふ【恐怖】fear, fright; horror

きょうみ【興味】interest　ー興味のある interesting

きょうれつ（な）【強烈（な）】intense, powerful, strong

きょたい【巨体】huge body

きょだい（な）【巨大（な）】huge

きらきら　[adverb describing a glistening quality]　ーきらきら光る to shine, to glisten

-きり　since...

ぎりぎり　ーぎりぎりと tightly, to the point of breaking

きりとる【切り取る】to cut off, to cut out

きる【切る】①to turn [switch] off　②➣でんわ（電話）

きれい（な）【綺麗（な）】clean; neat, lovely　ーきれいさっぱり completely

きれぎれ（に）【切れ切れ（に）】haltingly

きれめ【切れ目】cut, gap　ー切れ目を入れる to make a cut

-ぎわ【-際】ー...際の　by, near

きわめて【極めて】very, extremely

きんがく【金額】a sum [an amount] of money

きんじょ【近所】neighborhood　ー近所に in the neighborhood

きんじる【禁じる】to forbid, to prohibit

きんりん【近隣】neighborhood, vicinity　ー近隣の neighboring

く

くうかん【空間】space

くうき【空気】air

くぐらせる【潜らせる】to dip...into

くさ【草】grass

くさち【草地】grassy area　ー草地で in the grass

くし【駆使】free [full, extensive] use　ー駆使する to use freely [extensively]; to have a good command (of)

くしゃくしゃの　rumpled

ぐしゃり　ーぐしゃりと割れる to shatter, to crumble

くじゅう【苦渋】agony　ー苦渋に満ちた顔で with an agonized look on one's face

くずにく【屑肉】scrap meat, meat scraps

-ください【-下さい】[added when making polite requests] please do...

-くださる　ー...して下さる [honorific

form of …してくれる; used when the subject is of a higher status than the speaker] ➢ーくれる

くだらない【下らない】stupid, silly, nonsensical

くち【口】 ① mouth; lips ② opening, mouth ー口に出す to give voice, to speak; to put into words

くちびる【唇】lip

くちまね【口真似】mimicry ー口まね（を）する to mimic

くちょう【口調】tone

くつ【靴】shoe(s)

くっきり（と）distinctively, starkly

くつじょく【屈辱】humiliation

くばる【配る】➢き（気）

くび【首】 ① neck ② head

くま【熊・クマ】bear

くもる【曇る】to cloud [mist, fog] up

くら【蔵】warehouse, storehouse

くらい【暗い】dark ー暗くなる to get dark

-くらい【-位】 ① about, around ② at least

くらす【暮らす】to live, to get [go] along

グラビア photo pages (in a magazine)

くらべかた【比べ方】comparison

くらべる【比べる】to compare ー…に比べ（て）・…に比べれば compared to [with]…

くりかえし（て）【繰り返し（て）】repeatedly

くりかえす【繰り返す】to repeat

くる【来る】to come

くるま【車】car; vehicle

くるまる to be wrapped up, to be covered

くるむ to cloak, to wrap

ぐるり one's surroundings ーぐるりを見渡す to look all around

くれる¹ to give

くれる²【暮れる】to grow [get] dark

-くれる [added to verbs as an acknowledgment by the speaker that the subject's action benefits the speaker] ー…してくれる to be kind enough to do

くろ【黒】black

くわしい【詳しい】to know a lot (about)

-くん【-君】[suffix for personal names] ➢ ぼう（某）

くんずほぐれつ【組んずほぐれつ】ーくんずほぐれつする to wrestle violently

ぐんと much

け

け【毛】hair; fur

けいか【経過】ー経過する to pass, to go by (describing time)

けいさつ【警察】police

けいたいでんわ【携帯電話】cell phone, mobile phone

げいにん【芸人】performer, entertainer

けす【消す】to turn off, to put out

けっこん【結婚】marriage ー結婚する to marry, to get married

けっして【決して】ーけっして…ない never; not at all

-けど though

けぶかい【毛深い】hairy

けもの【獣】animal, beast

けりつける【蹴りつける】to kick hard, to give a hard kick

けれど but; though, although

-けん【-軒】[counter for houses and buildings]

けんお【嫌悪】hatred, dislike

けんがく【見学】visit, tour ー見学する to visit, to go and see

げんき（な）【元気（な）】fine, healthy ー元

気に lively, cheerfully

けんきゅうしつ【研究室】laboratory, lab

げんこう【原稿】manuscript

げんじつ【現実】reality —現実にする to realize

けんとう【見当】—見当がつかない cannot imagine [guess], to have no idea

げんに【現に】actually

けんめい(に)【懸命(に)】hard

こ

-こ【-個】[general-purpose counter]

-ご【-後】later

ご-【御-】[polite or honorific prefix; different form of お-]

こい【濃い】thick —濃くなる to thicken

こいつ this one

こいびと【恋人】boyfriend, lover

こう like this, in this way

こういうふうに【こういう風に】➤こんな

こうえん【公園】park

こうきしん【好奇心】curiosity

こうけい【光景】scene

こうご【交互】—交互に by turns, alternately

こうこう【高校】(senior) high school

こうこうせい【高校生】high school student

こうこがく【考古学】archaeology

こうじ【工事】construction (work)

-ごうしつ【-号室】(room) number...

こうして in this way, like this

こうしょうにん【公証人】notary (public)

こうそくどうろ【高速道路】highway

こうつう【交通】traffic, transportation —交通至便の favorably [conveniently] located (in terms of transportation)

こうどう【行動】action

こうはい【後輩】one's junior

こうふん【興奮】excitement

ごうまん(な)【傲慢(な)】haughty, arrogant

こえ【声】voice —声をあげる to cry out, to raise one's voice —声を出す to vocalize; to say something —声をかける to call out (to...), to talk (to...) —声を掛け合う to call out to each other

コード cord —コードを抜く to pull out a cord

コーヒー coffee —コーヒーを入れる to make coffee

こおり【氷】ice

こがい【戸外】—戸外で outdoors

こきょう【故郷】one's home, hometown, homeland

こぐ【漕ぐ】➤ブランコ

ごく【極】very

こくどう【国道】national highway

ここ(で)【此処(で)】here; this place —ここから out of here

ごご【午後】afternoon

こごえ【小声】low voice —小声で in a low voice

ここちよい【心地よい】pleasant

こころ【心】heart, mind —心をとらえる to attract

こころよい【快い】pleasant, comfortable

こし【腰】hip(s), lower back —腰(を)かける to sit down (on a chair)

-ごし【-越し】➤かべ(壁)

ごじゅう【五十】fifty

こす【越す】to move in (to a dwelling)

こすりつける【擦り付ける】to rub [nuzzle] against...

こする【擦る】to rub, to scrub

こだい【古代】ancient times —古代の ancient

ごたいまんぞく【五体満足】physical integrity　—五体満足で　safe and sound, in one piece

こたえ【答え】answer

こたえる【答える】to answer, to reply; to give an answer

こだね【子種】child

こちら　here; I, we

こぢんまり　—こぢんまり（と）した　small and cozy

こつ　the secrets (of…), the trick (of…)

こっそり　secretly, in secret

こっち　➤こちら

コップ　glass (for drinking)

こてい【固定】—固定する to fix　—固定された　fixed

こと【事】thing; matter; event

-ごと【-毎】every, each

ことば【言葉】word(s), phrase(s); wording; language

こども【子供】child, kid; baby

ことわり【断り】notice; permission

ことわる【断る】to decline, to turn down; to get permission

この　this

このまま　as [the way] it is; without doing anything

このむ【好む】to like, to prefer, to be fond of…

このよ【この世】this world, this life

このような【この様な】this kind [sort] of

こばなし【小話】short story

ごはん【御飯】rice

こびりつく【こびり付く】to get stuck (to, on…)

こぶし　one's fist

こぶとり（の）【小太り（の）】pudgy, plump, round

こぼれる【零れる】to spill out

こまかい【細かい】①sensitive　②picky　—細かく sensitively　—細かさ pickiness

こまわり【小回り】small turn　—小回りが利く　to be adaptable

ごめんなさい【御免なさい】I'm sorry.

こもりうた【子守歌】lullaby

こもる【籠る】to shut oneself up (indoors), to close oneself off

こや【小屋】hut, shed ➤かちく（家畜）

これ　this

これから　after this; from now on, in the future

これまで【これ迄】so far, till [until] now, up to now

-ころ【-頃】when…

ころがる【転がる】to drop, to fall　—ころがっている　to be lying around [about]

ころす【殺す】to kill

こわい【恐い・怖い】dreadful, terrible; scary

こわす【壊す】to destroy, to tear down

こわばる【強ばる】to stiffen, to freeze

こんかい【今回】this time

こんき【根気】patience, perseverance

コンクリート　concrete

こんけつ【混血】mixed parentage　—混血文化 hybridism

こんご（も）【今後（も）】after this, from now on, in the future

コンセント　outlet, (wall) socket; plug　—コンセントを抜く　to remove a plug from an outlet

こんど【今度】this time

こんな　such　—こんなふうに　like this

こんばんは【今晩は】Good evening.

こんや【今夜】tonight

 さ

さあ　[interjection used to focus atten-

あ
か
さ
た
な
は
ま
や
ら
わ

tion on the speaker] now, here; hey

サーカス circus

サークル circle

さいきん【最近】 recently, lately

さいげん【再現】 reproduction ―再現する to reproduce

さいご【最後】 the last ―最後の the last ―最後に（は）(at) last; finally; in the end ―最後まで to the end [last]

さいど【再度】 again

さいばん【裁判】 trial ―裁判にかける to put...on trial

さいみんじゅつ【催眠術】 hypnotism ―催眠術をかける to hypnotize

さえない【冴えない】 depressed, down

さかな【魚】 fish

さかば【酒場】 bar, tavern

－ざかり【－盛り】 the peak, the height ➤なまいき（な）（生意気（な））

さき【先】 ahead ―...の先に ahead of ...; beyond... ―先に first

さぎょう【作業】 work

さく【柵】 fence

さけ【酒】 alcoholic drinks; alcohol ―酒の席 banquet, party

さけぶ【叫ぶ】 to shout, to scream, to cry (out)

さげる【下げる】 ① to lower ➤あたま（頭）② to carry

ささえる【支える】 to support, to hold

ささやく【囁く】 to whisper

さしあげる【差し上げる】 [humble expression] to give ―...して差し上げる [humble expression] to do (for someone of higher status than oneself)

さしこむ【差し込む】 ① to thrust...into, to stick...into ② to come into

さししめす【指し示す】 to indicate, to point out

－させる to make (a person) do something

さそい【誘い】 temptation ―誘いをかける to tempt, to seduce

さそう【誘う】 to invite ―...を誘って with ...

さだまる【定まる】 to be settled ➤ちょうし（調子）

さっかく【錯覚】 illusion ―錯覚（を）する to have an illusion (that)...; to be confused

さっき a little [short] while ago; just now; just a moment ago

ざっし【雑誌】 magazine

さつじん【殺人】 murder

さつじんはん【殺人犯】 murderer

さっと quickly

さっぱり ➤きれい（綺麗）

さて well

さばきかた【さばき方】 how to slaughter [butcher] ―さばく to slaughter (animals); to dress (meat animals)

さびしい【寂しい・淋しい】 sad; lonely, lonesome ―寂しく sadly

ざぶざぶ [onomatopoeic word used to express a splashing sound]

さまざま（な）【様々（な）】 various

さます【覚ます】 ➤め（目）

さまよう【彷徨う】 to wander ―さまよわせる to let... wander

さむい【寒い】 cold

さむさ【寒さ】 cold, coldness

さめる【覚める・醒める】 ➤め（目）, よい²（酔い）

さらに（は）【更に（は）】 furthermore, moreover; even (more)

さる【去る】 to leave, to go away

さわぐ【騒ぐ】 to make noise

ざわめき buzz

さん【三】three ―三倍 three times, threefold

-さん [suffix for personal names]

さんか【参加】participation ―参加する to attend; to take part in

サングラス sunglasses

さんじゅう【三十】thirty

さんにん【三人】three (people)

ざんねん(な)【残念(な)】disappointed ―残念そうに disappointedly

さんびき【三匹】three (fish, etc.) ➤-ひき・びき・ぴき(匹)

さんぽ【散歩】walk, stroll ―散歩(を)する to take a walk, to stroll ―散歩に出る to go (out) for a walk

し

しあわせ【幸せ】happiness ―幸せな happy

しお【塩】salt ―塩をかける to sprinkle salt (on…)

-しか [followed by a negative] only, just

しかい【視界】one's sight, one's view

しかえし【仕返し】revenge

しかく【四角】square; rectangle ―四角の square; rectangular

しかける【仕掛ける】to set up

しかし but, however

しかた【仕方】way, manner, how to do

しかたなく【仕方なく】reluctantly

しかる【叱る】to scold

じかん【時間】① time ② hour ―時間をかける to spend (plenty of) time 時間をつぶす to kill time

しき【死期】one's end, one's time (to die)

しぎ【鴫】snipe, sandpiper (kind of bird)

しごく ➤ひげ(髭・鬚)

じこく【時刻】time

しごと【仕事】job, work

じこほぞん【自己保存】self-preservation

じざい【自在】―自在に easily; skillfully

しざん【死産】stillbirth

-じしん【-自身】himself, itself

しずか(な)【静か(な)】quiet ―静かにする to keep quiet

しずく【滴】drop

しせん【視線】one's eyes

した¹【下】―…の下で[の] under…, below…

した²【舌】tongue

しだいに【次第に】gradually

したしい【親しい】friendly; close

じっか【実家】one's parents' home

しつけ【躾】discipline

しつこい persistent ―しつこさ persistence

しっこく(の)【漆黒(の)】jet-black

じっさい(に)【実際(に)】actually, practically; in fact

じっと intently, fixedly ―じっと見る to stare [gaze] at… ―じっと耳をすませる to listen attentively [intently]

じつは【実は】in fact, actually

しつもん【質問】question ―質問する to ask a question

しつれい(な)【失礼(な)】impolite, rude

しでかす to do (especially bad things)

しぬ【死ぬ】to die, to be killed ―死んだ dead

しはつ【始発】the first train

しはらい【支払い】payment ―支払い書 written request for payment

しばらく【暫く】for a while ―しばらくして after a while

しばりつける【縛り付ける】to tie, to bind

しばる【縛る】to bind, to tie (up)

しぶしぶ【渋々】reluctantly

じぶん【自分】oneself ―自分で by [for]

oneself ―自分（たち）の one's (own)…

じへいてき（な）【自閉的（な）】autistic
―自閉的になる to withdraw into one's
shell

しべん（の）【至便（の）】very convenient
➣ こうつう（交通）

しぼう【脂肪】fat

しめきる【閉め切る】to close [shut] up;
to keep…closed [shut] ―閉め切った
closed-up

しめつける【締め付ける】to tighten

しゃがむ　to crouch, to squat (down)

じゃき【邪気】maliciousness; evil intent
―邪気がない innocent

シャキン　[onomatopoeic word used to
express the sound of someone sharp-
ening knives]

しゃべりかた【喋り方】one's way [man-
ner] of talking

しゃべる【喋る】to talk, to chat

じゃま【邪魔】disturbance, interference,
bother ―…の邪魔になる to disturb…

じゃらじゃら ―じゃらじゃら音を立てる
to jingle, to jangle

しゃりしゃり [onomatopoeic word used
to express a scraping sound]

じゆう【自由】freedom ―自由に freely;
as you like

じゅう【十】ten

-じゅう【-中】(all) through…

しゅうい【周囲】surroundings ―…の
周囲に　around…

しゅうがくりょこう【修学旅行】school
trip

しゅうかん【習慣】custom; habit

しゅうき【周期】―周期的な periodic

しゅうし【終始】from beginning to end

じゅうじゅん（な）【従順（な）】obedient

じゅうに【十二】twelve ―十二回目 the
twelfth time

じゅうにん【住人】resident

じゅうはち【十八】eighteen

じゅぎょう【授業】class

じゅくすい【熟睡】sound [deep] sleep
―熟睡する to sleep soundly

しゅじん【主人】storekeeper

しゅっしん【出身】(a person's) origin
―…出身である to come [be] from…

シュノーケル　snorkel

しゅふ【主婦】housewife

しゅるい【種類】kind, sort

しゅんかん【瞬間】moment, instant ―瞬
間的に instantaneously

じゅんとう【順当】―順当なら if things
had gone normally

じゅんび【準備】preparation(s) ―準備
する to prepare, to get ready

じょう【情】sympathy, pity

しょうがくせい【小学生】(elementary)
schoolchild

しょうがっこう【小学校】　elementary
school

しょうき【正気】balance of mind ―正
気を失う to go out of one's mind

じょうけん【条件】condition(s)

しょうしょう【少々】a little, a bit, slightly

じょうたい【状態】state, condition, situation

じょうだん【冗談】joke ―冗談を言う to
make a joke ―冗談半分に half-jokingly

しょうち【承知】―承知する to accept

しょうどく【消毒】disinfection ―消毒す
る to disinfect

じょうねつ【情熱】passion

じょうほう【情報】information

しょうめん【正面】the front

じょうりゅう【上流】upstream

しょくぎょう【職業】occupation

しょくご（に）【食後（に）】after a meal

じょこう【徐行】―徐行する to go slow(ly), to slow down

じょしゅ【助手】assistant ―助手席 the seat next to the driver, the front passenger seat

じょせい【女性】woman; girl

しょっちゅう　often

しょめい【署名】signature ―署名する to sign

じょやく【助役】deputy mayor

じょゆう【女優】actress

しらす・しらせる【知らす・知らせる】to let (a person) know

しられぬ【知られぬ】unknown

しり【尻】one's bottom [butt] ―尻に帆（を）かける to take to one's heels

じりつしん【自立心】sense of independence

しりょう【資料】materials, data

しる【知る】to know, to find out, to learn ―(…に)知られる to become known (to…)

シルエット　silhouette

しれる【知れる】to become known; to be knowable; to be nothing exceptional

しろ【白】white

しろい【白い】white

シロップ　syrup

しろめ【白目】the white of the eye ―白目をむく to open one's eyes wide

じんかく【人格】character, personality

しんぎ【真偽】whether it is true or not

しんけつ【心血】―心血をそそぐ to devote oneself

しんけん（な）【真剣（な）】serious; earnest

しんじる【信じる】to believe ―信じられる believable

じんせい【人生】(one's) life

しんせん（な）【新鮮（な）】fresh

しんちく【新築】―新築する to build a new house

じんちくむがい（な）【人畜無害（な）】harmless

しんつう【心痛】anxiety; (emotional) pain

しんぱい【心配】care, concern, worry ―心配する to worry, to be worried [concerned]

しんや【深夜】(in) the middle of the night

しんりがく【心理学】psychology ―心理学的に psychologically

す

す【巣】nest ―巣をかける to build a nest, to nest

すいすい　swiftly, smoothly

すいちょく（の）【垂直（の）】vertical ―垂直に vertically, straight up [down]

スイッチ　switch

すいでん【水田】rice paddy [field]

ずいぶん【随分】very; (very) much, a lot

すいりしょうせつ【推理小説】detective story [novel]

すう-【数-】a few, some, several

すうすう　[onomatopoeic word used to express the sound of someone breathing in their sleep]

すうねん【数年】a few years

すがた【姿】figure, shape ―姿を見せる to appear

すき（な）【好き（な）】favorite ―(…が)好きである to like, to prefer, to be fond of ―好きなように as one likes

すきま【隙間】gap, opening ―…の隙間に between…

-すぎる【-過ぎる】too…

すぐ soon, in no time; at once, immediately, right away ―…してすぐ as soon as…

すくう¹【掬う】to scoop up

すくう²【巣食う】[figurative] to lurk in one's mind

すぐさま ➤すぐ

すくない【少ない】few; small in number

すくなくとも【少なくとも】at least

すごく【凄く】very, awfully, terribly

すこし【少し】a little, a bit

すごす【過ごす】to spend (time), to pass the time

すじ【筋】plot (of a story)

すすめる【勧める・薦める】to advise, to suggest

スタミナ stamina

スタンド desk [table] lamp

-ずつ …each

すっかり（と） completely, entirely, fully; neatly

ずっと always

すでに【既に】already

すてる【捨てる】to throw away

すな【砂】sand

すなば【砂場】sandbox; sandpit

スピード speed

スプーン spoon

すべて【全て・総て】all, everything ―すべての all

すべらせる【滑らせる】to slide

すべりだい【滑り台】(playground) slide

すませる¹【済ませる】to finish, to get through with…

すませる²【澄ませる】➤みみ（耳）

すまん ➤すみません

すみ【隅】corner ―…の隅に in the corner of…

すみません I'm sorry.

すむ【住む】to live, to reside

する ①to do ②to make A into B ③to have sex ④➤かいもの（買い物）, かけごと（賭け事）, き（気）, におい（匂い）

するりと ―するりと消える to slip out of sight

すれちがう【すれ違う】to pass (in opposite directions)

すわる【座る】to sit (down)

せ

せ【背】one's back ―…を背に with… at one's back ―背を向ける to turn one's back

せい fault ―…のせいで due to…, because of…, owing to…

せいかつ【生活】life

せいじゅく【成熟】maturity ―成熟する to mature ―成熟した mature

せいにく【精肉】(butchered) meat ―精肉商 butcher's, meat shop

せいねん【青年】young man

せいぶつ【生物】living thing ➤やせい（野生）

せいめい【生命】life

セーター sweater

せかい【世界】world ➤ないめん（内面）

せき【席】➤さけ（酒）

せきぞう【石像】stone statue [image]

せく【急く】➤き（気）

せけん【世間】the world; people, the public

せすじ【背筋】spine

せっきゃく【接客】serving [attending to] customers ―接客する to serve [wait on] customers

セックス sex ―セックスする to have sex

ぜったい（に）【絶対（に）】absolutely ―絶対に…ない never

24

ぜっちょう【絶頂】orgasm ―絶頂に達する to reach orgasm

せっとく【説得】persuasion ―説得する to persuade

せつなさ【切なさ】painfulness

せのび【背伸び】―背伸びする to stand on tiptoe

せぼね【背骨】backbone

せまい【狭い】small, narrow

せまる【迫る】to approach, to draw near ➤ ゆうやみ（夕闇）

せりふ【台詞】lines; the words (from a play, etc.)

せわ【世話】care ―世話になる to receive a favor ―世話をする to take care of

せん【線】line

せんげつ【先月】last month

せんぜん【戦前】―戦前は in prewar times

ぜんぜん【全然】―全然...ない not...at all

せんぞ【先祖】ancestor(s) ―先祖の ancestral

せんたくき【洗濯機】washing machine, washer ―洗濯機をかける to run the washing machine

せんたん【先端】tip

せんぱい【先輩】one's senior

ぜんぶ【全部】all

そ

そいつ that (one)

そう¹【沿う】to go [run] along [parallel to]... ―...に沿って along, by, parallel to

そう² so, such

-そう to look, to seem, to appear; they say (that)..., I hear (that)... ―...しそうである almost..., to come near to...

ぞう【像】statue, figure

そういう such, like that, that kind of...

そうか I see.

そうこ【倉庫】warehouse

そうじき【掃除機】(vacuum) cleaner ―掃除機をかける to vacuum

そうぞう【想像】imagination ―想像する to imagine

そうだ That's right.

そうですね ➤ そうだ

そうにゅう【挿入】insertion ―挿入する to insert

そうやって like that, in that way

そくしん【促進】promotion ―促進する to promote, to encourage

そこ¹【底】the bottom

そこ² ―そこに・そこで there

そこなし（の）【底無し（の）】bottomless

そして and (then)

そそぐ【注ぐ】➤ しんけつ（心血）

そつぎょう【卒業】graduation ―卒業する to graduate (from)

そっくり ―...そっくりに just [exactly] like...

そっちょく（な）【率直（な）】honest, frank

そっと 1 gently, softly 2 alone; as it is

そと【外】outside ―...の外で（は）outside (of)

その that ―その場で on the spot, immediately

そのうえ【その上】besides, what is more

そのかわり【その代わり】instead

そのご【その後】after that, afterward; later

そのたび【その度】each time

そのとき【その時】then, at that [the] time

そのへん【その辺】around there; nearby, in the area

そのほか【その他】others　―そのほかの other

そのまま　just like that; (exactly) as it is

そのまんま　➤そのまま

そのもの　the very thing, itself

そば¹【蕎麦】*soba* [buckwheat] noodles

そば²【側・傍】―そばに　near, close to

そばかす　freckle(s) ―そばかす顔 freck-led face

そびえる　to rise, to tower

そふ【祖父】one's grandfather

そめる【染める】to dye, to color

そもそも　to begin with; in the first place

そら【空】sky

そりかえる【反り返る】to bend backward

そりゃ（あ）　[contraction of それは]

それ　it; that ―それだけで that alone

それが　however

それから　①and, (and) then　②after that, since then

それだけに　for that reason

それで　and, so

それとも　or

それに　and

それまで【それ迄】until then

それより（も）　rather than that

そんざい【存在】existence; human being ―存在する to exist

ぞんざい（な）rude, rough, impolite ―ぞんざいに rudely, roughly, impolitely

そんな　such, like that

そんなに　so, that; so [that] much

た

た【田】rice paddy [field]

–たい　―…したい to want to do

だい【代】generation

–だい【–代】[suffix for the range of a person's age in ten-year periods]

だいいち【第一】first (of all)

だいがく【大学】university

だいがくいんせい【大学院生】graduate student

たいくつ【退屈】boredom ―退屈する to be bored [tired]

たいした【大した】great ―大した…ではない not much of a [an]…

たいして【対して】➤たいする（対する）

たいしょう【対象】object, target

だいじょうぶ【大丈夫】okay, all right, fine

たいする【対する】―…に対して to, to-ward　―…に対する to, toward; for

たいそう【大層】very, terribly; a lot

だいたい【大体】①almost　②in the first place

たいてい【大抵】generally; usually, in general

だいのうじょう【大農場】big [large] farm

タイプ　(one's) type

だいぶ【大分】quite; fairly

たいへん【大変】very, very much; a lot ―大変な hard

たいよう【太陽】the sun; sunlight

たいりょく【体力】strength

たえる¹【耐える】to stand, to tolerate

たえる²【絶える】➤いき（息）

タオル　towel

たおれる【倒れる】to fall sick, to col-lapse

だが　but

たかい【高い】①high; tall　②loud (de-scribing sound) ―高く high　―高くなる to become louder

たがい【互い】each other; both ―互いに mutually; both

たかいびき【高鼾】―高いびきをかく to snore loudly; to sleep soundly

だがし【駄菓子】cheap sweets [candy]

だから so, therefore; that's why

−だから because, as, since

だきあう【抱き合う】to hug each other

だきしめる【抱き締める】to hug...tightly

だきすくめる【抱きすくめる】to hold [embrace]...tightly

だく【抱く】to hold; to hug

たくさん【沢山】a lot —たくさんの many, a lot of, a large number of

タクシー taxi

たくみ（な）【巧み（な）】skillful

−だけ [often used together with ほんの] just, only

たしか（な）【確か（な）】certain, sure, definite　—確かに certainly, surely, definitely; indeed

たしかめる【確かめる】to see, to check; to make sure

だす【出す】① to take out, to let [put] out　② to stick out (one's tongue)　③ ≻くち（口）、こえ（声）

−だす【−出す】—...し出す to begin [start] to do

たすけ【助け】help　—助けを呼ぶ to call for help

たすける【助ける】to help

たずさえる【携える】to carry

たずねる【訊ねる・尋ねる】to ask, to inquire

ただ【唯・只】① only, just, merely　② but, however　—ただ一つ only one

たたく【叩く】to pat, to tap

ただし【但し】but, however

ただしい【正しい】right, correct

たたせる【立たせる】to set [stand]... upright, to make...stand upright

だだっこ【駄々っ子】spoiled child

ただの【只の】ordinary

たたみ【畳】tatami mat

−たち【−達】[suffix added to form plurals]

たちあがる【立ち上がる】to stand up, to rise (to one's feet)

たちさる【立ち去る】to leave, to get [go] away

たちどまる【立ち止まる】to stop

たつ¹【立つ・建つ】① to stand　② ≻みこみ（見込み）

たつ²【経つ】to pass (by), to go (by) (describing time)

たっする【達する】to reach

たった only, just

たてもの【建物】building

たてる【立てる】≻おと（音）

たとえ¹【譬え】parable

たとえ² —たとえ...としても even if...

たとえば【例えば】for example [instance]

たどたどしい faltering, halting —たどたどしく falteringly, haltingly

たどる【辿る】to trace (a family tree); to follow

たな【棚】shelf

たにん【他人】others, other people; stranger ≻あかのたにん（赤の他人）

たのしい【楽しい】enjoyable, fun

たのしませる【楽しませる】to please

たのしむ【楽しむ】to enjoy, to have fun

たのむ【頼む】to ask, to beg —頼むから please; for God's sake

たび【旅】trip, travel —旅に出る to go on a trip

−たび（に）【−度（に）】—...するたびに every time one does...

たぶん【多分】probably, maybe

たべおわる【食べ終わる】to finish eating

たべる【食べる】to eat

たましい【魂】soul

たまたま【偶々】by chance; unexpectedly; accidentally ―たまたま…する to happen to do

たまらなさ　unbearableness

たまる【溜まる】to accumulate

だまる【黙る】to become quiet [silent]; to hush up ―黙って quietly, without saying anything ―黙っている to remain [keep] silent, to say nothing ―黙ったまま without a word, wordlessly

-ため(に)【-為(に)】in order to…; because of…, due to…

だめ(な)【駄目(な)】no-good ―駄目である　１ It doesn't work.　２ You mustn't …　３ No.; No way.

たよう(な)【多様(な)】various, diverse ―多様に　variously, diversely

-たら　if; when; once

たらい　(washing) tub

だらだら(と)　idly, lazily

だれ【誰】who

だれか【誰か】someone, somebody

だれの【誰の】―誰の…にも　everyone's …, anyone's…

だれも【誰も】―誰も…ない　nobody, no one ―誰の目も届かぬ nobody can see

だんかい【段階】stage, phase, step

だんせい【男性】man

だんだん(と)【段々(と)】gradually, little by little

たんなる【単なる】mere, simple

たんに【単に】merely, simply, just

だんりょく【弾力】―弾力のある　soft, springy

ち

ち【血】blood ➤ちまみれ（血塗れ）

ちいさい・ちいさな【小さい・小さな】small, little; tiny; short; young; low ―小さいうちは when (someone) was a little child ―小さく（＝小さい声で）in a low [small] voice

ちかい【近い】near, close to

ちがい【違い】➤みこみちがい（見込み違い）

ちがう【違う】to be different ―(…と)違った different (from…)

ちかく【近く】near ―…の近くで　near; in the neighborhood

ちかごろ【近頃】these days, nowadays

ちかづく【近づく】to get closer [near], to approach

ちかてつ【地下鉄】subway

ちかよる【近寄る】to come [get] near, to approach

ちから【力】strength, power, force ―力を入れて strongly; with emphasis

ちぎる【千切る】to tear (up, off), to break (up)

ちじょう【地上】the ground ―地上に above the ground

ちち【父】one's father

ちちおや【父親】one's father

ちちゅう【地中】―地中の in the ground, in the earth

ちほう【地方】region

ちまみれ【血塗れ】―血まみれの bloody ―血まみれになる to become covered with blood

ちゃわん【茶碗】(tea) cup; (rice) bowl

チャンス　chance

ちゃんと　properly

-ちゅう【-中】during, in

ちゅうがく【中学】➤ちゅうがっこう（中学校）

ちゅうがっこう【中学校】junior high school

ちゅうしゃ【注射】injection, shot ―注射薬 injection

ちゅうもん【注文】request ―注文をつける to make a request

ちょうし【調子】tone ―調子の定まらない unstable

ちょうしょく【朝食】breakfast

ちょうど【丁度】just; just like...

ちょくご【直後】―...の直後 immediately [just, right] after...

ちょくぜん【直前】―...の直前 just [right] before...

ちょっと　a little, a (little) bit, kind of, somewhat

ちょっぴり　a little, a bit

ちらりと　quickly, stealthily ―ちらりと見る to take a quick glance at, to catch a glimpse of

つい　① just, only　② in spite of oneself, unintentionally

ついで【次いで】and then

ついていく【付いていく】to go (along) with

つういん【通院】going to (the) hospital regularly ―通院する to go to (the) hospital (as an outpatient)

つうがく【通学】going to school ―通学の途中 on one's way to and from school

つうじあう【通じ合う】 to understand each other

つうでんひょうじ【通電表示】power indicator; ON light

つかいこなす【使いこなす】to use skillfully

つかう【使う・遣う】① to use　② ➤き（気）

つかまる【捕まる】to be caught, to be arrested

つかみあげる【摑み上げる】to grab up

つかむ【摑む】to catch, to grab, to grasp

つかれ【疲れ】tiredness, fatigue ―疲れを知らない never get tired

つかれる【疲れる】to get tired

つき【月】moon

つぎ【次】next ―次の next

つきあう【付き合う】① to stay with　② to go out with

つきさす【突き刺す】to stab, to jab

つきとばす【突き飛ばす】to push down, to knock over

ツキノワグマ【月の輪熊】Asian black bear (with a white crescent-shaped marking around its neck)

つきる【尽きる】to be focused [concentrated] on

つく¹【付く】① to have, to include　② to be attached, to be on...　③ ➤おち（落ち）, けんとう（見当）

つく²【就く】to take up, to enter (a profession)

つく³　➤いき（息）

つくえ【机】desk

つくりかた【作り方】how to make, way of making

つくる【作る】to make

つけまわす【付け回す】to stalk, to follow (a person) around

つける¹【付ける】① to bring...closer　② ➤ちゅうもん（注文）

つける²【着ける】to put...on ―つけている to have on, to wear

つける³【点ける】to turn on, to light

つたわる【伝わる】to be felt, to come across (to...)

つち【土】clay

つづき【続き】the continuation; the point where one has left off (writing

あ

か

さ

た

な

は

ま

や

ら

わ

or talking)

つつく【突く】to peck; to pick (at)

つづく【続く】to continue

つづける【続ける】to continue, to go on

-つづける【-続ける】―...し続ける to keep (on) doing

つっこむ【突っ込む】to thrust, to stick ...into

つつみ【包み】bundle, package

つつみこむ【包み込む】to encompass, to envelop

つな【綱】rope, string

つながり【繋がり】relation, connection

つの【角】horn ―角が生える to grow horns

つのぶえ【角笛】horn, bugle horn

つぶ【粒】grain

つぶす【潰す】 ➤ じかん（時間）

つぶやく to mumble, to murmur

つぼ【壺】pot, jar

つま【妻】wife

つまり in other words, that is (to say)

-づめ【-詰め】[suffix; used after verbs] to keep on doing

つめたい【冷たい】① cold ② cold-hearted

つめる【詰める】to stuff, to fill (up)

-つもり ―...つもりである to think, to believe

つよい【強い】strong

つらい【辛い】difficult, hard, painful

つり【釣り】fishing ―釣りをする to fish

-づれ【-連れ】a party of (people)

つれこむ【連れ込む】to bring (a person) in

つれさる【連れ去る】to take (a person) away

つれる ➤ -につれ（て）

つんと [mimetic word used to express

the sensation of a slight tug, bump, etc.] ―つんと触れる to bump [brush] up against

て【手】hand; arm ―手を振る to wave one's hand ―手を伸ばす to reach (for) ―手をやる to touch

であう【出会う】to meet, to come [run] across

ていねい(に)【丁寧(に)】carefully, with care

デート date ―デートする to go on a date, to go out

でかける【出掛ける】to go out

てがみ【手紙】letter

できる【出来る】① can do, to be able to do ② to be made (of [from]...)

てくび【手首】wrist

でし【弟子】apprentice ―弟子入りする to apprentice oneself (to...)

てつ【鉄】iron

てつだい【手伝い】help

でてくる【出てくる】to come out, to appear; to be found [discovered]

てのこう【手の甲】the back of one's hand

てのひら【手のひら・掌】palm

では well, then

デパート department store

デビュー debut ―デビューする to make one's debut

てまえ【手前】this side ―...の手前で before ―その手前 for decency's sake

でも but

-でも ...or something

でる【出る】① to get out (of), to leave ② to go out ➤ さんぽ（散歩）、たび（旅）③ to come forth [forward]; to come

out ④ to move ⑤ to appear (in a magazine, on TV, etc.) ⑥ ➤ はなし（話）

てわたす【手渡す】 to hand (over)

てん【点】 point

てんいん【店員】 salesclerk

てんかん【転換】 ➤ きぶん（気分）

てんじょう【天井】 ceiling

てんしん【転身】 ―転身する to start a new career

でんわ【電話】 telephone; (phone) call ―電話をかける to give (a person) a call ―電話を受ける to take a call ―電話（を）する to call, to make a call ―電話を切る to hang up, to end a call

でんわき【電話機】 telephone

と

-と and; with...

-ど【-度】 [counter for the number of times]

ドア door

-という【-と言う】 called..., named...

-というのに【-と言うのに】 though...; and yet...

といし【砥石】 whetstone

トイレ toilet; bathroom

どう how, what

どういう what (kind of)...?

どうぐ【道具】 tool

どうじ【同時】 ―それと同時に at the same time; meanwhile

どうして why

どうしても ① badly, by all means ② for the life of one; simply, just

どうせ anyway; after all

どうぞ please

とうちゃく【到着】 arrival ―到着する to get to, to arrive

どうでもよい one doesn't care; it doesn't

matter (that)...

どうとく【道徳】 morals, morality

どうぶつ【動物】 animal

どうも ① [used for emphasizing one's gratitude or apology] very, really ② ➤ どうやら ―どうもありがとう Thank you very much.

どうやら ―どうやら...らしい probably, likely; it seems (that)...

とおい【遠い】 far

とおく【遠く】 a distant place ―遠くに far, in the distance

とおす【通す】 to pierce

とおめ【遠目】 ―遠目には (when seen) from a distance

とおり【通り】 ―...の言うとおり as...says

とおりすがり【通りすがり】 ―通りすがりに as one passes (by)

とおる【通る】 to pass, to go through ..., to go past [by]

-とか or

とかい【都会】 city

とき【時】 time ―...の [...する] 時 when ...

どき【土器】 earthenware

ときおり【時折】 occasionally, at times

ときどき【時々】 once in a while, sometimes

とくい（な）【得意（な）】 proud, self-satisfied ―(...が) 得意である to be good [skilled] (at...)

とくに【特に】 especially, particularly

とくべつ（な）【特別（な）】 unique; special

とけい【時計】 clock, watch

とこ ➤ ところ（所）

どこ【何処】 ―どこに where ―どこまで how far, to what extent

どこか somewhere

どことなく　somehow, in some way

どこまでも　endlessly; to the (very) end

ところ【所】place, spot; point ➣ いま（今）, おもう（思う）　―…のところに where　―…するところだが would have done

–どころか　not only…(but also…)

ところで　and; now; by the way

ところどころ【所々】in places, here and there

とし【年】① age　② year

としおいた【年老いた】old, aged

とじこもる【閉じこもる】to lock oneself in, to hole up

–として　as…

とじる【閉じる】to close, to shut　―目を閉じて with one's eyes closed

–とすれば　if it's true

とちゅう【途中】on the [one's] way (to/from)　―途中まで halfway

どちら　which　―どちらかといえば rather

とっくに　long ago [since]; already

とっくり（と）　fully, well

とつぜん【突然】suddenly

どっち ➣ どちら

とても　very　―とても…ない hardly…, not possibly…

とどく【届く】to reach　―(…が)届かぬ does not reach [penetrate]

ととのう【整う】➣ かおだち（顔立ち）

となり【隣】next-door neighbor; next door　―隣の next, next-door, neighboring

どなりこむ【怒鳴り込む】to storm into (a room)

となりまち【隣町】neighboring town

とにかく　anyway

どの　which

どのくらい【どの位】how much

どのような【どの様な】what kind of…

とはいえ【とは言え】however

とびこむ【飛び込む】to jump [dive] in [into]

とびら【扉】door

トマト　tomato

とまどう【戸惑う】to be confused; to be at a loss

とまりがけ（の）【泊まりがけ（の）】overnight

とまる【泊まる】to sleep out, to stay overnight

ともだち【友達】one's friend

ともる【灯る・点る】to be lit

どようび【土曜日】Saturday

とらえる【捕らえる】to capture

トラック　(pickup) truck

とり【鳥】bird

とりあげる【取り上げる】to take away, to confiscate

とりすがる【取りすがる】to cling to…

とりだす【取り出す】to take out

とりのこす【取り残す】to leave…behind

とりはらう【取り払う】to remove, to take away

とりもどす【取り戻す】to get back

とる【取る】to take off, to remove ➣ れんらく（連絡）

どれ　which

どれも　all; every, each, any

とんでもない　① outrageous; terrible, awful　② [as a response] Not at all.

どんどん　rapidly; continuously

どんな　―どんな（ふうに）how　―どんな…も（みな）every; all　―どんな…も…ない not any…

どんなに　how; no matter how…

な

な【名】① ➤ なまえ（名前） ② fame ―名のある famous; honorable

ない【無い】there is [are] no [not]...

–ない [negation] not, no

ないしん【内心】one's mind, one's heart

ないぞう【内臓】the internal organs

ナイフ knife

ないめん【内面】the inside ―内面世界 (せかい) one's inner world

なか¹【中】the inside ―…の中に [を・で] in..., inside... ―…の中から out of... ―…の中へ into..., in...

なか²【仲】relations ―仲がよい close, friendly

ながい【長い】long

ながく【長く】(for) long, for a long time ―長くなる to lengthen, to take a long time

なかなか ―なかなか...ない (just) will not ..., not...easily

ながねん【長年】(for) a long time

ながほそい【長細い】long and narrow

なかゆび【中指】the middle finger

–ながら as..., while...

ながれ【流れ】stream

なき–【亡き–】late, dead

なきだす【泣き出す】to begin crying

なきまね【鳴き真似】mimicry ―鳴きまねをする to mimic

なく【鳴く】[verb describing the vocalization of animals] to moo; to low

–なければ ―...しなければいけない have to do, must do

なごむ【和む】to calm down, to relax

なし【無し】there isn't [aren't]...; no...

–なし（で）【–無し（で）】without...

なじむ【馴染む】to become familiar (with...)

なじる to accuse

なす【生す】➤ おそれ（恐れ・怖れ）

なぞ【謎】riddle, puzzle ―謎をかける to ask a riddle

なつ【夏】summer ―夏らしい summery

なっとく【納得】―納得する to understand; to accept

なつやすみ【夏休み】summer vacation

なでる【撫でる】to stroke, to pet

–など【–等】things like...

なな【七】seven ―七に七をかける to multiply seven by seven

なに【何】what ―何から何まで down to the smallest detail ―何をしているのか what one is doing

なにか【何か】① something ② somewhat ―...か何か ...or something

なにひとつ【何一つ】anything ―なにひとつ...ない not a thing

なにも【何も】anything ―何もない there is nothing

なにより（も）【何より（も）】better [more] than anything else

なので so

なのる【名乗る】to give one's name

なべ【鍋】pan, pot

なまいき（な）【生意気（な）】cheeky, impertinent ―生意気盛 (ざか) りである to be at the cheeky age

なまえ【名前】name

なみ【波】wave

なみうちぎわ【波打ち際】beach

なみおと【波音】the sound of waves

なみだ【涙】tear(s)

なめしがわ【なめし革】leather

–なら ➤ ほど（程）

ならぶ【並ぶ】① to be arranged, to be displayed [put] ② to be side by side ―並んで side by side

あ
か
さ
た
な
は
ま
や
ら
わ

なりたつ【成り立つ】to consist of, to be made up of

−なりに in one's own way

なりひびく【鳴り響く】to resound, to echo

なる【成る】① to become, to be ② ➤ じゃま（邪魔）, せわ（世話）, ノイローゼ

なるほど【成程】I see.; indeed

なわ【縄】rope, cord —縄をかける to arrest (a criminal)

なわばり【縄張り】territory, turf

なんかい【何回】how many times —何回も many times —何回か several times

なんきん【軟禁】confinement —軟禁する to confine

なんて【何て】what, how

なんでも【何でも】anything

なんでもない【何でもない】ordinary; there is nothing wrong with...

なんと【何と】what, how

なんど【何度】—何度も many times, again and again

なんとでも【何とでも】whatever

なんとも【何とも】quite, really

なんぼん【何本】—何本も many, a lot of

に

に【二】two

におい【匂い】① smell, scent, odor, flavor ② atmosphere —匂いがする to smell —匂いのよい fragrant, sweet-smelling

にぎりしめる【握り締める】to grasp, to hold tightly

にぎる【握る】to grasp, to hold ... in one's hand

にく【肉】meat

にくぎゅう【肉牛】beef cattle

にくや【肉屋】① butcher's ② butcher

にげさる【逃げ去る】to run [get] away

にげる【逃げる】to run [get] away

にこり —にこりとする to smile, to grin

にさん【二三】—二、三（の）a few, a couple of —二、三日 (for) a few days

にじ【虹】rainbow

にじっぷん【二十分】twenty minutes

−にしても even if, though; granting that

にじませる【滲ませる】to blur

にじむ【滲む】to be blurred; to run

にじゅう【二十】twenty

にだい【荷台】bed (of a truck)

−にち【−日】[counter for days]

にっき【日記】diary

−につれ（て） as...

にている【似ている】➤ にる（似る）

にどと【二度と】—二度と...ない never (again)

−には for, to

にばんめ【二番目】the second

にぶい【鈍い】stupid, dull

にもつ【荷物】things, belongings; bag

にやにや —にやにや笑う to smile knowingly, to grin

にゅういん【入院】hospitalization —入院する to be hospitalized

にゅうぎゅう【乳牛】milk cow, dairy cattle [cow]

にらむ【睨む】to stare (hard) at a person, to glare at

にる【似る】to be like..., to be similar, to resemble —似ている similar

にわとり【鶏・ニワトリ】chicken

−にん【−人】[counter for people]

にんげん【人間】person; human (being) —人間の human

ぬ

ぬく【抜く】to pull out ➤コンセント

ぬぐ【脱ぐ】to remove [take off]

ぬぐう【拭う】to wipe, to mop

ぬの【布】cloth

ぬのじ【布地】cloth, material

ね

ねいき【寝息】breath; the breathing (of a sleeping person)

ねいろ【音色】tone

ねえ Hey!, Look!

ねこ【猫】cat

ねころぶ【寝転ぶ】to lie [flop] down

ねすがた【寝姿】one's sleeping figure

ねつ【熱】fever, passion

ねっしん（な）【熱心（な）】earnest, eager, devoted —熱心さ earnestness, eagerness, enthusiasm

ねどこ【寝床】bed

ねむい【眠い】sleepy —眠くなる to become sleepy

ねむり【眠り】sleep —眠りに入る to go to sleep

ねむる【眠る】① to sleep; to go to sleep ② to lie, to be hidden

ねる【寝る】to sleep, to go to sleep; to lie down

ねん【年】year

-ねん【-年】[counter for years]

ねんじゅう【年中】all (the) year around; always

ねんまつ【年末】the end of the year —年末の year-end

の

ノイローゼ neurosis —ノイローゼになる to suffer from neurosis, to have a nervous breakdown

のうじょう【農場】farm

のうしんとう【脳震盪】concussion (of the brain) —脳しんとうを起こす to suffer [have] a concussion (of the brain)

のうどう【農道】farm road [path]

のうふ【農夫】farm worker, farmhand

ノースリーブ（の）sleeveless

のこす【残す】① to leave ② to keep, to preserve

のこる【残る】to remain, to stay; to be left

のせる【載せる】to put... (on...), to place

のぞく【覗く】to look, to peer

-ので because, as, since

のど【喉】throat —喉の奥で at the back of the throat

のどもと【喉元】throat; neck

-のに though, although; despite

のばす【伸ばす】to stretch (out); to reach for ➤て（手）

のべる【述べる】to state, to express, to tell

のむ【飲む】to drink

は

は¹【刃】blade

は²【葉】leaf

は³【歯】tooth

パーンチ ➤パンチ

はい [form of affirmative reply] yes

-ばい【-倍】...times, -fold

ハイキング hiking

ばいてん【売店】a stall, a stand

バイト part-time job —バイト（を）する to work part-time

はいりこむ【入り込む】to come [go] into

はいりょ【配慮】consideration, concern, care

はいる【入る】 ① to come [go, get] into, to enter ② to come in stock ③ ➤ ねむり（眠り）, ふとん（布団）, ふろ（風呂）

はえる【生える】 to grow ➤ つの（角）

はおる【羽織る】 to put on —はおっている to have...on, to wear

はか【墓】 tomb, grave

はがき【葉書】 postcard

ばかげた【馬鹿げた】 absurd

ばかな【馬鹿な】 foolish, stupid

ばかばかしい【馬鹿馬鹿しい】 ridiculous, absurd —ばかばかしく ridiculously

-ばかり only, just; all

はきけ【吐き気】 nausea, sickness —吐き気に襲われる to feel sick

はくしき【博識】 extensive knowledge

はくせい【剥製】 stuffed animal, taxidermy

バケツ bucket

ばけねこ【化け猫】 ghost cat

はこ【箱】 box

はこぶ【運ぶ】 to transport

はさむ【挟む】 to put...between, to insert

はし【橋】 bridge —橋をかける to build [construct] a bridge

はじきだす【弾き出す】 to estimate, to calculate

はしご【梯子】 ladder

はじめ【初め】 —初めは first

はじめて【初めて】 (for the) first time

はじめる【始める】 to start, to begin

-はじめる【-始める】 —...しはじめる to begin [start] to do

はしる【走る】 to run (away)

はず【筈】 —...はずがない it cannot be that...; there's no way that...

バス bus

はずかしい【恥ずかしい】 embarrassed

—恥ずかしそうに shyly

はだ【肌】 skin

はだか【裸】 naked body; nakedness —裸の naked, undressed —裸で naked, in the nude

はたまた or

はたらく【働く】 ① to work ② to act, to operate

はっきり（と） vividly, clearly

バッグ bag; handbag

はっくつ【発掘】 excavation

はつじょう【発情】 sexual excitement —発情期 the mating season

はっせい【発声】 vocalization —発声法 vocalization

ぱっぱと [adverb describing the action of sprinkling salt or pepper]

パテ paté

はな【鼻】 nose —鼻にかける to boast, to brag

はなし【話】 ① story ② conversation, talk —話をする to talk, to chat —話が合う to speak the same language —話が出る A story is told.

はなしあいて【話し相手】 someone to talk to

はなしかける【話しかける】 to talk to (a person)

はなす¹【話す】 to talk, to chat; to tell

はなす²【放す】 to let go, to release

はなれる【離れる】 to leave —離れて away, apart

ばにく【馬肉】 horsemeat

はは【母】 one's mother

はば【幅】 width

ははおや【母親】 one's mother

はぶく【省く】 to omit, to leave out

はまべ【浜辺】 beach

はめる【嵌める】 to put on

はもの【刃物】knife

はやい【早い・速い】[早い] early, soon;
　[速い] fast, quick

はやく【早く・速く】[早く] early, soon;
　[速く] fast, quickly

はやくち(に)【早口(に)】fast, rapidly

はやめる【早める】to hasten

はら【腹】stomach, belly ➤ふくれる(膨
　れる)

はらいおとす【払い落とす】to shake off

はらいきる【払い切る】to pay off

ばらし [colloquial expression] slaugh-
　ter, butchery

はらす【腫らす】to be swollen

ばらばら　―ばらばらに to pieces　―ばら
　ばらになる to be dismembered　―ば
　らばらにする to dismember

はり【針】needle

はるさき【春先】early spring

パン　bread

はんきょう【反響】echo　―反響する to
　echo

はんざい【犯罪】crime

はんたい【反対】the opposite　―反対の
　opposite

はんだん【判断】judgment　―判断(を)す
　る to judge

パンチ　punch

はんにん【犯人】criminal

はんのう【反応】reaction, response　―
　反応する to react, to respond

はんぱつ【反発】　―反発する to rebel
　against

はんぶん【半分】half　―半分冗談で half-
　jokingly

ハンマー　hammer

-ばんめ【-番目】[used for showing nu-
　merical order] ➤にばんめ

ひ【日】① day; time ② the sun, sun-
　light　―日に焼ける to get a tan

ひ²【陽】the sun　―陽[日]に焼けた sun-
　tanned　―陽[日]を受けて in the sun

ひ³【火】fire　―火にかける to put (a pot)
　on a fire

ひがし【東】east

ぴかぴか　―ぴかぴか(と)輝く to shine
　radiantly

ひからびる【干からびる】to dry up　―干
　からびた dried-up, shriveled

ひかり【光】① light, ray ② glow (in
　one's eyes)

ひかる【光る】to shine, to glitter

-ひき・びき・ぴき【-匹】[counter for
　animals, birds, fish and insects]

ひきあげる【引き上げる】to pull up, to
　pull out

ひきおこす【引き起こす】to draw up

ひきたつ【引き立つ】to look better　―
　引き立たせる to make...look better

ひきつける【引き付ける・惹き付ける】to
　attract, to charm

ひきつる【引き攣る】to become stiff

ひきぬく【引き抜く】to pull...out

ヒグマ【羆・樋熊】brown bear

びくん(と)　with a start [jump]

ひげ【髭・鬚】beard, mustache　―ひげ
　をしごく to stroke one's beard

ひこうき【飛行機】airplane

ひざ【膝】knee　―膝を抱く to hold one's
　knees

ひざし【陽ざし・日差し】sun, sunshine

ひそむ【潜む】to hide, to lurk

ひたい【額】forehead

ひたす【浸す】to soak

ひたすら　earnestly; just; (very) hard

ひだり【左】left

ひだりうで【左腕】left arm

びっくり　―びっくりする to be surprised

ひっくりかえす【引っくり返す】to turn [flip] over

ひっこし【引(っ)越し・引越】moving (house), move, removal　―引(っ)越しする to move　―引(っ)越し蕎麦 *soba* noodles (given out as a gift to neighbors after one moves into a new house)

ひっし(の)【必死(の)】desperate　―必死に(なって) for all one is worth

ひつじ【羊・ヒツジ】sheep

ぴったり(に) perfectly

ひっぱる【引っ張る】to pull, to tug

ひづめ hoof

ひつよう【必要】necessity, need　―必要な necessary　―必要(が)ない unnecessary

ビデオ　video; VCR

ひと【人】① person ② other people

ひといき【一息】―一息ごとに with each breath

ひとかげ【人影】(person's) figure

ひとがら【人柄】character

ひとけ【人気】―人気のない deserted

ひとたび【一度】once

ひとつ【一つ】one; [followed by a negative] not a single…

ひとでなし【人でなし】monster, brute

ひとばん【一晩】a night　――晩中 all night (long)

ひとびと【人々】people

ひとめぼれ【一目惚れ】love at first sight　―ひと目ぼれする to fall in love at first sight

ひとり【一人】one (person)　―ひとりで alone, by oneself

ひとりしばい【一人芝居】one-man play, monologue

ひとりむすこ【一人息子】one's only son

ビニール　vinyl, plastic

ひびき【響き】sound

ひびく【響く】to sound, to ring

ひもの【干物】dried fish

ひゃく【百】one hundred

ひやけ【日焼け】suntan　―日焼けする to get tanned

ひやり　―ひやりとする to feel cool

びょういん【病院】hospital

びょうき【病気】illness, disease

ひょうさつ【表札】doorplate, nameplate

ひょうじ【表示】display

ひょうじょう【表情】expression, look

ひらあやまり【平謝り】―平謝りに謝る to make a humble apology

ひらいた【開いた】open

ひらがな【平仮名】hiragana

ひらく【開く】to open; to cut open

ひらめく【閃く】to flash into one's mind

ひらや【平屋】one-story building

ひる【昼】noon

ひるね【昼寝】(afternoon) nap　―昼寝をする to take a nap

ひるま【昼間】daytime

ひれ【鰭】fin

ひろい【広い】big, large, wide

ひろいあつめる【拾い集める】to gather, to collect

ひろう【披露】―披露する to show; to tell

ひろげる【広げる】to spread (out), to open

ふ

ファンタジー　fantasy

ふいに【不意に】suddenly, all of a sudden

ふうっと　lightly

ふうみ【風味】flavor

ふえる【増える】to increase, to multiply

フォール fall —フォールを取る to score a fall

ふかい【深い】deep

ふかく【深く】deeply —深くなる to deepen, to grow deeper

ふかさ【深さ】depth; deepness —深さを増す to deepen

ぶかつどう【部活動】club activity

ふきとる【拭き取る】to wipe away [off]

ふきまわし【吹き回し】➣かぜ(風)

ふく¹【服】clothes

ふく²【拭く】to wipe, to dry

ふくむ【含む】to contain, to include; to absorb

ふくめる【含める】to include —…をふくめ(て) including…

ふくらませる【膨らませる】to puff out [up]

ふくれる【膨れる】to swell, to bulge out —腹がふくれる to be pregnant

ふくろ【袋】bag, sack

ふしぎ(な)【不思議(な)】strange, mysterious —不思議と・不思議なことに strangely, strange to say

ふじゅんぶつ【不純物】impurities

ふす【付す】➣いっしょう(一笑)

ふせぐ【防ぐ】to prevent

ふた【蓋】lid

ぶた【豚】pig, hog

ぶたい【舞台】scene, setting —…を舞台にする to set the stage (for a story) in…

ふたつ【二つ】two

ふたり【二人】two (people); the two of us [them]

ふだん【普段】usually —普段の usual, ordinary

ふち【縁】rim, brim; edge

ふつう¹【普通】usually, generally —普通の normal, ordinary —普通に normally

ふつう²【不通】interruption —不通になる to be interrupted

ふっきゅう【復旧】recovery —復旧する to return to normal

ふっくら —ふっくら(した) (soft and) puffy

ぷっくり —ぷっくり(とした) puffy

ぶつける to bump, to knock

ふってん【沸点】boiling point

ふと suddenly

ふとん【布団】bed; bedclothes, quilt, quilted bedding —布団に入る to go to bed —布団をかける to put on a quilt

ふへい【不平】complaint —不平をもらす to complain

ふみつぶす【踏み潰す】to trample, to crush underfoot

ふみわる【踏み割る】to break (by stamping on)

ふむ【踏む】to stamp, to step on, to tread on

ふゆ【冬】winter

プライバシー privacy

ブラウス blouse

ぶらさげる【ぶら下げる】to hang

プラスチック plastic —プラスチックの plastic

ふらつく to stagger —足元がふらつく to be unsteady on one's feet; to stagger

ぶらぶら(と) lazily, idly

ブランコ swing —ブランコをこぐ to play [swing] on a swing

フランス France —フランスパン French bread

ふりかける【振りかける】to sprinkle

ふりそそぐ【降り注ぐ】to pour on, to rain on

ふる[1]【降る】to fall; to rain ➤おおあめ（大雨）

ふる[2]【振る】to shake, to wave ➤て（手）, よこ（横）

ふる-【古-】old, used

ふるい【古い】old

ふるえ【震え】trembling, shaking

ふるえる【震える】to tremble, to shake, to shiver

ふるまう【振(る)舞う】① to behave, to act ② to treat, to entertain ―ふるまい behavior

ふれあう【触れ合う】to touch

ふれる【触れる】to touch, to come in contact (with…)

ふろ【風呂】bath; bathtub; bathroom ―風呂に入る to take a bath

ふろば【風呂場】bathroom

-ふん・ぷん【-分】[counter for minutes]

-ぶん【-分】the amount of…

ぶんか【文化】culture ➤こんけつ（混血）

ぶんがく【文学】literature

ぶんかさい【文化祭】Culture Festival

へ

へきえき【辟易】―辟易する to be annoyed [weary]

へこみ【凹み】dent

へた（な）【下手（な）】not good, poor, awkward

ベタ（な）conventional, tired (old)

べつ【別】―別に…ない not especially… ―別にする to separate… ―…を別にすれば except for…

ベッド　bed

へび【蛇】snake

へや【部屋】room

へん【辺】side (of a square) ―…の辺に around…

へん（な）【変（な）】strange

へんか【変化】change ➤かがく（化学）

べんきょう【勉強】study, preparation ―勉強する to learn; to study

へんしつしゃ【変質者】pervert

へんずる【変ずる】to change into

べんとう【弁当】lunch, box lunch

ほ

ほ【帆】sail ―帆をかける to hoist a sail ➤しり（尻）

ほう【方】① part, side ② direction ③ the one [used as a pronoun to distinguish among two or more people or things] ④ ➤-ほうがいい ―…の方へ toward, in the direction of…

-ほう【-法】way, method ➤はっせい（発声）

ぼう-【某-】a certain… ―某君 a certain person, a Mr. So-and-so ―某町 a certain town

-ほうがいい【-方がいい】―…する［した］方がいい should do, ought to do, had better do

ぼうし【帽子】hat

ほうぼくち【放牧地】pasture

ほうよう【抱擁】hug, embrace ―抱擁を交わす to hug [embrace] each other

ほえる【吠える】to bark

ほお【頬】cheek(s)

ほか（の）【他（の）】other; else ―他に some [any] other…, more…

ぼく【僕】―僕は・僕が I, myself ―僕の my ―僕に・僕を me

ぼくたち【僕達】―僕たちは・僕たちが we ―僕たちの our ―僕たちに・僕たちを us

ほけん【保険】insurance ―保険をかける to insure

ほこらしい【誇らしい】proud

ほこりっぽい【埃っぽい】dusty

-ほしい【-欲しい】―...してほしい to want (a person) to do

ほしうお【干し魚】dried fish

ほしゅう【補修】repair ―補修工事 repair work

ほしょう【保証】guarantee

ほそい【細い】narrow; thin, skinny ―細く narrowly

ほそう【舗装】pavement ―舗装する to pave ―舗装された paved

ほそながい【細長い】long and narrow

ほっと [sound of a sigh]

ぽつんと alone

ほてる【火照る】to flush, to burn ―ほてった burning

ほど【程】① extent, degree [indicates approximate amount of something] ② [followed by a negative] not so... as to... ③ as to... ―ほどの...である such a [an]...that... ―...なら...なほど the more..., the more...

ほとばしる to gush (out)

ほとんど【殆ど】almost; practically ―ほとんど...ない hardly ever ―ほとんどの most, almost all

ほほ【頬】➤ ほお（頬）

ホルモン hormone

ほん【本】book

-ほん【-本】[counter for long, thin objects]

ほんき（で）【本気（で）】really

ほんとう【本当】truth ―本当の real, true ―本当に really, truly ―本当は in fact

ほんの just, only, merely

ほんのう【本能】instinct

ぽんぽん（と）lightly

ほんもの（の）【本物（の）】real

ぼんやり ―ぼんやり（と）した dim ―ぼんやりと dimly

ほんらい（の）【本来（の）】natural, original

ま

ま【間】time; pause ―間を置く to pause (for a moment)

まあ well, er

-まい【-枚】[counter for thin, flat objects]

まいどあり【毎度あり】Thank you (for coming again).

まいよ【毎夜】every night

まうえ【真上】―真上に right above [over]..., just above [over]...

まえ【前】the front ―...の前で・前に in front of..., before... ―...の前に before... ―...前（の）...ago, ...before ―前に forward

まえもって【前もって】in advance, beforehand

まく【幕】curtain

まくら【枕】pillow

まし（な）【まし（な）】better (than...) ―ましである to be better than...

ましてや even more

まじめ（な）【真面目（な）】serious, earnest ―真面目に seriously, earnestly

ます【増す】➤ ふかさ（深さ）

また【又】① again ② also, as well ③ and (then)

まだ still ―まだ...ない not ...yet

またいとこ【又従兄弟】second cousin

まだまだ still; still [even] more

またも【又も】(once) again

41

またもや【又もや】➤またも（又も）

まち【町】town; city

まちあい【待合い】—待合い（室）waiting room, lounge

まちあわせる【待ち合わせる】to meet (a person), to wait for (a person)

まちいしゃ【町医者】doctor, general practitioner

まちがい【間違い】error, mistake —間違いなく surely, certainly, for sure

まちがう・まちがえる【間違う・間違える】to make a mistake

まちがった【間違った】wrong

まちはずれ【町外れ】the outskirts of (a) town

まつ【待つ】to wait (for)

まっか（な）【真っ赤（な）】bright red —真っ赤に bright red

まっくら（な）【真っ暗（な）】completely dark, pitch-dark —真っ暗になる to get completely dark

まっくろ（な）【真っ黒（な）】pitch-black, inky

まつげ【まつ毛・睫毛】eyelash(es)

まっさお（な）【真っ青（な）】deadly pale

まったく【全く】① [followed by a negative] not...at all ② quite, completely, absolutely ③ really, truly

-まで ① till, until, to; up to ② to; as far as ③ even

まど【窓】window

まないた【まな板】cutting board

まなぶ【学ぶ】to learn

まね【真似】mimicry —まねをする to mimic, to imitate

まねごと【真似事】—...のまねごと something like...

まねる【真似る】to mimic, to imitate

-まま as it is; with...

まもなく【間もなく】soon, before long

まゆ【眉】eyebrow(s) —眉を寄せる to furrow one's brow

まよい【迷い】hesitation

まよう【迷う】to hesitate

マラリア malaria —マラリアにかかる to get malaria

まるごと【丸ごと】wholly

まるで —まるで（...のような）(just) as if [though]...

まれ（に）【稀（に）】uncommonly, exceptionally

マレーグマ【マレー熊】sun bear, Malay bear

まわす【回す】to put...around

まわり【周り】one's surroundings; neighborhood —...の周りに around...

まわる【回る】① to move about, to go on rounds ②➤き（気）

まんざら【満更】altogether

マンション apartment (house), condominium ➤ワンルーム

まんぞく【満足】satisfaction —満足そうに with satisfaction

まんぷく（の）【満腹（の）】full —満腹する to become full, to have eaten enough

み

み【身】body —身をよじる to twist one's body, to writhe

みあげる【見上げる】to look up

ミイラ mummy —ミイラにする to mummify

みえない【見えない】invisible

みえる【見える】① to see, to show ② to look, to seem ③ can be seen; visible

みがき【磨き】polish —磨きをかける to polish, to give a polish

みぎ【右】right —右の right

みぎうで【右腕】right arm

みぎて【右手・右掌】right hand; right arm

みくだす【見下す】to look down on, to despise

みごと(な)【見事(な)】excellent; perfect

みこみ【見込み】prospect ―見込みが立たない to be incalculable

みこみちがい【見込み違い】miscalculation

みごもる【身ごもる】to become pregnant

みじかい【短い】short

みしらぬ【見知らぬ】strange, unfamiliar

ミシン sewing machine ― ...にミシンをかける to sew...on a sewing machine

みず【水】water

みずぎ【水着】swimsuit

みずぎわ【水際】beach; waterside

みずしぶき【水飛沫】spray of water ―水しぶきが上がる Water splashes.

みせ【店】shop, store

みせさき【店先】at the front of a shop

みせる【見せる】① to show ② ➤ かお(顔)

-みたい(な) (just) like...

みたす【満たす】to fill (up)

みだれ【乱れ】disorder ―乱れる to be disturbed

みち【道】road, street

みちびく【導く】to lead, to guide

みちる【満ちる】to be filled with ➤ くじゅう(苦渋)

みつかる【見つかる】to be found [discovered]

みつける【見つける】to find (out), to discover

みっつ【三つ】three

みっぺい【密閉】―密閉された closed (tightly)

みつめる【見つめる】to gaze at, to stare at; to face

みとめる【認める】to allow, to accept

みな【皆】① all; every, each ② [pronoun] everyone

ミニ mini

みぬく【見抜く】to see through, to detect

みみ【耳】ear ―耳にする to hear ―耳をすませる to listen intently

みみもと【耳元】―耳元で close to someone's ears

みょう(に)【妙(に)】unusually

みょうじ【名字】surname, family name

みる【見る】① to see, to watch, to look at ➤ じっと ② to judge, to think ―見に行く to go (and [to]) see ―見られる can be seen

-みる ―...してみる to try to do

みわけかた【見分け方】how to distinguish ―見分ける to distinguish

みわたす【見渡す】to look over

みんな【皆】➤ みな(皆)

む

むいしき(に)【無意識(に)】unconsciously

むかう【向かう】① to head for..., to go to... ② ➤ めん(面) ―...に向かう (heading, headed) to...

むかし【昔】the past, the old days [times] ―昔から(ずっと)...している to have always done...

むかしかたぎ(の)【昔気質(の)】old-fashioned

むかしばなし【昔話】folk tale

むきだし(の)【剝き出し(の)】bare, naked

むく【剝く】➤ しろめ(白目)

むくち（な）【無口（な）】quiet, reticent

むける【向ける】① to head for [toward] … ② to aim ③ to turn, to direct ➤ せ（背）—…に向けて to, toward

むこ【婿】husband; son-in-law

むこうぎし【向こう岸】on the opposite bank; across the river

むごん【無言】silence —無言の silent —無言で silently

むし【虫】insect, worm, bug

むじゃき【無邪気】innocence —無邪気な innocent —無邪気に innocently

むしゃくしゃ —むしゃくしゃする to get annoyed

むすこ【息子】son

むすめ【娘】① daughter ② girl, young woman

むだじに【無駄死に】useless death —むだ死にする to die in vain [for nothing]

むちゅう【夢中】—…に夢中である to be crazy about…

むね【胸】① chest ② heart, mind —胸を張る to stand with one's head held high

むら【村】village

むり（な）【無理（な）】impossible —無理をする to work too hard, to overwork oneself

むりやり【無理やり・無理矢理】forcibly —無理やり…する to force to do

め

め【目】eye —目が覚［醒］める・目を覚ます to wake up, to be awake

-め【-目】[suffix for order]

-めい【-名】[counter for people]

めい-【名-】great, famous —名女優 famous actress

めいれい【命令】order —命令する to order; to command

めいわく【迷惑】trouble —…に迷惑をかける to cause trouble for, to bother…

めかくし【目隠し】blindfold —目隠しする to blindfold

めがね【眼鏡】(a pair of) glasses, spectacles —眼鏡をかける to wear glasses; to put on glasses

-めく to look (like)

めくばせ【目配せ】winking —目配せする to signal with eyes, to wink significantly

めぐみ【恵み】blessing

めぐらす【巡らす】to turn

めしあがる【召し上がる】[honorific expression] to eat

めずらしい【珍しい】rare, unusual —珍しく unlike…, unusually

めだつ【目立つ】to stand out

めったに【滅多に】—滅多に…ない seldom, rarely, hardly ever

メデューサ Medusa

めん【面】① side, aspect ② face —面と向かって to a person's face, directly

めんどう【面倒】trouble —面倒な troublesome —…を面倒に思う to find… troublesome

めんどうくさい【面倒臭い】troublesome

も

-も also

もう ① already; now ② more; another ③ [followed by a negative] no longer, not…any longer, no more —もう一日 one more day —もう片方 the other (person) —もうしばらく a bit more [longer]

もういちど【もう一度】once again, one more time

もうける　to have (a child)

もくてき【目的】purpose, goal

もぐりこむ【潜り込む】to get into, to slip into

もし　if　―もしよかったら［よろしければ］if you like

もじ【文字】letter(s), character(s)

もしかしたら　possibly; perhaps, maybe

もしかすると　➤もしかしたら

もじどおり【文字通り】literally

もしも　➤もし

もじもじ　―もじもじする　to hesitate

もしや　if…; by any chance

もちろん【勿論】of course; naturally

もつ【持つ】①to have ②to last, to keep

もっていく【持っていく】to take (something to…)

もっと　more

もてる　to be popular (with girls)

もと【元】one's side　―…のもとで under …, with…

もともと【元々】originally; formerly, before

もどる【戻る】to go [get] back, to return

もの¹【者】person

もの²【物】thing, stuff; article, item

ものおと【物音】sound

ものがたり【物語】tale, story

ものごと【物事】things

–ものだ　used to do, would do

ものまね【物真似】mimicry　―物まねする to mimic

もよう【模様】pattern

–もらう　―…させてもらう to be allowed to do

もらす【漏らす】①to wet oneself ②➤ふへい（不平）

もんく【文句】complaint　―文句を言う to complain

もんだい【問題】problem, question

や

やがて　in time, after a while

やく【焼く】to broil, to grill

–やく【–薬】➤ちゅうしゃ（注射）

やくがくぶ【薬学部】college [school] of pharmaceuticals

やくざいし【薬剤師】pharmacist

やくそう【薬草】(medicinal) herb

やくそく【約束】promise, appointment　―約束（を）する to promise

やくば【役場】town hall [office]

やける【焼ける】to burn　➤ひ¹（日）

やさおとこ【優男】effeminate man; slender man

やさしい【優しい】tender, kindhearted; gentle, soft　―優しく gently, softly

やさしさ【優しさ】kindness, tenderness

やしなう【養う】to foster

やじり【矢尻】arrowhead

やすむ【休む】to rest

やすらか（な）【安らか（な）】calm, peaceful, tranquil

やせい（の）【野生（の）】wild　―野生生物 wild animal, wildlife

やせた【痩せた】thin

やつ【奴】guy

やはり【矢張り】①after all ②as expected

やまんば【山姥】(old) mountain witch

やみ【闇】darkness, the dark

やみくも（に）【闇雲（に）】at random, haphazardly

やむ【止む】to stop

やめる【止める】to stop

やる¹　①to do, to try ②to play ③to have sex

やる²【遣る】 ➤て（手）

やわらかい・やわらかな【柔らかい・柔らかな】 soft ―柔らかく softly

ゆ

ゆ【湯】 hot water

ゆうがた【夕方】 evening ―夕方に in the evening

ゆうかん（な）【勇敢（な）】 brave, courageous; heroic

ゆうき【勇気】 courage

ゆうじん【友人】 friend

ゆうはん【夕飯】 supper; dinner

ゆうひ【夕日】 the evening sun

ゆうめい（な）【有名（な）】 famous, well-known ―有名になる to become famous

ゆうやみ【夕闇】 dusk, twilight ―夕闇が迫る The dusk gathers.

-ゆえ【-故】 because of...

ゆか【床】 floor

ゆかい（な）【愉快（な）】 enjoyable, fun; pleasant

ゆがむ【歪む】 to become twisted [distorted] ―歪んだ twisted, distorted

ゆきとどく【行き届く】 to be careful, to be prudent, to be thorough

ゆっくり（と） leisurely

ゆび【指】 finger; toe

ゆびさき【指先】 fingertip

ゆびさす【指差す】 to point (at)

ゆめ【夢】 dream

ゆらりと precariously

ゆるす【許す】 to forgive, to pardon

ゆれる【揺れる】 to sway; to move

よ

よ【世】 world

よあけ【夜明け】 dawn

よい¹【良い】 good, nice, well ➤なか²（仲）―...すればよかった should have done

よい²【酔い】 drunkenness ―酔いが醒める to become sober

よいつぶれる【酔い潰れる】 to get dead drunk ―酔い潰れた falling-down drunk

-よう¹【-用】 for...

-よう²【-様】 manner (describing attitude)

ようい【用意】 preparation ―用意する to prepare

ようき（な）【陽気（な）】 cheerful ―陽気に cheerfully

ようす【様子】 condition; state ―(...な)様子である to look like...

-ようだ ―...のようだ to feel like...; it seems (that)..., it looks as if...

-ような ―...のような like...

-ように ① like, as if... ② May you [he, she]...! ―...のように見える to look like...

-ようのない ―...しようのない there's no way of doing

ようふく【洋服】 clothes

よかん【予感】 hunch, premonition

よく【良く】 ① well, right(ly) ② carefully ③ often; fully ―良くなる to get better

よくじょう【欲情】 sexual desire, lust ―欲情する to get sexually aroused

よくねん【翌年】 the next year

よくぼう【欲望】 desire, lust

よける【避ける・除ける】 to avoid, to ward off

よこ【横】 side ―横に beside..., next to; to the side, sideways ―横になる to lie ―横に振る to shake

よこたえる【横たえる】 to lay

よこめ【横目】 sideways [sidelong] glance
—横目で見る to cast a sideways [sidelong] glance, to look sideways

よごれる【汚れる】 to get dirty; to be soiled —汚れた dirty

よし【良し】 okay, all right

よじる to twist

よせくる【寄せくる】 surging

よせる【寄せる】 ① to attack (describing waves breaking on shore) ② to bring...close ③ ➤まゆ（眉）

よそ【余所】 somewhere else (other than home)

よそもの【余所者】 stranger

よなか【夜中】 midnight —夜中に at midnight; in the middle of the night

よのなか【世の中】 the world

よびかけ【呼び掛け】 calling, addressing

よびかける【呼び掛ける】 to call, to speak to (a person)

よぶ【呼ぶ】 to call; to address

よみち【夜道】 —夜道で on the street at night

よみとる【読み取る】 to read; to detect, to sense

よむ【読む】 to read

ーより（も） (even) more than..., rather than...

よる¹【夜】 night —夜に at night

よる²【寄る】 to come near [close]

よる³【因る】 —...によれば according to ..., as...tells it

よろこび【喜び・悦び】 pleasure

よろしい good, okay ➤もし

ーら [suffix added to form plurals]

らくてんしゅぎ【楽天主義】 optimism

らくらい【落雷】 stroke [bolt] of lightning

ーらしい ① to seem, to look (like) ② it seems (that)...; I hear (that)...; they say (that)...; it looks as if... ③ ➤なつ（夏）

ラジオ radio —ラジオをかける to turn on the radio

ラディッシュ radish

ーられる [added to the -nai stems of Group 2 verbs to form the passive voice]

り

りくつ【理屈】 logic; argument

りせい【理性】 reason —理性的な rational

りゆう【理由】 reason, cause

りょう-【両-】 both...

りょううで【両腕】 both (one's) arms

りょうしん【両親】 (both) one's parents

りょうて【両手】 both (one's) hands [arms]

りょこう【旅行】 trip, travel —旅行する to go on a trip, to travel

れ

れい【礼】 thanks —礼を言う to thank, to give one's thanks

れいき【冷気】 the chill (of...)

れいぞうこ【冷蔵庫】 refrigerator

レース lace —レースの lace —レース模様 lace pattern

レストハウス rest house

レスリング wrestling —レスリングをする to wrestle

ーれる [added to the -nai stems of Group 1 verbs to form the passive voice]

あ
か
さ
た
な
は
ま
や
ら
わ

47

れんあい【恋愛】love; romance —恋愛（を）する to love; to have a romance

れんじつ【連日】day after day

れんらく【連絡】contact —連絡を取る to contact, to get in touch with

ろ

ろうそく【蠟燭】candle

ろくがつ【六月】June

ろじ【路地】alley, lane

ろせん【路線】route, line —路線バス local bus

ロフト loft

ろんぶん【論文】paper, thesis

わ

わかい【若い】① young ② immature

わかき【若き】➤ わかい（若い）

わかる【分かる】① to know, to understand, to get ② (to be able) to tell that... ③ to turn out, to prove —分かりません I don't know.

わかれ【別れ】parting, separation

わかれる【別れる】to part, to leave, to say goodbye, to break up

わき【脇】side —...脇の by...

わく【枠】frame

わけ【訳】reason —わけのわからない incomprehensible —わけもわからず confusedly —...（という）わけではない it's not (the case) that...

わずらう【患う】to suffer, to be sick

わすれる【忘れる】to leave; to forget

わたし【私】—私は・私が I, myself —私の my —私に・私を me —私のもの mine

わたす【渡す】to pass; to give; to give out

わたる【渡る】to cross, to go over

わな【罠】trap —罠にかける to entrap, to ensnare

わに【鰐・ワニ】crocodile

わらう【笑う】to laugh; to smile; to grin

わる【割る】to divide; to break

わるい【悪い】① bad, not good ② be to blame ➤ きみ（気味）, きもち（気持ち）—悪くない not bad

われ【我】myself —我ながら I have to admit that... —我に返る to come to oneself [one's senses]

われる【割れる】to break ➤ ぐしゃり

ワンピース dress

ワンルーム —ワンルームの one-room —ワンルームマンション studio apartment

あ
か
さ
た
な
は
ま
や
ら
わ

Notes

1 **くまにさそわれて散歩に出る** さそわれて is the passive form of さそう
("to invite"). This sentence contains no grammatical subject, but that's
only because the meaning seems clear without it: if it were anyone but
the narrator, we'd need to be told. That's not to say, however, that there
is no difference between くまにさそわれて散歩に出る and くまにさそわ
れて、私は散歩に出る, because while we assume that the first sentence
is talking about the narrator, we could be wrong—we could always be
told later that this story is about someone else. Obviously, the second
sentence leaves no room for doubt.

　　On another note, you may have noticed that my translation of 散歩
に出る, "I set out on a walk," can be read as either past or present tense.
The ambiguity is intentional, and gives us a chance to reflect on an important characteristic of Japanese prose—its temporal flexibility. くまに
さそわれて散歩に出る reads like a statement in the present. Indeed,
our half-uncertainty about the subject makes this sentence feel, on
first reading, like the beginning of a story in a mythic, even allegorical,
unending present—something along the lines of "Having been invited
by a bear, one sets out on a walk." Something of this atmosphere clings
to the rest of the story, too, since much of it unfolds in the present. As
you keep reading, though, you will notice occasional intrusions of
what is normally considered "past tense," and the final sentence of the
story offers a perspective from which everything that precedes it—the
entire excursion with the bear—is unmistakably past. In other words,
while the events of the story would seem to be taking place in the past,
much of it (not all of it) is written as though it were taking place right
now, in the present, as we read. To a certain extent, then, it makes
sense to think of the difference between, for instance, くまにさそわれて
散歩に出る and くまにさそわれて散歩に出た as a rhetorical difference
rather than a clear difference in tense.

　　Unfortunately, English grammar makes it difficult, if not impossible, to follow the flow of a Japanese story closely as it slips from one
tense to another—at least not without changing the meaning, and
probably leaving readers confused. For the most part, then, the translations I provide here are in the past tense, and reflect my sense that
the events being recounted have, in fact, already taken place by the
time the story begins.

川原<ruby>かわら</ruby>に行<ruby>い</ruby>くのである　のである is a somewhat academic variant of のだ, a common sentence-ending phrase; in this case, it gives the statement the air of an explanation. のである and のだ are used in written Japanese. In the spoken language, people say んだ or, to be polite, んです.

歩<ruby>ある</ruby>いて二十分<ruby>にじっぷん</ruby>ほどのところにある川原<ruby>かわら</ruby>である　ところ means "place," and にある (particle に + be-verb ある) means "to be located in." である is a slightly stiffer way of writing (not saying) だ.

鴫<ruby>しぎ</ruby>を見<ruby>み</ruby>るために、行<ruby>い</ruby>ったことはあったが...弁当<ruby>べんとう</ruby>まで持<ruby>も</ruby>っていくのは　Besides marking the topic, は can signal a contrast. In this sentence, two contrastive は particles are used to emphasize the different circumstances under which the narrator visited the riverbank: "I had gone [to the riverbank] in early spring to see the snipes, but this was the first time I'd ever taken a lunch." You may sense that the second は seems to carry a little more of a punch than the first; this is because it also marks the point that the narrator most wants to make in this sentence: the focus here, after all, is *this* trip.

　　The の before the second は turns everything that precedes it in the clause—暑<ruby>あつ</ruby>い季節<ruby>きせつ</ruby>にこうして弁当<ruby>べんとう</ruby>まで持<ruby>も</ruby>っていく—into a noun phrase, which it needs to be in order for the sentence to be grammatical.

散歩<ruby>さんぽ</ruby>というよりハイキングといったほうがいい　というより is a fixed expression meaning "rather than" and is used to rephrase or better characterize what one has said. The pattern "-**ta** form of a verb + ほうがいい," meanwhile, corresponds to "had better" or "It would be better to (VERB)." So, literally, the sentence means "Rather than saying 'a walk,' it would be better to say 'a hike.'" The narrator seems to be qualifying the first sentence of the paragraph, くまにさそわれて散歩<ruby>さんぽ</ruby>に出<ruby>で</ruby>る.

2　くまは、雄<ruby>おす</ruby>の成熟<ruby>せいじゅく</ruby>したくまで、だからとても大<ruby>おお</ruby>きい　The で after くま tells us to expect more information about the bear.

三<ruby>みっ</ruby>つ隣<ruby>となり</ruby>の305号室<ruby>ごうしつ</ruby>に　It is, of course, "three doors down" from the narrator's point of view, i.e., the narrator's apartment.

越<ruby>こ</ruby>してきた　The auxiliary くる, here in the -**ta** form, tells us the direction of the move: the bear has moved closer to the narrator, not farther away. If the rent gets too high, the bear may 越していく "move away."

ちかごろの引越<ruby>ひっこ</ruby>しには珍<ruby>めずら</ruby>しく　"Following a custom that now seldom plays a part in a move" is an expansive translation: nothing in the original

corresponds directly to "following a custom." But basically that's the idea. Note that 珍しく (the adverbial form of 珍しい) modifies everything that follows it in the sentence, not just the first verb.

引越し蕎麦 "Moving buckwheat noodles" means nothing in English, but it means—or used to mean—a lot in Japanese: the tradition of bringing one's new neighbors *soba* as a present, now more or less extinct, dates back to the Edo period (1600–1867). Why *soba*? Because noodles are long and ideally one would like to have a long, friendly relationship with one's neighbors, and also because 蕎麦 is a pun on 側 ("nearby," "adjacent").

...を同じ階の住人にふるまい　ふるまい is the -**masu** stem of the verb ふるまう ("to treat"). The -**masu** stem is often used in place of the -**te** form in written Japanese. It means the same as the -**te** form.

渡してまわっていた　These are two verbs, 渡す ("to hand out") and まわる (回る) ("to go around"). Though the grammar of the sentence doesn't make it clear, we can assume that the bear distributed *soba* and passed out postcards to the same neighbors at the same time.

ずいぶんな気の遣いようだと思った　気を遣う means "to be thoughtful," "to show concern [for]," "to give consideration [to]." The pattern "-**masu** stem + よう" means "a way of doing" the action of the verb. I have translated 気の遣いよう in a slightly roundabout way as "display of solicitude."

くまであるから　であるから is the same as だから but more formal. The difference in this case is, perhaps, rather like that between "since he was a bear" and "insofar as he was a bear."

まわりに対する配慮が必要なのだろう　The のだろう, spoken with a falling intonation (CD 00:49), makes this more speculative than a straight 必要だろう, which is actually a fairly strong, definite statement. Note that nouns and -**na** adjectives take な before の, as 必要 does here.

3　その蕎麦を受け取ったときの会話で　As you may have sensed from the translation, で can indicate a cause or reason.

くまとわたしとは　The second と makes it clearer that the relationship between the bear and the narrator is being discussed.

満更赤の他人というわけでもないこと　わけではない is a phrase used to

神様

deny whatever precedes it—think of it as a less formal version of "It is not the case that…" Here the は has been replaced by も, which makes the statement a little less definite: "I wouldn't exactly say that…"

こと turns everything that precedes it in the clause into a noun phrase: "that we were not exactly complete strangers." You may remember seeing の used in the same way in the fourth sentence of this story. The difference between these two nominalizers is, generally speaking, that こと works well with abstract statements, while の tends to follow clauses whose meaning is more concrete. この地域では雨が全然降らなくなってきたことが、農家にとっては極めて深刻な問題です "The fact that it no longer rains at all in this region is an extremely serious problem for our farmers." 雨が降って来たのは、朝8時ごろだった "It started to rain around eight in the morning."

わかったのである のである makes the statement preceding it more emphatic and sets us up for the paragraphs that follow. Often のである lends an explanatory feel to the sentence it ends; here, it indicates that the narrator has reached a conclusion, and that the evidence on which that conclusion is based is about to be presented. It tells us, in other words, that the narrator is *about to* explain how she realized that she and the bear weren't exactly strangers.

5 **ご出身では** The bear is saying ではないでしょうか but he abridges it.

6 **以前くまがたいへん世話になった某君の叔父という人** This is a little tricky: the bear was helped out by 某君, whose uncle served as deputy mayor at the town hall. This deputy mayor is, we learn in the next sentence, the narrator's father's second cousin.

町の役場助役であったという であった is the past tense, obviously, of である. という indicates that everything preceding it is reported speech, although it is not as explicit as the English "someone said." It is perhaps closer to "evidently," "apparently."

わたしのものと同じであり Using もの here makes it possible to avoid repeating 名字 and also, perhaps, gives us the sense that the narrator is regarding her or his name from a slightly detached perspective. You can see this if you compare it to another option, which would be simply to write わたしのと同じ.

であり is almost the same as で, it just feels more "written."

…に当(あ)たる   The word 当たる is often used when explaining family relationships: タクシーの運転手(うんてんしゅ)は、実(じつ)はボスのまたいとこに当たる "As a matter of fact, the taxi driver is the boss's second cousin."

あるか無(な)しかわからぬような繋(つな)がり   Literally, "a relationship so tenuous you can hardly tell whether it exists or not." 無し is a throwback to classical Japanese; it means ない. The ぬ in わからぬ is one of two classical Japanese equivalents (the other is ず, as in わからず) of the negative ending ない. The old grammar gives this clause a charmingly archaic atmosphere that nicely matches the formality of the bear's speech, and feels just right for the off-kilter world the narrator is leading us into.

感慨深(かんがいぶか)げに   げ is a suffix that indicates that someone looks to be feeling, or that something gives the impression of being, a certain way: 楽(たの)しげに笑(わら)った "She laughed, looking as if she was having fun," 悲(かな)しげに頷(うなず)いた "She nodded sadly." げ attaches to nouns, the stems of -**i** adjectives, and the -**masu** stems of verbs, turning the element into a -**na** adjective. に in this example further changes the word into an adverb.

引越(ひっこ)しの挨拶(あいさつ)の仕方(しかた)といい、この喋(しゃべ)り方(かた)といい   といい…といい is a pattern used when listing the factors that contribute to a general impression. 座(すわ)った時(とき)のまっすぐな背筋(せすじ)といい、優雅(ゆうが)な動(うご)きといい、あの女(おんな)は明(あき)らかに尼(あま)さんか、バレリーナだったな "The way she sat with her back so rigid, and the grace of her movements…that woman had to have been either a Buddhist nun or a ballerina."

昔気質(むかしかたぎ)のくまらしいのではあった   The presence of the は here adds a note of hesitancy, as if the narrator is offering us the one bit of information that seems relatively clear in a generally unclear situation. This one は gives the sentence a very different nuance. Without the は, it would simply mean, "He seemed an old-fashioned bear." With it: "Whatever else you might say about this bear, he certainly had an old-fashioned air about him."

7   **散歩(さんぽ)のようなハイキングのようなこと**   Repeating のような conveys a sense of indeterminacy or intermediacy: the narrator and the bear were half-walking, half-hiking. 僕(ぼく)は悲(かな)しいような、嬉(うれ)しいような気持(きも)ちになった "I felt sort of sad, but also sort of happy."

ツキノワグマなのか、ヒグマなのか Repeating のか in this way conveys a sense of confusion: not being knowledgeable about animals, the narrator isn't sure what type of bear she is dealing with, and is throwing out whatever species come to mind.

面と向かって訊ねるのも Again, の turns what precedes it into a noun phrase. も replaces が, softening the statement and making it seem as though the narrator is considering various options.

8 **僕しかくまがいないのなら** The particle しか, followed by a negative, means "only"; in this case, "If I'm the only bear." If you haven't yet learned this particle, you may find it helpful to think of it as meaning "other than": "If there are no bears *other than* myself…"

なら ("if"), as you can tell from the translation, expresses the bear's presumption about the present situation: "If I really am the only bear…" The addition of the の, which isn't grammatically necessary, makes the statement sound more emphatically hypothetical, rather like the "really" in "If I really am the only bear."

ええ This ええ suggests, perhaps, that the narrator has interjected, and the bear is responding, clarifying.

漢字の貴方 貴方 is a polite way of saying "you." When the same word is written in hiragana, it feels less courteous, and can sometimes even seem blunt.

ひらがなではなく漢字を思い浮かべてくだされ!ばいいんですが 思い浮かべてくだされば is the conditional (-**ba**) form of 思い浮かべてください, so the phrase literally means, "If you would do me the favor of calling to mind…" ん is a contraction of の, which here softens even further the bear's polite, indirect request.

まあ、どうぞご自由に何とでもお呼びください The ご in ご自由に is an honorific prefix, as is the お in お呼びください. Polite speech comes with practice. At first it's enough to be able to recognize it when you see it.

9 **との答えである** This sort of との is more or less the same as という, though it isn't used very often in spoken Japanese.

10 **大きくよけていく** The auxiliary いく indicates movement away from the narrator.

すれちがう人影はない 人影 looks like it ought to mean "the shadow of a person," and in some cases it does. Here it stresses that there is really no one around—not that there is no shadow, but that there is "no sign" of anyone.

16 **もしあなたが暑いのなら** The の here adds a more speculative note to the question, much like "should happen" in the translation, "If you should happen to feel hot." Grammatically, it is not required.

国道に出てレストハウスにでも入りますか でも is often used in this way when people make suggestions: いつかコーヒーでも一緒に飲みませんか "Why don't we have coffee together sometime?" でも makes the suggestion softer.

17 **などと、細かく気を配ってくれる** などと can be thought of as an abbreviation of などと言って. など suggests that the narrator is only reporting some of many things the bear said.

When くれる is appended to another verb, it means that someone has done, or not done, something—usually a good thing—for or to the object of the verb, who is either the speaker or someone to whom the speaker feels related in some way. It sounds very tricky when it is explained, but it's not. There are similar phrases, admittedly somewhat antiquated, in English: "I beg the favor of a reply," "He was good enough to write back," and so on. ‐てくれる is a bit like that.

暑さには強いほうなので さ is a suffix added to the stems of adjectives to turn them into nouns. In this case, it turns 暑い ("hot") into 暑さ ("heat"). は, meanwhile, is contrastive: it lends the nuance of "the same might not be true of other things, but as far as heat is concerned…" The ほう that follows 強い means "side," i.e., "on the strong side."

18 **遠くに聞こえはじめた水の音** 聞こえる is a verb that means "to become audible"; はじめる is an auxiliary meaning "to begin to (VERB)." Literally, then, the subject of this sentence is "the sound of water in the distance that began to become audible."

22 **シュノーケルが答える** This is an example of a type of metonymy, fairly common in Japanese fiction, whereby people are referred to by the name of something they are wearing. "The snorkel" is, that is to say, simply shorthand for the man wearing the snorkel.

26 <u>ちらりとうかがった</u> ちらりと conveys a sense of brevity: 車窓からちらりと見えた景色はとてもきれいだった "The scenery I glimpsed from the train window was really lovely."

<u>くまの顔を正面から見ようとはしない</u> This is 見る in its volitional form, followed by とする. The pattern "volitional form of a verb + とする" means "to try to (VERB)." Here は is added for emphasis: "He didn't *even* try to look at the bear's face straight on."

<u>何も言わずに</u> ず is a negative ending deriving from classical Japanese. ずに is equivalent in meaning to the -**naide** form of a verb, though with some restrictions.

<u>こぶしをぶつけてから、走って行ってしまった</u> 行く is the same auxiliary いく were saw earlier (paragraph 10), again expressing movement away from the narrator. The しまう that attaches to its -**te** form expresses completion of the action of "running off."

28 <u>しばらくしてから</u> This sentence refers to the quotation that precedes it, not the one that follows it, though both are spoken by the bear.

29 <u>小さい人は邪気がないですなあ</u> The なあ here is a drawn-out version of the emotive particle な, used at the end of sentences. It gives the statement a slow, mild, perhaps reflective air.

31 <u>そりゃいろいろな人間がいますから</u> そりゃ is a contraction of それは.

<u>子供さんはみんな無邪気ですよ</u> さん gives this expression a polite, respectful feeling that seems subtly off-kilter and fits this old-fashioned, well-mannered bear very well.

33 <u>細長い四角の辺をたどっているように見える</u> ように見える turns everything that precedes it into a simile: "It looks as though…"

<u>くまの目にも水の中は人間と同じに見えているのであろうか</u> のであろう is the である equivalent of のだろう (see paragraph 2).

34 <u>三倍はありそうなものだ</u> The pattern "-**masu** stem + そう" generally means "seems like he/she/it may (VERB)." 泣きそうな顔をしていた "He had a look on his face like he might cry." "あり + そう" is slightly different from most instances of this pattern, because here the statement concerns what is already present, rather than what seems likely to happen in the future: "It looks as though there must be…" In this case, the fish

"looks like it has" about three times as much mass as the little fish swimming near the bank.

The は here strengthens the statement: "It looked as if it were at least three times the size."

37 <u>おことわりしてから行けばよかった</u>のですが　おことわりする is a humble way of saying ことわる, which in this case means "to give notice," "to let someone know something in advance." The のです gives the sentence an emotional resonance that it wouldn't otherwise have, and makes the statement more persuasive. You often see のです/んです, or the informal んだ, used in this way when the speaker is making an excuse.

つい足が先に出てしまいまして　つい suggests that someone has done something unintentionally, perhaps without even realizing it: その時点ではもうかなり酔っていたので、ついしゃべってしまった "I was pretty drunk by then, so I told her the whole thing."

39 **さしあげましょう**　さしあげます is a humble equivalent of あげる ("to give").

40 **くまは担いできた**　The auxiliary くる here means just what it looks like it ought to: the bear has *come* carrying the bag over his shoulder.

小さなナイフとまな板が出てきた　This くる is different from the one we just saw, but its meaning is no more surprising: here, a small knife and a cutting board *came* out of the cloth bundle.

43 **パテとラディッシュをはさんだ<u>もの</u>**　The もの in this clause means "something," but in terms of the nuance it communicates, it's more like the "sort of" in "a sort of sandwich," which seems to be what the bear is, in fact, eating.

You'll notice, by the way, that there is no verb in this sentence, which consists, basically, of a list of what the two picnickers ate. The implied verb is 食べた, taken from the previous sentence. The effect of this verbless catalog is similar to that of the list that follows a colon. "Then we ate our lunches: the bear, a sort of sandwich; me, a rice ball."

ゆっくりと食べ<u>おわる</u>と　おわる, like the はじめる we saw earlier (paragraph 18), is an auxiliary verb. It means "to finish," as in "to finish eating."

44 **オレンジの皮を<u>いただけます</u>か**　いただける is the potential form of いた

だく, which is a humble way of saying もらう ("to receive"). "Noun + を +いただけますか" is a polite way of asking for something.

46　少し離れたところに置いてある魚　When ある is combined with the -te form of a verb in this way, it suggests that the object of the verb continues to exist in whatever state the action of the verb has put it in, and often that it was put in that state in preparation for something that will happen later. In practice, this means that the ある can have various different nuances: 置いてある means "sitting there, where it was put"; 取ってある means "set aside" (for some future purpose); 話してある means "has been explained" (for some future purpose).

…を引っくり返しに行き　"-Masu stem + に + movement verb" means to move in some way (to go, to come, to walk, to run, etc.) in order to carry out the action of the verb. Here, "to go flip" the fish.

47　お使いください　Once again, we encounter the polite "お + -masu stem." This is different from the おことわりして we saw a bit earlier (paragraph 37), and the same as the お呼びください that appeared even before that (paragraph 8): the pattern "お + -masu stem + する" is used to make an ordinary verb humble, and refers to an action by the speaker. "お + -masu stem + ください," an honorific construction, is a polite way of asking someone to do something.

僕はそのへんをちょっと歩いてきます　If the bear were pointing, そのへん would refer to the particular direction or area toward which he was pointing; if he isn't pointing (and there's no reason to believe he is), it simply means "in the area."

　　歩いてきます means "to take a walk and come back"—it's kind of the opposite of the English "to go for a walk."

子守歌を歌ってさしあげましょうか　–てさしあげましょうか is a politer, humbler way of saying –てあげましょうか ("Shall I…?").

49　子守歌なしでも眠れそうだ　なしで is a fixed phrase, equivalent to がなくて, that means "without." Here も has been added as a softener.

50　木の影が長くなっており　おり (-masu stem of おる) is a more formal, written form of いて. Like "and," it creates a brief pause that allows for the introduction of new information more or less closely related to what we have already been told.

53 またこのような機会を持ちたいものですな　Adding な to the end of a sentence that ends with です is unusual in everyday spoken Japanese—unless you want to sound antiquated and quaint, you should probably steer clear of imitating this bear's speech. The もの here gives the bear's statement a warm, emotional touch: we get the sense that he has really enjoyed his outing with the narrator, and means what he says.

54 わたしも頷いた　The も here would seem at first glance to indicate that the bear has nodded, and now the narrator is nodding, "too." But this isn't necessarily the case: in effect, the も simply indicates that the narrator is agreeing with the bear.

大きく手を振って　In contexts like this, waving a hand back and forth in front of you is a way of denying or declining something that has been offered or said—the equivalent, perhaps, of saying "No, not really," or "Please, don't even mention it!"

56 と答えるのだった　This is the past tense of のだ. It does something so subtle to the sentence that it's hard to pinpoint its effect: it lends a note of objectivity to the statement, perhaps suggesting that the bear's response follows the pattern of politeness he has already established and confirms the narrator's impression of him.

57 では　The narrator is saying something like では、失礼します or では、さようなら but abbreviates the main content of the sentence.

60 人間と同じ発声法なのである　This is the same as のだ, of course, just more formal and prosy.

61 抱擁を交わしていただけますか　As always, this bear is very polite. Note again the use of the potential form いただける (see also paragraph 44). If the bear had said 抱擁を交わしていただきす, he would be being polite, but pushy: "I am going to take the liberty of hugging you."

66 熊の神様のお恵みがあなたの上にも降り注ぎますように　When you add ように to a verb that ends a sentence, particularly one in the -masu form, the statement turns into a prayer or an expression of a wish. 早く元気になりますように "May you recover your health soon."

今夜のうちに　うち is often used in talking about time. Here it means "within" the night.

召し上がるほうがいい　召し上がる is an honorific verb meaning "to eat" or "to drink." In paragraph 1 we saw the pattern "-**ta** form of a verb + ほうがいい" and the literal renderings "had better" and "It would be better to (VERB)," both of which are somewhat strong. Here it is the bear talking, and—appropriately enough—he uses the dictionary form before ほうがいい instead of the -**ta** form, making the suggestion sound considerably less forceful. Compare: 今夜のうちに召し上がったほうがいい "You'd better eat it tonight." 今夜のうちに召し上がるほうがいい "It might be best if you eat it tonight."

67　部屋に戻って魚を焼き、風呂に入り、眠る前に少し日記を書いた　Many dictionaries (including the one in this book) will tell you that 部屋 means "room," and it often does. But it means "apartment" ("flat," "pad," etc.) almost as frequently.

1 <u>こぢんまりとした公園</u> Words like こぢんまり are classified as adverbs that attach to the words they modify with と. This makes a lot of sense when you're dealing with a verb that expresses some sort of action: 自宅でこぢんまりと営む探偵社 "the small detective agency she runs out of her own house." It also makes sense with phrases like こぢんまりとした公園, as long as you remember that in this case する doesn't mean "to do," it means "to give an impression of…" "to have" a certain characteristic, and so on: あの店員、本当にきれいな目をしているね "That clerk has such lovely eyes, don't you think?" こぢんまりとした公園 is a park that exhibits the qualities of being こぢんまり. If you find this confusing, though—as I do—you may find it helps to think of こぢんまり as being both an adverb and an adjective: as an adverb, it attaches to verbs with と; as an adjective it attaches to nouns with とした. Sometimes these pseudo-adjectives can be negated; when they can, you do it by turning とした into としない. One example: すかっとした気分 "a feeling of release"; すかっとしない感じ "a feeling of vague dissatisfaction." (The situation with these と adverbs is further complicated, by the way, by the fact that in some cases you don't even need the と: こぢんまりした公園 would also be correct.)

<u>高い建物に囲まれており</u> As we saw in 「神様」(paragraph 50), おり is a formal, written version of いて: it creates a brief pause, after which new information on the same topic is introduced.

<u>車の音や人のざわめき</u> The や tells us that the noises mentioned here are just a few of many that could actually be heard. If you replace the や with a と, these sounds become the *only* sounds.

<u>消え去る</u> A compound verb that might be translated, almost literally, by "vanish clean away."

<u>だれかの忘れた子供用の小さな靴</u> The first の in this clause could easily be replaced by が. This would, however, lead to a subtle difference in meaning. In the sentence as it is now, の creates a stronger bond between だれか and 靴; if の were replaced by が, there would be a stronger bond between だれか and 忘れた.

2 <u>夕飯の時間になって</u> になって leads into the next clause, preparing us to hear how the situation changed once dinnertime rolled around. This

pattern is often used when talking about things that happen at a certain time: 8時になって、やっと結婚式の会場に忍び込むことに成功した "At eight, we finally managed to sneak into the venue for the wedding."

僕は 僕 is a first-person pronoun used by boys and men. It is less formal than 私 and less macho than 俺.

両親が帰って<u>くる</u>まで くる tells us that this sentence is being written from the point of view of home: his parents *come* back home. This is true, interestingly, even though the narrator is actually still killing time at the park. It's as though he's imagining home, wanting to be there.

時間をつぶしてい<u>なければいけなかった</u> Just in case you haven't learned it already, –なければいけない is a fixed expression meaning "must," "have to." It attaches to the -nai stems of verbs and -i adjectives, and in the form でなければいけない to -na adjectives and nouns. Here it attaches, in the past tense, to the -nai stem of the -te iru form of つぶす ("to kill [time]"), indicating that the narrator had to stay at the park, killing time.

3 **一人でブランコをこぐ<u>の</u>にあきると** の is a nominalizer and has the same function as こと (but see「神様」paragraph 3).

<u>まるで</u>何かから<u>呼ばれた</u>ように まるで lends a bit more force to the ように at the close of the clause. Perhaps the difference is something like that between the English phrases "It felt like I had been summoned" and "It felt for all the world as though I had been summoned." 呼ばれる is the passive form of 呼ぶ ("to call," "to summon").

その公園の隅<u>には</u>砂場があった The は establishes "in the corner of the park" as the new topic, shifting it from the 僕 of the previous sentence.

その一画はいつも<u>忘れられていた</u> 忘れられる is the passive form of 忘れる ("to forget"). The verb is in the -te ita form to emphasize that that corner of the park always remained in the state of "being forgotten."

4 **音<u>もなく</u>** なく turns this phrase into an adverb that modifies にじませる. The も strengthens the statement: "without so much as a sound."

世界を赤<u>く</u>にじませる夕方 にじませる is the causative form of にじむ ("to bleed" [the way ink bleeds on paper]).

話し相手<u>もなく</u> Once again, なく turns the phrase into an adverb. Here

it modifies 遊んだ. And again, も strengthens the statement: "without so much as a friend to talk to."

だれが置いていったのかわからない　The の lends a subtle emotional nuance to this statement, making it more forceful than it would be without it.

自分の足に砂をのせていく　The いく here gives a sense of the passage of time: little by little, the narrator keeps piling more sand on his feet. This is different from the いく used in, for instance, phrases like トンネルに響いていく "to echo *down* the tunnel" or 隣の町に引っ越していく "to move *away* to the neighboring town."

小さな粒が足の指の隙間に入り込んでいくのが心地よかった　The いく in this case is directional: the sand works its way *down into* the spaces between the narrator's toes. The の that follows it is a nominalizer.

5　砂の中に深く手をつっこむという遊びもした　This という sets off the clause before it—砂の中に深く手をつっこむ—and clarifies its relationship to the word 遊び. Everything before という is the "game" the boy plays. You might expect this to mean that the game is *called* "stick your hand deep down in the sand," but that's not the case.

地中のどこまでが砂なのだろうかと　地中のどこまで serves as the subject of this clause, which is essentially a question meaning "To what depth did the sand go?" The のだろうか expresses the narrator's curiosity and speculation, almost like "Gee, I wonder…" と can be thought of as an abbreviation of と思って.

確かめたくなったのだ　確かめたくなった ("started wanting to find out") breaks down as follows: -**masu** stem of 確かめる ("to find out") + auxiliary adjective たい ("to want to [VERB]") in the -**ku** form + auxiliary verb なる ("to become") in the -**ta** form. のだ turns the sentence into an explanation of why the narrator started playing his new digging game.

6　最後には　は is used here for emphasis. If 最後に means something like "in the end," 最後には might be more along the lines of "until finally…"

肩まで入るのではないか　This is a rhetorical question and conveys the narrator's surprise.

砂場にも底はあるんだから、そんなはずがあるか　あるんだから is a colloquial equivalent of あるのだから. This is the same の (or ん) that

むかし夕日の公園で

we've seen several times already. そんなはずがあるか is a blunt rhetorical question. The father is not asking whether his son is "certain" his arm went in so deep; he is expressing his skepticism.

8   それは何回目のことだったかすでに忘れてしまった　それは…のことだった is a phrase used, mostly in written Japanese, to set the scene for some past event. Since in this case we don't yet know what the event was, there is an element of suspense: "I no longer recall how many times I had stuck my arm in the sand by the time it happened."

夕日のために　This ために means "because of," not "for the purpose of."

指先に何かの当たる感触がした　This の could be replaced by a が without changing the sentence all that much. Grammatically, the difference is similar to that between "I felt something brush against my fingertips" (何かが当たる) and "My fingertips felt the brushing of something" (何かの当たる)—though in English that second sentence sounds a bit odd. The author may have used の here to avoid repeating が twice in quick succession, since the sentence ends with 感触がした.

9   それが何なのかを確かめようと　"-Masu stem + よう" in this case indicates the narrator's intention. 確かめようと can be thought of as an abbreviation of 確かめようと思って. The combination "-masu stem + よう + と思う" means "I'm hoping to (VERB)," "thinking I would (VERB)," and so on. In this context it's "hoping to figure out what it was."

中指の先端がかろうじて触れるほど深いところに　ほど (and its near-identical twin くらい) is used in various ways and has various shades of meaning which will come with practice. It is used in sentences like this one to express the extent of something: a depth, a distance, an amount of time. One literal translation of this clause might be: "at the place deep enough down that the tip of my middle finger just barely touched [the object described in the next clause]."

ふっくらとして弾力のあるもの　This is the same の that appeared a few lines above (paragraph 8), in the phrase 指先に何かの当たる感触. Here we see another characteristic of this type of の: it strengthens the connection between the verb (ある) and the noun that precedes it (弾力). 弾力のある and 何かの当たる both function as single units—adjectival phrases—modifying the nouns (もの and 感触) that follow.

指に何かが絡みつくのを感じた　This is another nominalizing の.

10　**それは女の子の髪の毛であるように思えた**　This である could be replaced by a の without really changing the sense: それは女の子の髪の毛のように思えた. This would, however, alter the mood of the sentence because である has a distinctly formal, written feeling to it.

11　**今度は**　This は is contrastive: "this time (as opposed to the last time)."

いくら深く腕を入れても　いくら is a slightly more formal way of saying どんなに, or "how much." "いくら + -te form of a verb + も" means "no matter how much (SUBJECT) (VERB)." いくらがんばっても、彼には無理だった "No matter how hard he tried, he simply couldn't do it."

指先は何も見つけられない　This は establishes a shift in topic from 僕 (at the beginning of the paragraph) to 指先. 見つけられる is the potential form of 見つける ("to find").

12　**どれも窓を閉め切っていて**　閉め切る is a compound verb formed by tacking 切る onto 閉める. When 切る is used in this way, it means that the action of the verb has been carried out thoroughly, all the way, as much as possible. In this case, all the windows have been shut. Note, however, that this is not a passive construction: it's almost as though the buildings have shut their own windows, though presumably it was the workers who shut them. The continuative -**te ite** form shows that the windows remain in the closed state in which they have been put.

巨大な壁のように僕とその砂場を切り取っていた　The -**te ita** form, like the -**te ite** form in the previous clause, indicates that the situation (being cut off from the surrounding city) is ongoing, though in this case you might think of it as an ongoing action rather than simply a state: the buildings were "*cutting* the sandbox and me *off* from the surroundings like an enormous wall."

13　**砂の中へ入れていた右手**　The -**te ita** form here might seem to suggest that the narrator is in the process of putting his hand in the sand, but in fact it tells us that he has already put it there, and still has it there—another "continuing state" usage of -**te iru**.

魚がくちの先端でつついたような、小さな感触だった　This sentence has a parallel structure: 魚がくちの先端でつついたような and 小さな both modify 感触. The comma (、) makes this clear.

14　**手首をつかまれた**　つかまれる is the passive form of つかむ ("to grab").

手首がしめつけられる　しめつけられる is the passive form of しめつける ("to tighten," "to squeeze").

周囲にはだれもおらず　おる is a formal, written equivalent of いる. ず is a negative ending meaning –なくて or –ないで. The combination gives us, in this context, the meaning いなくて, where the **-te** form indicates a reason for what follows.

声はただ建物に囲まれた公園に反響するだけだった　囲まれる is the passive form of 囲む ("to surround").

15 **無理やり広げさせられた**　広げさせる is the causative form of 広げる ("to spread open"), and 広げさせられる the passive of the causative. These conjugations are tricky until you get used to them.

手のひらに、小さなだれかの指先の感触がした　You may find it difficult, at first glance, to determine precisely what 小さな modifies here: is it だれか, だれかの指先, or 感触? Is the person buried in the ground a "small person"—a child? Is it someone (again, probably a child) with "little fingers"? Or is it the sensation that's small? To tell the truth, it's hard to tell even on the second or third glance, and grammar doesn't help. You just have to decide, as I have, which interpretation you think works best.

どうやら文字を書いているらしいと僕は気づいた　どうやら...らしい is a set pattern indicating that the speaker has come to a somewhat tentative decision based on circumstances or hearsay. Here the narrator is judging from what he feels in his hand.

16 **ここからだして**　The **-te** form of a verb can be used in informal situations to encourage someone to do something. これも入れておいて "Put this one in, too." 食べてみて "Try some."

17 **そう書いた**　Here そう means そのように.

19 **残念そうに僕の右手首をはなした**　This そう is similar to らしい, at least in terms of when it is used: it tells us that the narrator is making a judgment based on something directly perceived. 重そうな石 is "a heavy-looking rock"; 嬉しそうな笑い声 is "a delighted-sounding laugh."

それ以来　This is one of a few words—以降 and 以後 are two others—that can be used to mean "after" or "since." Unlike 以降 and 以後, which

can be used in talking about past, present, or future times, 以来 can only be used in discussing past events. It's the same, in this sense, as "ever since": ヘビに咬まれて以来20年泣き続けている女性 "A Woman Who's Been Crying For 20 Years, Ever Since She Was Bitten By a Snake" (this was the headline of an article in *Kokusai Jiji Shimbun*, September 6, 2006).

砂場には近寄らなかった　This は emphasizes that it was the sandbox the narrator avoided, not the swings or the jungle gym or the park as a whole.

公園が壊されてマンションになるとき　壊される is the passive form of 壊す ("to destroy").

中に何かが埋まるような深さはなかった　埋まる means "to be buried under," "to be covered in," "to be filled in," and so on. In this context, it reads almost like a potential form: there wasn't enough sand in the sandbox for anything to be buried there, so nothing could be buried there. The は marks 深さ as the topic, if only for a moment, but also suggests that while the sandbox was a bit deep, it wasn't *that* deep.

1　**赤さびた鉄看板を真上に載せた**　鉄看板 functions as one word, "iron signboard." を...に載せた is a transitive construction ("placed on top of..."), but since there is no subject the effect is similar to the intransitive or the passive.

コンクリートの平屋で　で tells us that more information will be given about the noun it follows.

だんだんと近づくにつれ　"Dictionary form of a verb + につれ（て）" is a pattern meaning "as (SUBJECT) (VERB)," e.g., 暑くなるにつれ "as it gets hotter," 子どもが成長するにつれ "as a child grows."

誰の耳にもききまちがえようのない　誰の耳にも literally means either "anyone's ears" or "no one's ears," depending on whether the sentence or clause ends with a positive or negative phrase. Here the expression means "no one's ears," i.e., "that no one's ears could possibly mistake."

　　The pattern "-**masu** stem + ようのない／ようがない + noun" means "a (NOUN) that it is impossible to (VERB)," e.g., 救いようのない失敗 "a mistake that can't be salvaged."

あの...声がきこえてくる　あの...声 works with the previous clause to emphasize the voice's peculiarity: "that voice." あの in this case carries the nuance of "that everyone is familiar with."

2　**さあ、牛かい?**　かい is a casual, chatty form of か.

牛ならこうだ——な　な is an exclamation similar to "Hey" or "Get it?" or "Listen..."

じっさいこの肉は、いい声で鳴いたんだ　んだ is a colloquial form of のだ and adds a personal, explanatory, even reflective tone to the sentence it ends.

3　**肉屋は町にここ一軒しかなく**　なく is the conjunctive form of ない. The combination of the particle しか and ない means "only" or "nothing but" when it follows a noun. When it follows a verb, it means "There's no choice but to (VERB)": やるしかない "We just have to do it."

かならず肉屋主人の口まねを耳にした　肉屋主人 (usually 肉屋の主人) reads as one word: "the proprietor of the meat market," i.e., the butcher. 口まね, from 口 ("mouth") and まねる ("to mimic"), means "imitating with the mouth" and refers to the butcher's mooing.

農道の先に 先 has several meanings, both spatial and temporal, but basically it suggests either "before" or "beyond."

小太りの主人が、声をあげながら目を真っ赤に染め 目を真っ赤に染め is a transitive phrase that seems like it ought to mean "dyeing his eyes bright red," but in effect it is more like an intransitive or passive construction: "his eyes dyed bright red…"

必死になって頬をふくらませていたりした This is an instance of the pattern "-**tari** form + する" (here the -**tari** form of the -**te iru** form). It tells us that the butcher's puffing up of his cheeks is only one of several states in which the children might have seen him as they were passing by his shop.

目配せしあいながら あう (合う) is used to form a wide variety of compound verbs describing actions that are undertaken mutually, or in concert, by two or more parties. 囁き合う "to whisper to each other"; 泣き合う "to cry together"; 話し合う "to discuss," "to talk something over"; 理解しあう "to understand each other."

肉を売るのと同じくらい One function of の is, as we have seen, to turn what comes before it into a noun phrase. Here it turns 肉を売る, "sell meat," into a noun phrase meaning "selling meat."

いや This is an exclamation similar to "Or rather," "I might even go so far as to say…," etc. A different いや, also an exclamation, means something like "I don't want to" or "No!"

家畜の物まねに心血をそそいでいる 口まね is "imitating with the mouth." 物まね is "imitating something." This sentence has a touch of humor in Japanese because 心血をそそぐ, "to pour one's heart into," is usually associated with more serious endeavors than 物まね.

ようにみえた This refers all the way back to それ以上の熱心さで: "It *looked* to us children *as though* he were pouring his heart into…with even more enthusiasm than…"

4 **大農場の家畜小屋と思いこんだことだろう** 思いこんだことだろう could also be written as 思いこんだだろう. The こと makes the statement subtly more speculative. The difference between the two phrases is like that between "She might well have gotten the impression" and "She would have gotten the impression." の, by the way, fulfills the same function as こと and could replace it in this sentence.

肉屋おうむ

5 　牛に豚、羊に鶏　Here に means "and." You hear this a lot on trains when the snack cart comes around: お茶にコーヒー、ビールにおつまみ "tea and coffee, beer and snacks…"

珍しく甲高いいななき声が店先から響いてくれば　珍しく modifies the entire clause, not just the adjective 甲高い. The くる in 響いてくる indicates the direction the sound is traveling: coming, not going. When you call into the depths of cave, your voice does the opposite: 響いていく.

には…とわかるのだった　には highlights the fact that the housewives were able to read the signs, while someone else (a stranger, for instance) might have overlooked them. わかるのだった suggests that this was a recurring event, with の making it clear that the sentence is an explanation, i.e., the housewives knew what meat the butcher had in stock based on the sounds that came from his shop.

7 　乳牛と肉牛じゃな、声のふるえがちがうんだよ　Grammatically, じゃな is a contraction of ではな. では emphasizes that the two kinds of cows are different; な is like "you know" and makes the tone more colloquial. Forget the grammar, though: the main thing is that old men used to talk this way (think Shūkichi in Ozu's film *Tokyo Story*) and still do in manga and anime.

9 　どっちかといえば　どっち is colloquial for どちら. Literally, this useful phrase means something like "If I had to say one way or the other"; it can also be used to mean "To tell the truth," "Given the choice," etc. どっちかといえば、あまり行きたくない "To tell the truth, I'd rather not go."

音色がやさしいんだ　んだ gives the statement a personal, explanatory tone (see also paragraph 2).

ここんところに　ここん is a contraction of ここの.

10 　再現してみせる「おうむ男」として世間に知られていた　"-Te form of a verb + みせる" is a pattern used to suggest that a difficult action will be accomplished, perhaps with flair, despite the odds. It often expresses the speaker's confidence or a feeling of triumph.

11 　おうむ男が肉屋に転身したのは　の turns what comes before it into a noun phrase, as we saw earlier (paragraph 3). Here this phrase becomes the topic of the sentence: literally, "the Parrot Man's taking a new job as a butcher."

サーカスで死んだ馬を、市場へもっていった<u>の</u>がきっかけだったらしい
Once again, の is used to create a noun phrase. The structure of the sentence is simpler than it may look: 転身したのは…がきっかけだったらしい is the main message ("The occasion for the change, it seems, was…"). サーカスで死んだ馬を、市場へもっていった ("his having taken a horse that had died in the circus to market") is the occasion.

精肉商の親方 精肉商 is another word for "butcher."

弟子入りを決めた彼は 弟子入りを決めた modifies 彼, which then becomes the topic of the sentence.

ぼくたちの町に店をかまえたのは二十年も前のことになる The も in 二十年も前 suggests that twenty years is a long time. 二十年も前のこと literally means "something that happened a good twenty years ago."

12 **奥さんが店先へ姿をみせる<u>こと</u>は<u>滅多に</u>なかった** こと turns what precedes it into a noun phrase, just as の did in previous cases (paragraphs 3, 11). 滅多にない is a useful phrase meaning "hardly ever."

くしゃくしゃの髪をした、顔色の悪い女<u>で</u> で tells us that more information will be provided about the noun it follows.

こんな女性にひと目ぼれした<u>なんて</u> なんて stresses the narrator's disbelief and/or scorn. こんなおもしろい映画を観ないなんて、信じられない "I can't believe you won't watch such a good movie!"

ぼくたちには<u>とても</u>ほんとうだとは<u>思えなかった</u> とても modifies 思えなかった and has something like the effect of "just" in English.

けれど主人はいつも陽気にふるまっていた<u>し</u> し is a conjunctive particle meaning "and," often used when giving reasons for something. 今日は暑いし、どっちかといえばあまり行きたくない "It's hot today, and to tell the truth I don't really want to go."

自分で店を開いてから、<u>奥さんとのあいだに</u>息子<u>まで</u>もうけていた In Japanese, babies are born "between" their parents. 奥さんとのあいだに means the same as 自分と奥さんのあいだに. まで tells us the narrator finds it hard to believe the butcher was prepared to go "that far."

年は少なくとも五つ<u>は</u>上だったと思う The second は stresses that he was *certainly* five years older, if not more.

13 **いつだって** This is a colloquial equivalent of いつも or いつでも.

大口をひらき、こんなふうに叫ぶ　こんなふうに is another, more collo-quial way of saying このように.

15　町に住む誰の目にも...明らかだった　This 誰の目にも is similar to the 誰の耳にも we saw earlier (paragraph 1). Literally, it means "to any eye," i.e., "It was clear to any eye that things were going well at the Parrot Meat Market."

肉屋おうむがうまくいっていることは　Again, こと turns what precedes it into a noun phrase (see also paragraph 12).

運河脇の草地でレスリングのまねごとをした　運河脇 reads as one word meaning 運河の脇.

彼に勝てるもの　This もの is 者, meaning "person."

17　と嬉しげにいったものだ　げ is the same suffix we saw in「神様」(para-graph 6), and again に turns the phrase it attaches to into an adverb. ものだ, meanwhile, lends a note of nostalgia to the statement. 小さい頃、僕はよく大人の口まねをしたものだ "When I was little, I often used to imitate the adults."

18　古トラック　This is treated as one word. The difference between 古トラック and 古いトラック is one of rhythm and feeling, rather than meaning.

助手席にすわるのはラー　Japanese slips easily back and forth between what people tend to think of as past and present tenses. Here すわる indicates that the situation being described took place many times, and makes the scene feel more immediate. 助手席にすわったのはラー, by contrast, would give the impression that a particular ride in the truck is under discussion, rather than a recurring event.

荷台にはぼくをふくめ、運のいい子どもが二、三人、膝を抱いて屈んでいる　The は in 荷台には functions like the word "while" in the translation, creating a juxtaposition that is almost, but not quite, a contrast.

19　解体用の小屋へとみちびいていく　The と here subtly highlights the move-ment from pasture to hut by turning what precedes it into something like a quote. Imagine the farmers thinking, "Onward! On toward the butchering hut!"

シャキン、シャキン　This spine-tingling onomatopoeia (擬音語 in Japa-nese) precisely captures the sound of a blade being sharpened: the

swish of the metal being drawn fast along the sharpener, then the faint clang as it is lifted away, vibrating.

21 <u>おまえさんらはむだ死にじゃないぞ</u>　おまえ, used mostly by men in casual speech toward intimates who are socially equal or inferior, is one of many words that mean "you." The さん gives it a formal, even respectful feel, and the ら makes it plural. The ぞ at the end of the sentence is a particle, also used mostly by men, that lends strength to an assertion. Here it reinforces the butcher's words of encouragement, "Your deaths won't be wasted, hear?"

22 <u>やわらかいもので撫でるような、あたたかな声でいう</u>　Both やわらかいもので撫でるような and あたたかな modify 声.

23 <u>おまえさんらのおかげで</u>　おかげ means "thanks to" and indicates the speaker's gratitude toward the person or thing that contributed to the situation he considers favorable (see also せい in paragraph 31).

24 <u>ビニールの幕へと横たえる</u>　Again, the と stresses the motion of moving the cows (see also paragraph 19).

　<u>おうむの親子、農場の親方たちは</u>　おうむの親子 and 農場の親方たち both serve as the topic of this sentence. 農場の親方たち might seem to mean that there are several head farmers; in fact it refers to the head farmer and the people who work under him.

　<u>ていねいに拾いあつめ</u>　拾いあつめる (拾い集める) is a compound verb and is read as one word.

　<u>塩と脂と、まるで自分たちの指をかじっているような味がした</u>　塩と脂と sort of hangs in the air grammatically, as if something has been abbreviated: 塩と脂とがまざった味がして、まるで…

25 <u>おたくの息子</u>…　Everything that follows, up until the end of the paragraph, can be thought of as the notary's words, more or less. The narrator is indirectly reporting the words, so he does not use「　」.

　<u>まったくとんでもないことをしでかしてくれた</u>　In this case, くれる is obviously not being used in a positive sense. Consider it a sort of irony.

　<u>やつ</u>　One of many words used as a second-person pronoun, やつ can express either scorn or affection for the person being spoken of.

今後二度とおもてを<ruby>歩<rt>ある</rt></ruby>けんようとっくりと<ruby>思<rt>おも</rt></ruby>いしらせてやる　歩けん is a contraction of 歩けぬ (= 歩けない). 思いしらせてやる means something like "give him something to think about" and here expresses the speaker's anger toward Laa. This "-**te** form of a verb + やる" pattern can be used with any number of verbs to mean "to give someone something" in an ironic sense, or sometimes "to do something to someone." This isn't a pattern you'll want to practice much in actual speech.

26　ラーは<ruby>勝手<rt>かって</rt></ruby>にひとの<ruby>寝床<rt>ねどこ</rt></ruby>にもぐりこんだりしない　ひとの means "other people's" or "another person's." もぐりこんだりしない is another instance of the "-**tari** form + する" pattern seen in paragraph 3, but here する is negated. It implies that, not only does Laa not creep into other people's beds, he doesn't do things *like that*. He's not that sort of guy.

…ほどの<ruby>臆病者<rt>おくびょうもの</rt></ruby>なの<u>だ</u>　のだ gives what comes before it the air of an explanation.

ハンマーを<ruby>打<rt>う</rt></ruby>ち<ruby>付<rt>つ</rt></ruby>けたみたいな、おおきなへこみが<ruby>残<rt>のこ</rt></ruby>っていた　ハンマーを打ち付けたみたいな and おおきな both modify へこみ. みたいな is a colloquial equivalent of ような.

たしかにレスリングに<ruby>似<rt>に</rt></ruby>ていなくもなかった　This is a double negative: sex wasn't exactly like wrestling, but then it wasn't wholly unlike it, either. The も serves a function not entirely unlike that of "either" in that last English sentence.

27　ひら<ruby>謝<rt>あやま</rt></ruby>りに<ruby>謝<rt>あやま</rt></ruby>り　ひら謝りに謝る originally means "to kowtow," but it can be used figuratively: it's about as likely that the butcher really got down and kowtowed (especially given the vaguely non-Japanese setting of this story) as it is that he literally apologized a thousand times.

<ruby>息子<rt>むすこ</rt></ruby>を<ruby>五体満足<rt>ごたいまんぞく</rt></ruby>でとりもどすため　五体満足 refers to "the five parts of the body": the head, two hands, and two feet.

<ruby>不平<rt>ふへい</rt></ruby>ひとつもらさ<u>ず</u>　This is the same ず we saw in「むかし夕日の公園で」 (paragraph 14), except that here it is equivalent to –ないで and indicates circumstance. Compare the translations.

28　<ruby>顔面<rt>がんめん</rt></ruby>をかぼちゃのように<ruby>腫<rt>は</rt></ruby>らせ　腫らせる is the causative form of the intransitive verb 腫る ("to puff up"), which is itself a literary variation of another intransitive verb, 腫れる, meaning the same thing. To further add to the complexity, this causative functions here more like a passive

or intransitive: Laa's face is puffed up because of the beating he got, not because he has found some way to make it grow.

なにもいわず This is the same ず we saw a moment ago (paragraph 27).

31 **主人が命を落としたのは...のせいだという意見がある** せい indicates that someone or something is responsible for a bad event or situation. おかげ (paragraph 23), by contrast, is normally used when the event or situation is good. Compare: 牛たちのおかげで俺たちはもうしばらく生きていける "Thanks to the cows, we can go on living a bit longer." 俺たちのせいで牛たちはもう死んでしまった "Thanks to us, the cows are already dead."

というものもいた This is another 者 (see also paragraph 15).

慰謝料分 分 is a handy suffix: 一食分 "enough for one meal," 一人分 "enough for one person."

連日無理をした 連日 and 無理 are read as two words, sort of like this: 連日、無理をした. 連日 is a noun acting as an adverb.

33 **すまん、ほんとうにすまん、と彼はいっているようだった** すまん is a contraction, used mainly by older men, of すまない, which is an informal version of すみません ("I'm sorry").

なにが起きているのかよくわかっていない様子で The の here makes the statement a bit stronger: rather than offering us an objective, outside perspective on Laa's confusion—彼はなにが起きているかよくわかっていない—this sentence makes it seem as though we are listening in on his thoughts. Laa looks as though he is thinking なにが起きているのかよくわからない. The difference might be compared, perhaps, to that between "Laa had no idea what was happening" and "Laa really had no idea what was happening." The addition of one little の might not seem all that important, but it changes the nuance of the sentence considerably.

35 **おまえさん、むだじに、じゃないぞ** Note that when Laa speaks (or at least parrots), he does so only in hiragana.

38 **何度も何度もくりかえしささやいた** くりかえし (繰り返し) is an example of a noun acting as an adverb.

39 **一年とかからなかった** This is a set phrase, more or less, and means ex-

actly the same thing as 一年もかからなかった: "It didn't even take a year." と is sometimes used in this way when an expression of quantity (an amount, a distance, a period, and so on) is followed by a negative form. This usage gives greater strength to the negative.

まったく疲れを知らず This is the same negative ず we saw earlier (paragraph 27). Here 知る is the same as the "know" in "he knew no want."

証人の娘の腹はぷっくりとふくれていた Imagine a pregnant woman's stomach. That's what ぷっくりと is like.

ぼくたち家族は Here 家族 is used in apposition with ぼくたち, in the same way that, for instance, "students of Japanese" can be with "we": "we students of Japanese."

40 **ラーと娘の子どもは...二番目の子どもは元気に産声をあげ** The first は establishes ラーと娘の子ども as the topic of the sentence. The second is contrastive: the second child, who "cried out vigorously" when it was born, is being contrasted with the first, who died at birth.

渋々とながら This is a bit unusual, I'd say. Ordinarily it would be 渋々ながら.

42 **若き父親** 若き is the classical Japanese equivalent (classical grammar again!) of the adjective 若い when it's used to modify a noun. The Japanese for "the good old days" makes use of this good, old grammar: よき日の思い出 "memories of the good old days."

44 **身をよじる幼いからだは** This might seem a bit strange at first glance, since both 身 and 体 often mean pretty much the same thing, but 身をよじる functions as one word: technically it's a noun plus を plus a verb; in practice it's basically just a verb meaning "to squirm."

いまは亡き祖父 This is the same classical conjugation we just saw (paragraph 42): 亡き for 亡い, meaning "dead."

1　**二十代になる直前の娘というものは**　というものは is a dressed-up version of plain old は, used to make a universal statement about the nature of the noun that precedes it.

すっかりおさめているつもりになっているものだが　When つもり follows a verb in the -te iru or -ta form, rather than one in the dictionary form, as is usual, it indicates that the speaker believes she or he has succeeded in doing something. Compare these two examples: 明日、ちゃんと宿題を提出するつもりです "I fully intend to turn my homework in tomorrow, as we are supposed to." あの宿題は昨日出したつもりですけど "I believe I handed that homework in yesterday." In the sentence from the story, the narrator is using this pattern after a verb in the -te iru form to suggest that, as a general rule, women just under twenty tend to think they know everything.

On another note, people often equate が with "but," but it doesn't always have this meaning. This is a nice example of a non-contrastive が, the function of which is to help establish a topic of conversation. (We'll encounter more of these.) The ものだ here is similar to the one we saw in paragraph 17 of「肉屋おうむ」, except that here, instead of conveying nostalgia for something that used to happen a good deal in the past, it helps turn the sentence into a general statement that applies to all times: "a young woman in her late teens tends to be…"

そしてたいていは　Compare this sentence to the one that opened the story: in the opening sentence, we were being told about 二十代になる直前の娘というもの, so that phrase was marked with a は. Here the emphasis is on "in most cases," so that's what gets the は.

むしゃくしゃしたりいらいらしているものだ　If this sentence were put into textbook Japanese, it would read むしゃくしゃしたりいらいらしたりしているものだ. It's less of a mouthful without the second したり, and the sentence makes sense without it, so Yoshimoto left it out. The ものだ at the end is the same kind we encountered a moment ago.

その匂いをかぎとることができる存在というのも稀にはいる　The という のも here makes sense when you pair it with the end of the fourth sentence: 異常に鋭敏な感性を生むことがある. There are extraordinarily sensitive people, and there are people who can sniff those special peo-

ple out. The の, as you may remember by now, is a nominalizer. By the way, don't be tricked by 稀にはいる: it's 稀には、いる not 稀に入る. The は emphasizes the rareness.

2 **薬学部に通っていた** The narrator's use of 通う ("to commute") tells us that she is living at home with her parents. My translation of 薬学部 as "college of pharmaceuticals" uses "college" in the British sense of the word, to mean an academic department of a larger institution.

六月だというのに The Japanese school calendar begins in April, so the year is just beginning—hence the implied "only," which I have made explicit in my translation of this phrase. だというのに is a more emphatic version of なのに.

その夕方 Sometimes a phrase like その夕方 (その日, その朝, etc.) is used to set the scene for a past event whose precise timing, in relation to the present, is unimportant. The effect is the same as that of the それは we saw in paragraph 8 of「むかし夕日の公園で」. Note also the position of その in the sentence: it appears after a modifying phrase. We haven't come across this yet, but it's actually quite common. The first sentence of paragraph 4 of this story includes another example: 田島というその青年.

うっすらと輝く消えかけた虹を見つけた When かける is used to form a compound verb, as it is here, it often means "to start to (VERB)." Unlike compound verbs formed using 出す, the action described using "-**masu** stem + かける" often ends up going unfinished. 僕らがちょうど夕食を食べかけていた時に、停電が起こった "We were just tucking into dinner when the blackout happened." (The rice left uneaten until the candles are lit is 食べかけのご飯 "half-eaten rice.") かける can have other meanings as an auxiliary verb, as in 見かける "to catch sight of," 呼びかける "to call out to." You'll get lots of practice with かける in the last story in this collection.

3 **予感は当たっていた** The verb is in the -**te ita** form, rather than the -**ta** form, because the narrator is looking back from some later time, after the events in the story are over, and judging that her premonition *had been* correct. 予感は当たった would be appropriate if the story were being narrated as if it were unfolding in the present, not narrated retrospectively; in that case, the phrase would mean something like "My hunch proved correct."

私^{わたし}はその日^ひ…青年^{せいねん}に連^つれ去^さられるようにして軟禁^{なんきん}され At first glance, ようにして might seem to suggest that the narrator is herself doing something, and in a sense she is—she's being led off. But the real effect of ようにして is to smooth the connection between 連れ去られる and 軟禁され and to make it a modicum less clear what happened: the narrator might have been led off, or she might have been *sort of* led off. The difference is clear if you compare the sentence as it is here to, say, 私はその日…青年に連れ去られて軟禁され…

4 年^{ねん}に半分^{はんぶん}はエジプトに行^いっている人^{ひと}だ This は is doing the same work as the one we saw in paragraph 12 of「肉屋おうむ」(年は少なくとも五^{いつ}つは上^{うえ}だった). It stresses that the young man Tajima spent at least half, if not more, of every year in Egypt.

ちょっともてそうな家庭^{かてい}教師^{きょうし}のお兄^{にい}さんタイプの青年^{せいねん} In this case, お兄さん doesn't mean "older brother"; it's a sort of affectionate, casual way of referring to, or calling out to, a young man, usually around college age.

9 あぶないからひとりで歩^{ある}かないほうがいいよ This is still Tajima talking. In Japanese, you will generally start a new paragraph whenever a character speaks, just as in English. The similarities end there, though, because often the interjections telling us who is speaking ("he said," "she stated") get their own paragraphs, too. And if the same character continues speaking after the "he/she said," as Tajima does here, the second part of the quotation also starts a new paragraph.

送^{おく}ってあげようか? This is the informal form of 送ってあげましょうか?

10 あんたがあぶなくないという保証^{ほしょう}がどこにある あんた is a contraction of あなた that you sometimes hear women, and male transvestites on TV, using. It can be uttered in a wide variety of tones that make it mean anything from "darling" to "you jerk."

11 犯人^{はんにん}はまだつかまってないんですか? つかまってない is another contraction, this time of つかまっていない. People talk like this all the time, particularly in informal situations.

12 私^{わたし}は言^いった This refers back to the quotation in the previous line.

13 うん Depending on the context and how it's said (or grunted?), うん can have either a positive or a negative meaning. Here Tajima is agreeing

ミイラ

with the narrator: "Yeah, they haven't caught the culprit yet." Note that while in English people tend to respond to negatively phrased questions like "They haven't caught the culprit yet?" by repeating the negative—"Nope, they haven't"—in Japanese this would have the opposite meaning: "Nope, they have caught him."

16 首だけ見つからないって　This って is an informal equivalent of ということだ or そうだ, both of which indicate that the preceding information is hearsay.

18 知らされているものだ　First of all, 知らされている is the passive form of 知らす (a variant of 知らせる, "to make known"). It's in the -**te iru** form here because the narrator is suggesting that this is a habitual situation: "We are almost always given some sort of advance notice of the things that are going to happen in our lives." Second: ものだ is the same "general statement" ものだ that we encountered in the first paragraph of this story. It turns the whole sentence into a kind of universal statement.

ほんとうは読み取っていた　Though it may not look like one, this is a contrastive は. The tricky bit is that the statement it's contrasted with is only implied. The idea is that, *unlikely as it seems*, the narrator *actually was* (ほんとうは) aware of what was happening.

19 …に一瞬おびえ　Note that the author uses the -**masu** stem of おびえる instead of the -**te** form, even though she used the -**te** form in the previous clause (比べ方をして). This is deliberate, of course: the -**masu** stem speeds up the tempo of the sentence.

理性的な判断をしたつもりになった　This is the same sort of つもり we saw back in the first paragraph. Here it follows the -**ta** form of a verb because it refers to a particular judgment that the narrator made, not an ongoing state of affairs. Often when つもり is used like this, it implies that the action of the verb preceding it may not actually have been carried off without a hitch, as the person who did it believes it was. That's the case here, obviously.

私は彼を選び彼と並んで歩きだしたのである　と並んで does not mean "line up with…and…" but rather is used adverbially to mean "side by side with." 歩きだす (歩き出す), meanwhile, is a compound verb meaning "to start walking." You can tack 出す onto lots of other verbs in this way; 言い出す ("to start talking") in paragraph 21 is another example.

ミイラ

人間には発情期はない It's easier to understand what's happening in this clause if you compare it to 人間<u>は</u>発情期<u>が</u>ない. This latter version is a plain statement of fact, without any nuance or emphasis. In the clause as it appears in the story, には quietly emphasizes the word 人間, and the は after 発情期 makes the statement a tiny bit stronger: "*People don't, of course, have a mating season.*"

もしも私が野生生物だったら もしも is a more tentative, speculative version of もし. Compare: もし雨が降ったら、どうする? "*What will you do if it rains?*" もしも雨が降ったら、どうする? "*What will you do if it should happen to rain?*"

生命の危険を読み取って This is, obviously, an incomplete sentence. It is also an inversion and has to be read in conjunction with the preceding sentence in order to make sense. If we were to re-invert the inversion, we would end up with something like this: もしも私が野生生物だったら、生命の危険を読み取ってとっくに逃げ去っていただろう.

22 **僕達はこのまま別れちゃいけないと思うんだ** You can tell from the use of the masculine first-person pronoun 僕 here that this is Tajima speaking. The next sentence—目が真剣だった—is about him, too. ちゃ in 別れちゃいけない is a contraction of ては.

23 **私は言った** Notice that in this case the attribution *precedes* the quotation. In Japanese, you can do it either way: "'Blah blah blah,' he said"—or—"He said: 'Blah blah blah.'"

24 **また会う約束をするとか? そういうこと?** The とか that ends the first of these two brief sentences accomplishes the same thing as "or something" in English: it suggests various other possibilities without specifying what they might be. "You think we should agree to get together again or something?" would be another, more literal translation.

27 **人気のない夕方の路地** Note the difference between にんきのない ("unpopular") and ひとけのない ("with no sign of human presence," "deserted"), both of which are written 人気のない. You can generally figure out which reading you want from the context.

私を抱きすくめた This is a compound verb made up of 抱く ("to hug") and 竦める ("to render immobile"). It's a subtly ominous hug.

ついていかなかったら、いずれはつけまわされて殺される This is the first

of three separate thoughts, all running through the narrator's mind, that have been stuck together here, separated only by commas, to form a single sentence. If the sentences weren't joined in this way—if there were a period after 殺される, then another after 長くなってしまう—it would be a little more difficult to figure out where the narrator's thoughts end. Splicing the sentences together like this also conveys a sense of the narrator's agitation, the rapidity of her thoughts.

早くすませて**しまおう** This is the volitional form of しまう.

彼と体の一部を触れあわせ**ていたかった** Note that it says 触れあわせて いたかった rather than 触れあわせたかった. The difference seems slight, but it's much more graphic this way: the narrator is saying, literally, that she wanted to *be in the state of having* a certain part of her body in contact with a certain part of his.

今まで感じたこと**の**ない気持ちが悪い熱 As we saw in「むかし夕日の公園で」(paragraph 8), の can replace が in certain constructions. Yoshimoto is probably using の here because the sentence is much easier to read this way—感じたことがない気持ちが悪い熱 is difficult to parse.

ミイラ

29 見せたいもの**って** This って means というのは but is more informal. Here it marks 見せたいもの ("the thing you wanted to show me") as the topic. See paragraph 16 for another use of って.

32 私の内心を見抜いた**かの**ように The かの here makes the clause sound a little less definite. The difference between 私の内心を見抜いたように and 私の内心を見抜いたかのように is like that between "seeming to have seen into my heart" and "as if he had seen into my heart."

33 彼の欲望は挿入よりも何よりも見る、ということに**つきていて** If より can be translated as "more than," よりも means "even more than." Tajima is interested in "entering" the narrator, and in all sorts of other things, but he's "even more" interested in looking at her. The basic meaning of the verb つきる, which appears here in the **-te ite** form, is "to be exhausted" in the sense of "to run out." So while Tajima is happy to do other things with the narrator, you could count the activities that *really* excite him on just one finger: he likes to look, and that's it. End of story.

私を楽し**ませ**ようという考えはあまりないようだった 楽しませよう is the volitional form of the causative form of the verb 楽しむ ("to enjoy").

Notes to pp. 82–84 • 83

あまりのしつこさに思わず何回も<u>絶頂に達した</u>　絶頂に達する, like "to climax" in English, can also be used outside the context of sex to mean "to peak," "to hit a zenith."

普通のセックスで普通に気持ちいい<u>というものではなくて</u>　というものではなくて is used to say that what comes before it isn't an adequate, or even an appropriate, description of the situation—or rationale, or whatever it is the speaker is trying to explain. This is a neat example how the basic S-O-V structure of Japanese allows speakers to execute sudden about-faces, starting out seeming to say one thing, but then changing direction with the verb.

しかし、なんと<u>言えばいいのだろう</u>　"-Ba form + いい" can be used in a few different ways, but essentially it means just what it appears to mean: "would be good if…" Here it is as if the narrator is looking for the best word to describe the pleasure she felt. "Twisted" doesn't seem quite right, so she keeps trying to explain the sensation in the paragraphs that follow.

34　その腕の妙に<u>細いこと</u>… All the ことs in this paragraph could be replaced with の, but the effect would be different. The ことs make the narrator's description sound more objective.

35　やわらかく水を<u>含んだ</u>砂が体の下で<u>揺れるようす</u>　含む covers a wide spectrum of meanings: to contain, to hold in one's mouth, to be infused with, to be saturated with. In this sentence, it has the last of these meanings: sand saturated with water. The word ようす that ends this grammatically incomplete sentence is similar, in this context, to "the way" in English, as my translation suggests. Concluding the sentence in this way—without bringing in a verb, and thus diluting the purity of the description—calls up the particular feeling that the narrator is recalling all the more vividly.

もう<u>どうでもよくなって</u>　どうでもいい is a fixed expression meaning "I really don't care," "It doesn't matter," "It's all the same to me," "Whatever," and so on. Here the -i adjective いい is in its -ku form, and is followed by the auxiliary verb なる ("to become") in its -te form. One literal rendering of the clause would be: "I had already become indifferent, and…" It's important, by the way, not to confuse どうでもいい with 何でもいい, which means "Anything is fine with me."

36　私は親に連絡も<u>取らせてもらえず</u>　取らせてもらえる is the causative

form of 取る (from 連絡を取る "to contact") in its -**te** form, followed by the receiving verb もらう in its potential form. The combination means "to be allowed to contact." Since the phrase is negated with ず here, it becomes "not to be allowed to contact." The も strengthens the statement the way the "even" does in the translation.

一晩中彼の好きなようにされた 好きなようにする is a set phrase meaning "to do whatever one likes." The use of the passive here conveys the narrator's displeasure.

37 **私は幼いなりに** なりに follows nouns and -**i** adjectives, and is used to suggest that the subject does whatever it does in a manner appropriate to it, "in its own way." 私なりに, for instance, can mean "in my own way," "as best I can," and so on.

自分をどんなふうに扱っても許せるか否か か否か is just another way of saying かどうか. It has a slightly archaic feel that makes this phrase stand out a bit, and seem a bit self-conscious—both of which are appropriate, since the narrator is giving us a sort of statement of her dating policy.

それが許せる人としか恋愛をしてこなかったつもりだった しか…ない, as you may recall from paragraph 8 of「神様」, means "only." Here it is used in combination with the particle と ("with"). The meaning of 許せる人としか恋愛をしてこなかった, then, is "I had only had relationships with people I could allow to do those things." してこなかった is used, rather than simply しなかった, in order to emphasize that this was the narrator's policy over a period of time leading up to the point about which she is speaking. (The sentence ends with だった because the narrator is now looking back on the events of the story, telling us what happened after the fact.) This sounds complex, but it isn't really—no more complex, at any rate, than the difference between "I only had relationships" and "I had only had relationships."

The つもり, which again follows the -**ta** form of a verb, tells us what the narrator believes about her past actions, not what she intends to do in the future.

こんなふうにただセックスするためにしか存在しない関係なんて しか…ない can also be used in combination with ために to mean "solely for the purpose of…" The particle なんて expresses the narrator's surprise.

彼のスタミナにおそれをなしての質問だった おそれをなす is a set phrase

meaning "to be awestruck." The pattern "**-te** form + の + noun" is used to express the idea that a state (indicated by the **-te** form) gives rise to something (the noun, that is). Here we can think of 彼のスタミナにおそれをなしての質問 as "a question my awe of his stamina gave rise to."

38　彼は時計をかくしてしまった　It's not clear (nor does it need to be) whether "the clock" Tajima has hidden is really just one clock or several, or a watch or several watches and clocks. It's also unclear when exactly he hid them: Did he do it progressively, each time she tried to steal a look at another clock or watch? Or all at once? Needless to say, depending on how one imagines the scene, one could come up with several different translations of this clause.

…をもちろんトイレにもプライバシーはなかった　にも has the same effect as the "even in" in "I had no privacy, even in the toilet."

ほとんど見知らぬ他人の前でならできるとは　It's not unusual for なら ("if") to appear after certain particles (mostly で, に, and の), as it does here.

セックスとは全く不思議なものだ　Both this とは and the one in the preceding clause serve as abbreviations of というものは or ということは.

時間が経過して行くにつれて　The auxiliary verb 行く here expresses progression into the future. See paragraph 1 of「肉屋おうむ」for a note on the use of につれて.

40　親が警察に電話する前に家に電話しないと　This indirect quotation trails off in an implied warning, just like its English translation: "I'd better call home before my parents call the police, or else…"

突然彼はそう言い　This そう refers back to the quote in paragraph 39.

42　私は言った　As we have seen, quotations are often set apart in a new paragraph in Japanese, and in many cases this is also true of interjections, like this one, that help us keep track of who's talking. This is common in Yoshimoto's prose. Until you get used to it, the free-floating position of these interjections can make it hard to figure out whether the attribution points to the quote that precedes it or the one that follows. But eventually you do get used to it. Here the narrator is speaking both lines.

47　**君は僕が楽しんで作ったと思うかもしれないけど**　Like と並んで in paragraph 19, 楽しんで here is used adverbially. It helps to think of it as a set phrase meaning "with pleasure."

思い出したくもない　The も here strengthens the statement. Compare: 思い出したくない "I don't want to think about it." 思い出したくもない "I don't even want to think about it."

自分が殺したのでもないのに　This looks a bit complex, but it's not really. 自分が殺したのでもない is just a way of negating 自分が殺したのである. Here, too, the も makes the statement a little stronger and emotionally resonant than it would otherwise be: less "I hadn't killed it myself" than "It wasn't as though I had killed it myself." Tajima's use of the のである ending here gives the statement a slightly formal feel, as compared with, say, 自分が殺してもいないのに, which would also mean something like "It wasn't as though I had killed it myself."

On another note, it is one of the misfortunes of the English language, at least from the perspective of Japanese, that you usually have to specify whether you're talking about a "he," a "she," a "they," or an "it." I used "it" here so that I wouldn't have to assign the cat a sex (I did decide that there is only one), but this grammatical objectification of the animal weakens our sense of Tajima's evident fondness for his pet. It would also have been possible to decide on a sex.

自分が殺したのと同じ重みの思い出ができてしまった　重み is a noun meaning "weight," formed by attaching the suffix み to the stem of the -**i** adjective 重い. み can be attached in this way to a number of -**i** adjectives. It is very similar to another nominalizing suffix, さ, which we encountered in paragraph 17 of「神様」; but while さ simply turns adjectives into nouns, み implies an extent. Compare, for instance, the two nominalized forms of the adjective 厚い ("thick"): 厚みのある生地 makes perfect sense as "thick cloth"; 厚さのある生地 doesn't, because it means "cloth with thickness," and no matter how thin a cloth is, it still has thickness. Because nominalized adjectives formed using み carry this implication of extent, and because perceptions of extent are subjective, they lend themselves to metaphorical usages. Tajima's use of 重み here is an instance of that.

50　**はくせいにしたり、毛でセーターを作る人とあまり変わらない気持ちなんじゃない?**　なんじゃない? is a colloquial version of なのではないだろう

か／でしょうか that is spoken with a rising intonation (CD 13:20). You might think of it as a distant cousin of the English "Don't you think?"

51 私は言った。間をおいて彼は言った。 This is a good example of how an attribution of a quote in one line can refer to either the preceding or the following line: here, of course, 私は言った points back to the preceding line, while 彼は言った refers to the one that follows.

52 いっしょにいてくれないか。今、家に電話していいから。 The から at the end of that second sentence seems puzzling until you realize that the order of the two sentences has been inverted: he's asking if she'll be willing to stick around *because* he's agreeing to let her call home.

55 よく親に怒られたが 怒られる is the passive form of 怒る, a verb whose basic meaning is "to get angry," but means "to be given a scolding," "to get yelled at," and so on when it is used in the passive. The が after it doesn't mean "but"; it helps prepare the way for the discussion that follows by telling us that the preceding clause ("I used to get chewed out by my parents [for this]") is background information.

私にはそういういやに冷たい面があった そういういやに冷たい面 refers to the "cold side" of the narrator's personality, exemplified by her words in paragraph 53: むりよ. The そういう points us back to her behavior in this paragraph.

そういうことを思うんじゃない "Dictionary form of a verb + んじゃない" is used with a strong falling intonation (CD 14:30) to express fairly strong disapproval, generally for something that the person being addressed has just done.

とたいそうしかられたりした Here's how this breaks down: quotation particle と + adverb たいそう ("terribly") + passive form of しかる ("to scold") in its -**tari** form, followed by した.

この時もそうだった この時 refers to the scene that was put on hold when we got into this little digression about the clerk, and specifically about the narrator's blunt rejection of Tajima's request that she spend another day with him.

59 ぐしゃりと割れ This is a brilliant instance of 擬態語 (words that mimic actions, states, or emotions; not to be confused with 擬音語, words that imitate sounds). ぐしゃ captures the hard-on-the-outside-but-soft-on-

the-inside feeling of something collapsing, caving in, being pounded in, or mashed, while しゃり has a nice gravelly feeling—only it seems a bit more dusty, or sandy, than gravel. (Gravel, incidentally, is じゃり in Japanese.) As a whole, the word gives us a vivid image of the brittle statue cracking against Tajima's forehead, then breaking to bits in the narrator's hands.

彼の顔が血まみれになった　まみれ is a suffix that attaches to a very small number of nouns, all dirty, that can mean "plastered with," "coated with," "drenched with," and so on. 泥まみれ is "plastered with mud"; 垢まみれ is "covered with filth."

60　私の中に眠っていた愛情という概念の全てが沸点に達した　This sentence, and the one after it, are classic Yoshimoto Banana: they seem easy enough on the surface, but are brilliantly, beautifully, richly confusing. If you should happen to feel bewildered, don't let it worry you. As my translation should suggest, you have to do a lot of work if you want to try and pin this sentence down, and it's less interesting when you do.

61　ごめんなさい、何ていうことを!　ていう is a colloquial form, a sort of contraction, of という. Obviously, a verb has been omitted after the を. Literally, the sentence means something like "I'm sorry, what a [horrible] thing [for me to do]!" Or, to be even more floridly literal: "I'm sorry, [I've done] something that prompts me to say: What [the hell am I doing]!" (Bear with me: this literal-mindedness will come in handy soon.)

63　いいんだ、悪いのは僕だ　Tajima is responding to the narrator's apology, two lines up. She says she's sorry; he says, "No need to apologize, *I'm* to blame." The は is contrastive.

65　思うところがある　This ところ doesn't quite mean "place," though in some ancient etymological way it is presumably related to that standard usage of the word. Think of it as a distant relative of the word "part" when it appears in the phrase "There's a part of me that thinks…" In this case, there is a certain part of the narrator that is thinking of something that necessitates her taking a short trip.

68　にしても　Ordinarily, you would expect to see それにしても here, not にしても, which generally isn't used on its own in this way. Yoshimoto's

careful, sparing use of extremely informal language is part of what makes her prose feel so intimate, as if her narrators are addressing you, the reader, directly.

69 細く街灯の光が入っている中で　The pattern "dictionary form of a verb + 中で" or "-**te iru** form + 中で" tells us that the action that follows (in this case it's not much of an action: Tajima has just gotten up and is sitting there, staring at her stomach) happens or is happening in the midst of something—in this case, light pouring in from outside.

内臓まで見ているかのように　The pattern "dictionary/-**ta**/-**te iru** form of a verb + かのよう" is used to say that someone or something looks as though she/he/it were doing whatever the verb is, though this may not actually be the case. The か emphasizes the fact that an analogy is being drawn, or that the appearance described could be deceiving. Compare these two sentences, for instance: 先生が私の名前をころっと忘れたように見える "The teacher seems, all of a sudden, to have forgotten my name." 先生が私の名前をころっと忘れたかのように、何も言わずに曖昧な笑いを浮かべている "The teacher remains silent, a vague smile hovering on her lips, as if she has suddenly forgotten my name."

不思議とこわくはなかった　The と here turns 不思議 into an adverb, much like に does in other contexts. The narrator is surprised at her own lack of fear—she's so calm that she herself finds it odd. The は tells us that while she wasn't afraid, she was feeling other things.

70 顔の傷の血もすっかり固まっていた　The も is here because the scab is *another* change: earlier it wasn't raining, now it is; earlier the cut was still oozing blood, now it has hardened.

雷の音が大きく鳴り響く中で、最後の時間を過ごした　The compound verb 鳴り響く suggests both the first boom and the reverberations of the thunder.

71 面白いおちがついたのだが　おちがつく is a set phrase meaning "to have a good punch line," "to end with an unexpected twist in the story."

72 その後帰国してからは　The は creates a contrast with the first half of the sentence: Tajima came down with malaria abroad; back in Japan, he had a breakdown.

73 そのまんまの職業につくなんて、大した人じゃなかったんだ　そのまんま

is a colloquial variation of そのまま ("just like that"). "大した + noun + ではない" is a pattern meaning "not much of a (NOUN)." In this case, the tense is past, so the meaning becomes "turns out not *to have been* all that much of a…"

74 服の上からでもわかる   In Japanese, as in English, clothes are worn in layers that go from bottom to top: 下着 is "underwear"; 上着 is an "overcoat." So when you notice someone's physique "through" their clothes in English, in Japanese you are looking from "above" their clothes at the underlying form. That's why we have 上から here.

75 もう二度と…することはないだろう   "二度と…verb in the -**nai** form (or some other negative form)" is a pattern used to indicate that the speaker firmly intends never to do the action of the verb again, or expects that the action of the verb will never again take place. 私は二度と彼と口を利かないつもり! "I'm never going to talk to him again, as long as I live!"

　　現実とは違う位相に飛び込んでしまったのだ   The は in 現実とは違う makes it clear that what's important about the "different dimension" is precisely its difference from reality. If this were simply 現実と違う, the qualities of that other dimension might themselves be important.

　　お互いがとまどうほど強烈な力が働いたのだろう   The topic of the sentence is still ふたり, established in the last sentence. Don't get confused by the two がs here: the second one marks the subject of the sentence; the first marks the subject of the subordinate clause.

76 しかし今の   This しかし isn't setting up a contrast with the previous sentence, as it might seem—the progression is not "Sometimes I wonder. But…" It's the beginning of the narrator's thought, part of what she's wondering. The contrast here is with the seemingly natural assumption that the life she is living is unquestionably the correct and happy one.

77 もしかしたら…かもしれない   It's easy to get a grasp on もしかしたら if you break it down into its constituent parts: もし + か + したら. All the elements suggest hesitancy, uncertainty, questioning—hence the meaning, "Could it be that…?" "It might just be that…" This phrase isn't always followed by かもしれない, but it's generally be followed by something similar. もしかしたら、このへんで財布を見つけていないでしょうか "You wouldn't, by any chance, happen to have found a wallet around here, would you?"

ミイラ

78 **あの猫のように、ミイラにされてしまった異次元の私を** This sentence and the next are both grammatically incomplete, because they are connected with the very short sentence—想像する—that opens the paragraph.

79 **それはそんなに悪いことにはどうしても思えなかった** 思う generally takes と (変だと思った "I thought it was odd") or を (いろんなことを思っている "I'm thinking all kinds of things"), but it can also take に, as it does here. In this case, it means "think of…as…" or "think that…is…" When 思う (or some variation of it: here, it's the potential 思える) is in the negative, the に will frequently be followed by a は, which strengthens the denial: "I can think all kinds of things, but the one thing I can't think, try as I might, is that it's a bad thing."

1 **わたし、寝たくないの** This の can serve two purposes: it either gives what precedes it an explanatory air, or stresses the speaker's emotional involvement in what she or he is saying. It used to be that this の was considered characteristic of "feminine" speech, though children used it, too. These days, you'll find that young men (even those who aren't all that young—myself, for instance) use it as well.

2 **嫌々をしながら** If this were 嫌々ながら, without the を and the **suru**-verb stem し, the clause would mean "grudgingly," "unwillingly." The を changes this: 嫌々をする literally means something like "to do *No, no!*" and refers to the way very young children shake their heads when they don't like something.

これは、文字通り ... という意味である This これ points to the quotation that opens the story: わたし、寝たくないの. Specifically, it's aiming at the word 寝る, which, like the English *sleep*, can mean either "to sleep" (in the sense of doing what people do when they're really tired) or "to sleep with" (in the sense of getting it on). The word 眠る, which also came up in 「神様」and 「ミイラ」, doesn't have the latter meaning.

恐れているのかもしれない の can be added to phrases like this one to convey a sense of the speaker's involvement in whatever she or he is saying. Here the subjective resonance seems to imply the presence in the narrative of some individual who is personally implicated in the story—we sense, in other words, that the sentence speaks from the perspective of someone in the story, that we are momentarily inside the head of a character. We are about to meet that person: Anzai, the second of the two characters in this story.

横になってしまったら、おかしなことをされるのではないかと This の is a nominalizer, plain and simple—there's no emotional nuance. The と at the end of the sentence points us back to the first part of the sentence, helping us piece the inverted pieces together: 横になってしまったら、おかしなことをされるのではないかと恐れているのかもしれない. Inversions of this sort are more typical of speech than of formal prose, so again the effect is to make us feel that we are inside the head of a character.

3 **安西も男だから** This も means "too" in the sense of "like all other men." Hence the English translation: "Anzai is a guy like any other."

若い娘と朝まで過ごすことになって　Depending on the context, 娘 can mean "daughter," "girl," or "young woman." We'll see more of the meanings as the story progresses. "Dictionary form of a verb + ことになる" is a set pattern meaning "to end up" doing the action of the verb.

甘い気分にならないわけではない　わけではない is a pattern used to negate the statement that precedes it. When the preceding statement is already negative, as it is here, the resulting double negative acquires a sense of ambivalence. Compare: 行きたいわけではない "It's not that I *want* to go." 行きたくないわけではない "It's not exactly that I *don't want* to go."

安西も、そんな娘に襲いかかれるほどの人でなしではない　This も is similar to the one we encountered a moment ago, but also a little different. You might think of it as gesturing to the existence of other men like Anzai—a group of men who aren't brutes, of which Anzai is a member. Setting aside the question of what the も actually means, the effect of it is more to soften the statement than anything else: 安西は would be talking very clearly about Anzai; 安西も is still talking about Anzai, but at the same time it situates him in a broader context.

ほど retains the meaning of "extent" here: Anzai was not such a brute as to (literally, "a brute to the extent that he would") try and have his way with a girl in that state.

先輩から…と命令された　から in this case could be replaced by a に without changing the meaning.

おい、お前、送ってやれや　This is the first of numerous instances of overtly "masculine" speech that we will encounter in this story. お前 is a second-person pronoun used, usually by men, to address someone the speaker either sees as an equal or looks down on. (You may remember seeing this in「肉屋おうむ」.) やる is a verb meaning "to give," but unlike あげる or the honorific 差し上げる, it suggests that the person doing the giving stands in a position superior to that of the person receiving the gift. Here it is being used as an auxiliary verb: "*Do her a favor* and see her home." (This, too, appeared in「肉屋おうむ」.) The や at the end comes from a regional dialect; it gives the sentence a different mood, but doesn't alter the basic meaning. "Will yuh?" might be a decent translation of it in this context.

その手前もある　…の手前がある is a handy way of saying that the person being discussed has to consider how some other person or group

of people will view her (let's just assume it's a "her") if she performs a certain action. 世間の手前があるから is a good translation for the British phrase, "We must keep up appearances."

4　高いびきだ　Don't be fooled by the い here—it's part of いびき "snore," not 高い. You want to split this up, in other words, into たか/いびき, not たかい/びき. The だ at the end of the sentence may seem odd at first; the meaning should be clearer if you think of it as an abbreviation of をしているはずだ. Leaving out verbs in this way helps gives the prose a chatty, colloquial feel.

それが雷のおかげで面倒なことになった　それが doesn't point back to a particular word in the preceding sentence or sentences; it's an interjection that refers generally to the situation in which Anzai has found himself, indicating that something about it is unexpected. See paragraph 23 of「肉屋おうむ」for a note on おかげで.

5　帰り道が途中まで一緒なのと　の turns this clause into the first half of an explanation. な precedes it because 一緒 is a noun. The と simply means "and." This is what tells us to read 帰り道が途中まで一緒 as the first item in a list of reasons that is about to be expanded.

いわゆる人畜無害な人柄ゆえに　And here's the continuation of the list. The two reasons, you will notice, don't line up the way they normally would in English—there's no need to maintain the same degree of rigid parallelism, making sure that each of the two reasons can be combined with the ゆえに ("because of") at the end, or inserting a similar word meaning "because of" after the first reason. In English, a sentence of this sort would probably be structured something like this: "Because of A, and because of B," or "Because of A and B." Here 帰り道が途中まで一緒 can be left dangling, grammatically unconnected to what follows, because the overall meaning of the sentence makes its connection to the clauses that follow perfectly clear.

…を預けられた安西なのだ　This is a splendid example of one of the neat things the grammatical structure of Japanese allows us to do. Everything that precedes 安西 has been turned into a long adjectival phrase modifying his name: right now, he's the sort of Anzai who has, for certain reasons, been put in charge of a drunk freshman. Why would one write a sentence this way? At least in part, to avoid having

to end on a verb. No matter how you conjugate them, Japanese verbs always end, when they appear at the conclusion of a grammatically complete sentence, in either an "u" sound or a "ta." This means writers have to juggle sentence structures if they want to avoid having a dull, monotonous string of repeated sounds at the ends of their sentences. If you glance back over the first few paragraphs of this story, you'll see that Kitamura has been ending his sentences in all kinds of different ways. And he'll continue to do so, too, as you'll see in the next line.

ある路線が不通で This ある is different from the verb ある ("to exist"). It means "a certain...," as in "a certain track."

6 **切れ切れに** Since this is an adverb, we would expect it to be followed eventually by a verb. In this case, however, 言う (or some similar verb) has been omitted, and all we get is the quotation itself. Omissions of this sort have no effect on our understanding of what is being said, of course, and help keep the writing concise. You encounter this sort of thing in newspapers all the time.

7 **先輩の、とこで、休ませて、ください** 休ませる is the causative form of 休む ("to rest"). ください turns it into a request: "Please let me rest."

8 **当たり前ならタクシーを使うところだが** This is a somewhat unusual use of 当たり前, which isn't a word you expect to see used in a conditional statement. The idea is, I think, that Anzai would have used a taxi "if this were the sort of thing he was used to doing." ところ means something like "situation" here: this is *the sort of situation* in which Anzai would have used a taxi, had he been used to using them.

まだ学生の安西には、そういう気がまわらなかった The compound particle には stresses the fact that Anzai, inexperienced student that he is, didn't know how to handle the situation. Perhaps someone else, older and more polished, would have done better. 気がまわる (気が回る) is a set phrase used to describe someone who is attentive to detail and makes sure that other people have what they need. そういう気 refers to the kind of thoughtfulness that would have prompted Anzai to get a taxi. Literally, that kind of 気 did not 回る, or "come around."

金がないわけでもない This is the same ambivalent double-negative usage of わけではない that we saw in paragraph 3. The も makes the statement even more hesitant.

それだけに This looks like it ought to mean "that's all," but in fact it's closer to "to that extent" or "precisely for that reason"—hence the somewhat roundabout translation, "being that type." Anzai is less able to think on his feet precisely because he's that type of guy, a spoiled rich boy. The に tells us that それだけ modifies everything that follows; if the clause read それだけ小回りのきかないところもある, then それだけ would only modify 小回りのきかない, and the meaning would be "That's how bad he was at thinking on his feet."

交通至便の自分のワンルームマンションに 交通至便 is a fixed phrase meaning, more or less, "conveniently located near the station," or maybe in some cases "near a bus stop." 至便 means "the most convenient." This is not, by the way, a traditional four-character compound, or 四字熟語—it comes out of real estate advertising.

9 **安西はいった** This refers, obviously, to the quotation in the next line. We saw in「ミイラ」how flexible Japanese is when it comes to attributing quotations: the attribution can come before or after the quote. This is another example.

10 **頼むから、静かにしててくれよ** 頼むから is a fixed expression that covers a range of meanings from "Can you do me a favor and…?" to "Please, please, I'm begging you!" してて is a contraction of していて. 静かにして would be a command: "Be quiet"; 静かにしていて is "Keep quiet." くれ is the blunt imperative form of くれる, but when it's used as an auxiliary verb, as it is here, it becomes a much less formal version of ください. Finally, よ makes the request more emphatic. This combination of くれ and よ is typical of informal "masculine" speech, and you'll notice that when Mitsuko speaks, she doesn't talk this way at all—she's much more formal, and sounds more "feminine." This makes it easier to identify who's speaking, even without attributions. In the real world, men and women—especially young men and women—don't always speak in such radically different styles.

11 **美都子は黙ったまま、部屋に入り** "-Ta form of a verb + まま" is a pattern used to indicate that a situation remains or has been left unchanged. Here Mitsuko enters the room "in the unchanged state of having kept quiet," or "without a word." Ordinarily, when entering someone else's home, you say お邪魔します (literally, "I will interrupt"). Mitsuko doesn't say that.

百物語

床に膝を抱いて座ったかと思うと "-**Ta** form of a verb + かと思うと" is a pattern meaning "No sooner had…than…" or perhaps, to be slightly more literal, "By the time one realized that…was already…." The subject cannot be the speaker; it must be a second or third person. Usually what follows is an expression of the speaker's/writer's surprise.

13 どうしたんですか、<u>あたし</u>? あたし is a first-person pronoun used mostly by women, or by people representing themselves as feminine in gender.

14 不思議なことに This に turns the noun phrase 不思議なこと into an adverbial phrase that modifies the clause or clauses that follow it. The same construction can be made, of course, using other noun phrases: 驚いたことに ("surprisingly"), for instance, appears in paragraph 82.

15 美都子<u>は夏らしくノースリーブのミニワンピース、色は黒である</u> Once again, Kitamura omits a verb. Mitsuko, presumably, is 夏らしくノースリーブのミニワンピースを着ている. But since we know that anyway without being told, Kitamura doesn't tell us. 夏らしく becomes, as a result, a free-floating adverb, with no verb to modify.

黒と、柔らかな女の肌の色を<u>引き立</u>たせていた 引き立つ means "to look good," "to look better," "to stand out," and so on. 引き立たせる is the causative form of this verb. The lace pattern (レース模様) showed to great advantage (引き立たせていた) the black (黒) and the color of Mitsuko's skin (肌の色).

16 心理学のサークル<u>の中で</u>も …の中で means "among," and …の中でも "even among." There are several psychology clubs at the university, and the club Anzai and Mitsuko belong to is one of those. The も suggests that these clubs exhibit a certain general tendency (their memberships are predominantly male, as we learn in the next clause), and that this tendency is particularly evident in their club.

安西達<u>のところ</u>は女性が特に少ない This ところ is close to "place" in meaning but isn't quite that specific—there is no actual "place" involved. Indeed, the word is used here precisely as a non-specific, even abstract stand-in for サークル.

顔立ちの整っている美都子は We saw in paragraph 8 of「むかし夕日の公園で」and again in paragraph 27 of「ミイラ」that の can replace が in certain constructions, in order to clarify the sentence structure,

making it immediately apparent that the noun before the の is an element in an adjectival clause, not the subject of the verb that follows it.

酒の席には殆ど顔を見せなかった には sets up a contrast between drinking and non-drinking parties or other get-togethers. Mitsuko doesn't usually participate in the former.

それが、どういう風の吹き回しか This is another hazy, non-specific それが like the one we encountered in paragraph 4. Rather than pointing back to some particular word in the sentences that precede it, this type of それが tells us that the narrator is going to comment on the state of affairs just described, giving us some new information that contrasts with what came before—in this case, the fact that Mitsuko has broken her rule of non-appearance at drinking parties.

風の吹き回し is a set phrase literally meaning "the blowing of the wind"; in the pattern どういう風の吹き回しか, it means, roughly, "as chance would have it," or "by some twist of fate."

17 コーヒーをいれてやる This is the same auxiliary verb やる we saw in paragraph 3.

18 わたし、それまで起きていたいんです Notice that Mitsuko speaks more politely than Anzai. This is one of the characteristics of "feminine" speech.

22 かえって目立つよ かえって is an adverb used to indicate that the action of a verb or the state of an adjective happens or exists in a way that might seem contrary to one's expectations. Mitsuko may think she can avoid being stared at if she goes home on the earliest train, but Anzai disagrees: that would make it more obvious, not less, that she was returning from a night on the town.

23 それはいいんです This is a good sentence for considering the difference between は and が. If a が had been used here, the meaning would be "That's exactly how I like it." With a は, the meaning becomes: "That doesn't bother me."

24 うちの人が電話かけてくるのか うちの人 means "someone from home," "someone in your family." うち is often used to mean "my family" or "my," but in this case Anzai is obviously referring to Mitsuko's parents, not his own. It is common, by the way, for people to omit the を in

phrases like 電話をかけてくる in informal speech, because the meaning is perfectly clear without it. Indeed, you don't even need to think of this as an omission—it's probably more accurate to say that speakers of Japanese (like speakers of any language, I suspect) tend to add as little as possible to their sentences unless they have a good reason (such as wanting to sound formal) to do otherwise.

28 **とにかく、始発で帰る、朝まで寝ないと決めている**　とにかく can have at least three different but related meanings: the casual "at any rate," the more vehement "come what may," and the all-encompassing "every last one." This is an instance of the second meaning.

そう<u>か</u>。それじゃあ……　The か in そうか seems like it ought to turn this little exclamation into a question, but it doesn't—in actual usage, そうか isn't all that different from なるほど.
　　それじゃあ is a contraction of それでは.

<u>そこで</u>、何かで読んだ言葉がひらめいた　そこで here means "at that moment," or simply "and." 何か means "something," probably some book or magazine. The word that "flashed into Anzai's mind," of course, is the one that appears in the next line: 百物語.

31 **聞いたことない? 百本、蠟燭<u>つけといて</u>ね、お化けの話、<u>するんだよ</u>**　つけといて is a contraction of つけておいて. するんだよ, a contraction of するのだよ, is typical "masculine" speech—though again, in real life, women, especially young women, often talk this way, too. Besides these contractions, note the absence of particles: 聞いたこと(が)ない? 百本、蠟燭(を)つけといてね、お化けの話(を)するんだよ.

一つ話す<u>たびに</u>、一本消す　"Dictionary form of a verb + たびに" is a pattern used to say that "each time" or "every time" the action of the verb takes place, the action of some other verb also takes place. The agent of the second verb can be the same as that of the first, but it doesn't have to be. The pattern "noun + の + たびに" is also used, e.g., 食事のたびに "Every time I have a meal..."

本物のお化けが出て来る<u>んだって</u>　んだって is a colloquial equivalent of のだという and indicates that what comes before it is hearsay. It breaks down grammatically as a contraction of the explanatory のだ + って (see paragraph 16 of「ミイラ」for an explanation of って).

33 **女の子<ruby>って<rt></rt></ruby>、恐い話が好きだろう** In this case, って means というのは, which is used when the speaker wants to make a general statement about something.

34 **でも百本の蠟燭<ruby>なんて<rt></rt></ruby>あるんですか** As we saw in paragraph 12 of 「肉屋おうむ」 and again in paragraph 37 of 「ミイラ」, なんて can be used to express surprise and/or scorn. In this case, it's surprise/disbelief.

35 **<ruby>そりゃあないさ<rt></rt></ruby>** そりゃ（あ） is a contraction of それは. さ is a rather informal particle that can appear either in the midst of a sentence or at the end, and can have all sorts of different effects. Often it just serves as filler, much like "like" in English. Depending on the context and tone of voice, it adds a different sort of spice. In this case, Anzai is trying to emphasize, and confirm, that he and Mitsuko are on the same wavelength: this さ accomplishes something similar to the "of course" in "Nah, of course not." She's skeptical; he agrees that she's right to be.

第一、百だとしたら、二人で話して五十ずつ In this context, 第一 is more or less the same as "for starters." The sudden ending of the sentence with the words 五十ずつ is another instance of Kitamura's omission of inessential verbs. Indeed, more than just a single verb has been omitted here: a whole phrase, such as 話すことになる, would have been necessary.

36 **<ruby>いぶかし<rt></rt></ruby>げに** See paragraph 6 of 「神様」 for a note on げ.

37 **どうするんです** We saw in paragraph 28 that そうか doesn't function as a question, despite the か. This is a good example of a sentence that actually *is* a question, and yet doesn't have a か. You can tell it's a question, naturally, because どう is a question word. If you were to read this sentence aloud, you would probably want to do it with a rising intonation, though even the rising intonation can be dropped if you want the query to sound angry or aggressive. Listen to how Matsunaga-san does it (CD 05:52).

38 **とにかく明かりのあるところは全部点ける<ruby>のさ<rt></rt></ruby>** In my note to the とにかく in paragraph 28, I suggested that this word has at least three meanings. This is a good example of the third, "every last one," which only becomes relevant when とにかく is used in connection with words such as 全部 or すべて. Indeed, this is less a meaning than a function: とにかく simply strengthens the sense of inclusiveness. The のさ at the

end is the same old explainer の that we've seen in many sentences up to now, followed by さ (see paragraph 35).

そういうわけさ In this case, そういうわけ means something like "That's the idea," "That's how we'd do it." You can sense, I'm sure, how the わけ here relates to the word's basic meanings of "reason," "cause."

40 **カーテンを……** This sentence is, obviously, incomplete. We can tell from the previous sentence, however, that Mitsuko is asking (注文^{ちゅうもん}をつける) Anzai to do something to the curtain, presumably close it. In the following paragraph, Anzai completes the sentence for her.

42 **完全主義者^{かんぜんしゅぎしゃ}だなと、いささか面倒^{めんどう}に思^{おも}いつつ、安西^{あんざい}は立^たち上^あがって** When つつ appears in contexts like this one, it is a conjunction used to indicate that the actions expressed by two verbs are taking place at the same time, and are being performed by the same person. Often, it implies some sort of disagreement between the two actions, as is the case here: Anzai finds it a bit of a bother to have to stand up and close the curtain, but he stands up anyway. つつ attaches to the -**masu** stem of the verb. In this usage, it can be replaced by ながら.

43 **机^{つくえ}の上^{うえ}のスタンドから懐中^{かいちゅう}電灯^{でんとう}にいたるまで** スタンド is an abbreviation of 電気^{でんき}スタンド, "light stand," i.e., "lamp." "Noun A + から + noun B + にいたるまで" is a fixed pattern meaning "everything from A to B."

46 **演技^{えんぎ}なのか、それとも酒^{さけ}のせいか** せい first appeared in「肉屋おうむ」(paragraph 31). せいか (=せい + interrogative particle か) is one of many patterns used for expressing a cause, the result of which is generally bad—or perhaps it would be more accurate to say that the combination of cause and result is bad. In this case, the narrator is suggesting that Mitsuko's furrowing her brow could be the result of having drunk too much (酒のせい), and the bad part of the situation is more the overdrinking than the furrowed brow.

48 **美都子^{みつこ}は、思^{おも}いのほか巧^{たく}みな語^{かた}り手^てだった** This 美都子は establishes Mitsuko as the topic of discussion for the next two paragraphs, until 安西は changes the topic again. She's the one talking in the following line, and she's the one who lets her eyes wander around the room in the sentence after that.

50 **いくつめかの物語^{ものがたり}を終^おえた後^{あと}、視線^{しせん}をさまよわせている** いくつめか can

百
物
語

be broken up into three parts: いくつ ("how many"), the suffix め (目), and the interrogative particle か. A clumsy literal rendering of the meaning of this clause would be "after finishing a story—what number in the series was it, I wonder?" In actual usage, though, the meaning is closer to "after finishing a certain number of stories…"

55 **そいつも、切るの** こいつ, そいつ, and あいつ are three pronouns used to refer in a very casual, sometimes less-than-polite way, to people or things. They are distinguished, based on the perceived closeness or distance to the speaker, in the same way that これ, それ, and あれ are.

57 **美都子はにこりともしなかった** にこりともしない is a set phrase meaning "didn't even grin." It can also be understood, however, by breaking it down into its constituent elements: にこり is an adverb that attaches to the verb する with a と; も is added for emphasis.

学校の机の因縁話をすると 因縁 is a noun meaning "karma." Here the character 話 has been stuck on to it, forming a single compound noun that is read いんねんばなし. There are, unfortunately, no hard and fast rules to guide our readings of combinations like this—you just have to give yourself time to develop an instinctive feel for them, or check a dictionary.

66 **早口に小話めいた怪談をして** めく is a suffix that attaches to nouns, the stems of adjectives, and sometimes adverbs, and turns them into verb phrases. It means "to seem like," "to appear to be," and so on. In contemporary Japanese it tends to be used in the -**ta** form, as it is here.

67 **さあ。これでこいつだけだぞ** Similar as they may seem, さあ and さ are really quite different: As we saw in paragraph 35, さ is an informal particle that can either be inserted in the middle of a sentence or tacked on at the end, and can express a wide variety of different meanings. さあ is an exclamation that either stands on its own, as it does here, or appears at the beginning of a sentence; it has only two basic meanings. Often it expresses an emotion—surprise, confusion, or enthusiasm are the most common; in other instances, it acts as a sort of invitation to the listener. In this context, it has the latter meaning: Anzai is attempting to create a sense of intimacy, subtly stressing the fact that he and Mitsuko are about to be plunged, together, into darkness.

これで is similar in some ways to the interjection それが, which we

百物語

encountered earlier (paragraphs 4 and 16). これ refers to the current situation, rather than to a specific word or object that appears in the preceding text.

68 安西は、その手に最後の光を渡した   その手 refers, of course, to Mitsuko's hand.

69 いろいろと話が出ましたけれど   This sentence would make sense if the と were replaced by a な, but it would make a slightly different kind of sense: as the sentence stands, いろいろ serves as an adverb modifying 出ました; if the と were changed to a な, いろいろ would turn into an adjective modifying 話. Even so, the meaning is closer to "We've heard all kinds of different stories" than to "Stories have emerged variously," since "emerging variously" in this context is just another way of saying "emerging in different forms, as different stories." Hence my translation.

とすれば、自分て恐くありません?   Ordinarily, とすれば would follow a statement, rendering it hypothetical: "If it's the case that…" Mitsuko is using it as a conjunction instead, so that the meaning becomes: "If that's the case…" Indeed, you may already have noticed that the story shifts here from third-person limited-omniscient narration to first-person narration: Mitsuko is now telling her story as it comes to mind. The polite language (e.g., –ましたけれども in the first line, and –ませんか in this one) serves as an immediate clue.

70 それって、凄く、恐くありませんか   って can serve as a topic marker, as we saw in paragraph 29 of「ミイラ」. Here it is equivalent to は.

71 それどころじゃない   This is a set phrase that means, literally, "That's not the full extent of it," "Far from it." In this context, we can think of it as meaning "That's not the worst of it."

何をしているのかどころか、どうなっているのかも分からない   どころか is a conjunction used to express surprise at the extremity of a situation. Basically, it works like this: "statement A どころか statement B" means "You might expect statement A to be the case, but in fact statement B." The particular meaning changes depending on whether one or both of the two statements are positive or negative. Here the pattern is "…どころか…も…ない," and the meaning "Not only…, (but)…not even…": "Not only do you have no idea what you're doing, you don't even know what's happening to you."

寝ている間は魚になっていた<u>って</u> This って is a little different from the ones we encountered earlier, in paragraphs 31 and 32—it functions as a conjunction meaning "even if" and is equivalent to としても.

73 **一人で寝る<u>ようにいわれたのです</u>** "Dictionary (or -**nai**) form of a verb + よう（に）いう" is a phrase meaning "to tell someone to (VERB)" and expresses an indirect command. ようにいわれる is the passive form of this phrase and means "to be told to (VERB)."

74 **泊まりがけの修学旅行も<u>行かせてはもらえなかった</u>** We saw in paragraph 7 that if ください is appended to the causative form of a verb, the resulting combination means "please let me" perform the action of the verb. A similar thing is happening here, except that ください in the previous pattern has been replaced by もらう, changing the meaning from "please let me" to "to be allowed to" perform the action of the verb. In this case, we are working with the base combination 行かせてもらう ("to be allowed to go"). もらう is in the potential form, もらえる, but in the negative past tense もらえなかった. And finally, a は has been inserted for emphasis between 行かせて and もらえなかった.

<u>合宿のある部活動はいけない</u>といわれました 合宿のある部活動 means "club activities with overnight training sessions," or "club activities that involve overnight training sessions." いけない is not quite the potential form of いく（行く）; think of it instead as an adjective meaning "no good," "that will not do"—a roundabout word for "bad."

<u>とにかく</u>、よそに泊まるのは駄目だといわれたのです This is the first of the three meanings of とにかく that I listed in paragraph 28: "at any rate."

ええ、父親にです This is another grammatically incomplete but nevertheless complete sentence, like 仮にですよ (paragraph 71). As you might expect, sentences like these have a very colloquial feel.

75 **納得できないでしょう?** Notice that many of the sentences in Mitsuko's story have no explicit subjects. This is completely intentional, and extremely effective: she seems to be telling a story about someone else, but at the same time, she seems to be talking about herself. This 納得できないでしょう is about as close as she will come to stating outright that the story is her own (if, in fact, it is): the form of this question, after all, suggests that she is seeking confirmation of the appropriateness of

something she herself feels. *She* is (probably) the one who couldn't accept the prohibitions to which she was being subjected.

76 <u>そうしたら、父親が学校まで来ました</u>　そうしたら means just what it seems it ought to mean: "And with things like that…," "The situation was like that when…" Culture Festival takes a *lot* of preparation, and it's not unusual for students to stay at school until very late, perhaps even overnight. The girl in this story (Mitsuko herself?) feels humiliated because her father seems to be treating her like a child, coming to bring her home when everyone else is allowed to stay.

友達に<u>あわす顔がない</u>　あわす顔がない is an idiom meaning "to be unable to face" someone—though 合わせる顔がない is, in my experience, the more common phrasing. 合わす is simply a variation on 合わせる, so I suppose either one is fine.

自分の部屋に閉じこもった<u>きり</u>　きり is a particle used when something happens, and then, for a long period, the situation remains unchanged.

77 <u>その家には、特別ないい伝えがあるというのです</u>　Written in kanji, this would be 言い伝え. The いい is "to say," not "good." The verb 言い伝える means "to pass a story on"; 言い伝え is a noun derived from this verb, and denotes the story that is passed on.

78 <u>大体、《何》になるのだ、と聞きました</u>　Often 大体 is used to mean "generally." The usage here is a little different: it means something like "anyway" or "in the first place." The presence of the 何 in the phrase 《何》になる<u>のだ</u> is enough to make it a question; the のだ makes it a very emphatic question—though Mitsuko would have sounded even more confrontational if she had said 《何》になる<u>のよ</u>.

ところが父親は、《あるもの》<u>としか</u>分からない　としか can be broken down into the quotation particle と and the particle しか. The father only understood that it was "a certain thing." See paragraph 8 of「神様」 for a note on the use of しか, and paragraph 37 of「ミイラ」 for しか used with the と that means "with."

79 <u>わたしのことなら、子供の頃、母の実家にいったことがあるではないかと</u>　"If this is actually me you're talking about, well, I stayed at mom's parents' house when I was a child, didn't I?" The logic here, if it isn't clear yet, is "Grandma and Grandpa, then, can attest to the fact that I

didn't turn into anything strange when I slept, so what you say can't be true."

80　父の代、祖父の代と男ばかりが続いたから問題はなかったのだ　The と turns what precedes it into an adverbial clause. The usage here might become clearer if you think of it in terms of 代々と "generation after generation." This is the same usage of と that we saw in paragraph 69 of「ミイラ」(不思議と).

そんないい伝えなど馬鹿げたものだと思っていたそうです　This など expresses the speaker's contempt for the noun it follows. The meaning is the same as なんて, but なんて is stronger.

母は一笑にふし　一笑にふす is a set phrase meaning "to laugh off," "to brush something aside with a laugh."

81　蛇の髪は忌まわしいとはいえ　とはいえ (or in slightly more formal language, とはいえども) is a conjunction meaning "although."

その姿が知れています　知れる may look like the potential form of 知る, but in fact it isn't—the correct form is 知られる. 知れる is a separate word in its own right, and means "to become known," "to be knowable," or, in the -**te iru** form, "to be nothing exceptional." Mitsuko's usage of it here is tantalizingly ambiguous.

知られぬ恐怖の底無しに比べれば　See paragraph 6 of「神様」for a note on ぬ and 無し.

それも甘いものに思えます　The most familiar meaning of the adjective 甘い is "sweet," but this is only one of its meanings. Unfortunately, its meaning in this context is about as tricky to translate into English as it would be to translate "cheesy" into Japanese. One thing we can be quite certain of, however, is that a Medusa is not "sweet." The idea is, essentially, that anyone who thinks a Medusa is as bad as the "bottomless depths of an unknown terror" is drastically underestimating the unknown.

82　自己保存の本能というのは強いものです　This is the same というのは we saw in the first paragraph of「ミイラ」. Again, it is used to make a universal statement about the noun that precedes it.

83　先祖の女達はどうして来たのか　We're used to seeing どうして as a single word meaning "why," but if you break it down into its constituent

百物語

parts, it turns into two words: the question word どう and the verb する in the -**te** form. Read as two words, the phrase means something like "how doing" or "in what way"—and that's what it means here. 来る is the same auxiliary verb we encountered in paragraph 40 of「神様」, except that in this context it means "to come" in temporal rather than physical terms. How, in other words, did they get along all those years?

夫に寝姿を見せぬようにして来たのでしょう　This ぬ is the same classical negative ending that we encountered a moment ago. We could rewrite the underlined words using modern grammar as 見せないようにして. The meaning of both phrases is the same, but the one with ぬ sounds more literary.

戦前はその地方の名のある家だったといいますから　First, the topic of the sentence is implied, not stated, but it is clearly something like "the family" or "our family." Second, a note on 名のある家, which is what marks the implied topic, in a thinking-backwards sort of way: if you translate the ある into kanji, you get 名の有る家. Flip the first two kanji in this phrase, and you end up with 有名, or "famous." That's exactly what 名のある家 means: 有名な家, a well-known family.

そういういい伝えを知っても来る婿があったのでしょう　A 婿 is a man who marries into a woman's family. This could happen for various reasons; often, though, it would happen when the bride's family was much better off than the groom's. That, presumably, would be the case here: Mitsuko's family was a 名のある家 before the war, so there would have been no shortage of men eager to come join the family.

84　それを思うと、娘は毎夜の眠りが恐くてならないのです　The pattern "adjective/verb in the -**te** form + ならない" is used to indicate that someone feels something very strongly, often to the extent that the emotion is uncontrollable. The emotion in question is expressed by the verb or adjective. In this case, the young woman feels "helplessly frightened."

85　語り終えて　You're probably familiar with the auxiliary verb 終わる, meaning "to finish" as in 読み終わる ("to finish reading"). 終わる is intransitive; 終える is its transitive equivalent. In practice, both expressions usually translate as "to finish (VERBing)."

87　すうすうという寝息が聞こえ出した　すうすう is an onomatopoetic rendering of the sound of someone (in this case, Mitsuko) breathing

deeply in her sleep. See paragraph 19 of 「ミイラ」 for a note on the use of 出す as an auxiliary verb.

体が、その一息ごとに強ばるのを、安西は感じた　ごとに, much like たびに (see paragraph 31), means "each time" or "every time" and is used in the patterns "noun + ごとに" and "dictionary form of a verb + ごとに." 一息ごとに is an example of the former, and means "with each breath (Anzai heard)…"

88　馬鹿なと笑おうとしたが　This と is the quotation particle, and 馬鹿な the thought being quoted. Which is really just another way of saying that the と turns what precedes it into an adverbial phrase—we saw this in paragraph 80. On its own, 馬鹿な means "Ridiculous!"

百物語

1 **枕にカヴァーをかけ** It will soon become clear, if it isn't already, that this story—not only the short excerpt printed here, but the entire thing—revolves around the different meanings (and there are heaps of them) of the verb かける. It's a word story, in other words, not a plot story. And as luck would have it, it's not really a grammar story, either.

主婦の仕事にはあまり縁のないわたしでも 縁がない is a set phrase whose nuances vary quite a lot from context to context. Here it simply suggests that the narrator tends not to do very much (or have very much to do with) housework.

朝食のトマトには This は sets up a contrast with the previous clause: the narrator isn't very involved with housework, but she *does* put salt on her tomato. If you find yourself wondering whether salting a tomato really counts as housework, as it would have to for this contrastive は to make sense, you've understood an important part of Tawada Yōko's quirky sense of humor.

ラジオをかけたまま This is the same "-**ta** form of a verb + まま" seen in paragraph 11 of「百物語」. The narrator has turned the radio on, and left it on.

このまま静かにしていれば 静かにする means "to keep quiet." In the -**te iru** form, it means "to keep keeping quiet."

誰の邪魔にもならない The に here is part of the phrase 邪魔になる ("to get in the way"). The も forms a set with 誰 to mean "anybody."

迷惑だって人にかける橋なのだから The だって here means でも.

自閉的になるよりはまし まし is a -**na** adjective that means "better (than something else), but not wholly satisfactory, either." It is often used in this pattern, よりはまし.

そういう悪いことばかりして ばかり is a particle that follows nouns and means "only" or "nothing but."

尻に帆かけて逃げる 尻に帆(を)かける is an idiom equivalent to the English "take to one's heels," "show a clean pair of heels." It is often used in the -**te** form as an adverbial phrase, and frequently the verb it modifies is 逃げる, as it is here.

日が暮れかけた頃に　The auxiliary verb かける, which means "to begin to (verb)," has already appeared several times in this book, notably (pardon the pun) in paragraph 2 of「ミイラ」. It will appear several more times in this story, each time with the same "to begin to (but not necessarily finish)" meaning.

いつかは死んでしまうのだから　いつかは is a word in its own right that means "eventually." The addition of the は makes it more forceful than an ordinary いつか, suggesting the speaker's certainty or determination that the action expressed by the verb will, indeed, eventually take place.

面白いことは今のうちにやっておこう　今のうちに is a set phrase meaning "now, before it is too late," "now, while you still can." おこう is the volitional form of the auxiliary おく.

わたしの中に巣食った掛け言葉の習慣　I translate 掛け言葉 as "punning" because that seems to be what the narrator means here, and because the narrators of many of Tawada Yōko's other fictions—to which this self-referential sentence seems to be pointing—also pun frequently and brilliantly. But the particular type of linguistic wizardry denoted by the word 掛け言葉 (or 掛詞, as it is generally written) isn't really a pun—and indeed, the term is often and better translated as "pivot word." Unlike a pun, which is made by playing on the different meanings of a single word or on two words with the same pronunciation, a pivot word is created by overlapping the last syllables of one word with the first of the next. It's difficult to do this in English, but here's an attempt: "Work on the new mine was just beginn/ing/ots of gold haunted the owner's dreams." You can see how the "ing" functions like a pivot linking "beginning" and "ingots." Pivot words have none of the humor of puns, because there is really no overlapping of meaning, only sound.

物語という布地にミシンをかけた方がいい　"Noun A + という + noun B" is a pattern used to equate two nouns. It can be translated in a number of different ways: "noun A as a noun B," "noun A that is a noun B," "noun A of a noun B," etc.

ひとり欠けるともう一人芝居はできない　This is a wacky, wonderful sentence—utterly typical of Tawada Yōko. There is no explicit subject, of course, but the placement of the sentence at the very end of the story

かける

suggests that it is referring, in a cleverly self-reflexive way, to the narrator: when she (or he) drops out of the story—when the story ends up "short one person"—there's no story anymore; the "one-man play" is over. It's a brilliant ending. The peculiar thing about the sentence is that the verb 欠ける ("to be short on," "to lack") is used to say that *part* of something is missing—one member of a group, for instance. Ordinarily you wouldn't say that a person is 欠けている if there was only one person to begin with. So we are left wondering who is left behind after that "one person" goes missing. Perhaps, come to think of it, there were originally two people involved in this "one-man play"—not just the narrator, but the reader? When the narrator makes his (or her) exit, the reader is left hanging, at loose ends, like an audience gazing up at an empty stage. This observation, too, seems characteristically Tawada Yōkoian—that it takes at least two to put on a one-man play.

かける